EVE GOT A BAD RAP

EVE GOT A BAD RAP

What Lies Have You Believed?

by I. M. REDEEMED

XULON PRESS

Xulon Press
2301 Lucien Way #415
Maitland, FL 32751
407.339.4217
www.xulonpress.com

ISBN-13: 9781545629826

PREFACE

YOU'RE ABOUT TO EMBARK ON A JOURNEY with me through my lifetime of rags to riches, danger to safety, despair to delight, sad to funny, loneliness to love and lies to truth.

Let's look beyond the veil. Examining over fifty years of my life has revealed life-changing keys. Has your life been altered due to a pattern of lies? Can you remember the first time you were talked out of experiencing your full capacity? Go back to that moment and identify the deception. Do you see it? Perceiving a false reality can cost us everything! Is that a price we're willing to pay?

Small thinking robs us of our potential. Some people hit rock bottom before looking upward. Others lead incredibly awesome lives, yet they feel empty. If there is a lack, there is a lie. Hopelessness is a lie!

Modern society has exploded with intelligence, yet poor coping skills continue. Everything imaginable is at our fingertips, yet we are not satisfied. Where do we look when we've already looked everywhere? Drugs are not enough, so more drugs are added. Thrills are not thrilling enough. Extreme sports are not extreme enough. Why do we doubt that we have already been given the fullness of life?

Who will teach others that their own precious lives are passing by while they feed on violence-based movies, television shows and video games? Domestic violence has not diminished. Child abuse has not diminished.

There's a plethora of philosophies, self-help seminars, cultural adjustments and social programs, yet anger remains unbridled. Wouldn't you think that we would have figured it out by now?

Poverty has been examined, yet God's provision is often ignored and high school dropout rates continue to increase. Peer pressure promotes bullying, atheism, gender confusion, suicide, witchcraft, gang membership, school shootings and racial unrest. We need peer partners not peer pressure. Children need to know that there is a power bigger than themselves and there is hope and safety. A shift needs to occur where all eyes and ears are on deck. We are all the watchmen who must look out for each other's well being.

Humans succumb to peer pressure and political correctness. We should embrace diversity. Diversity is good, yet it has been taken out of context and in some instances has caused more problems than solutions. The youth, especially, yearn to be accepted. Under stress they strive to fit in, but the truth is only a breath away. They have already been made accepted in the beloved.

Self-righteous criticism does not affect true change. Judgmental attitudes were never the answer! People are tired of the fake. It's time for a radical change. Why do we simply follow the crowd? Whose voice are we following? Let in the light. Hope breaks through where there was no hope. A way is made where there was no way. We must begin by speaking a new sound!

This story is for everyone, but especially for women to rise up and discover their true identities and value. It exposes deception and traps. The door is thrown open for escape. This story may be shocking to those who are living sheltered lives, but it will stretch you in ways that you never thought possible. These words are a friend to those hanging on by a thread. You are not alone.

This testimony is raw and unapologetic. The memories were once too painful to recall, but now thankfulness outweighs the pain. I am free. Freedom is a gift and a choice. What will you chose? Will you dare to look deeper?

DEDICATION

I DEDICATE THIS BOOK TO THE ONE WHO MADE me free. I'll introduce him later in the story. To John, my love, who encouraged me to write: The things you did to make this possible are too vast to list. Thank you for supporting my endeavors and sharing your life with me. You are a cheerful giver. To my children: You teach me new things every day. I love watching seed bear fruit. Abide with the vine. Grow in grace and truth.

To others who pressed me to write: Wendy, her Mother and Debra. To all my rescuers who helped me come to the knowledge of the truth and deliverance: Tonia, Tom and Sue, Mike and Tari. Many more can be named, and you know who you are. Thank you Tomberlin for believing in the book and encouraging me to press forward in writing and speaking engagements. Special thanks to Tom. Many keys herein I learned from him. Thank you for a relationship of divine purpose.

Special thanks to the editors

John, who patiently combed through *all* the early drafts. Sue, who brings peace and honor to every situation. Karen, thank you for your prayers regarding every line. Thank you for allowing this to be one of the published works that you have edited with expertise and wisdom. Brittany, thank you for carving out precious time while working and meeting the demands of your family. Thank you for your insight that comes through as a professional educator and as a woman of depth. Thank you for your encouragement and heart for the book.

Thank you to those who made publishing possible.

CONTENTS

Chapter 1

VICTIMIZED OR MESMERIZED?

HANDS ARE GRIPPED TIGHTLY AROUND MY throat by the person I *should* be able to trust. His legs are straddled across my thighs pinning my arms against my body. I'm rendered helpless. No sound can be made. My eyes are closed. I cannot bear to *look* at the evil. It's getting darker and darker as my life fades. My bowels and bladder lose control as my body and spirit begin to separate. From deep within, a silent scream goes out for help. Suddenly, his hands…we will talk more about that later.

My eyes creak open, afraid to look. I'm afraid to move at all. How did I get here? This was not my first or my last cry for help. Often we don't understand the beginning until closer to the end. How many times have I heard someone say this, "If I only knew then what I know now!" Many people have been on a journey similar to mine. Some of them found victory, some did not. Will you?

Let's start at the beginning. Why was I born in the late 1950's to a particular set of parents? Why was I raised in a particular location of the world? Mom and Dad were handsome, loving, and full of passionate ideas. They worked hard, yet succumbed to the deception of poverty. They seemed to accept it as their *lot* in life. How did *they* get there? How does anyone foresee a trap?

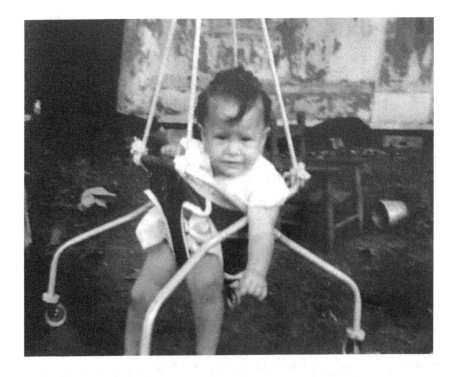

My primitive baby walker is hanging from a tree so I couldn't flee. Later, I fled. Go with me along my path. There were some good times along the way, but also some false promises that blinded me to the road hazards. Were there any red flags? Personally, I didn't see any until it was too late. If you ask most people, they will tell you that they saw warnings. Be alert to the voice that protects you. Most people admit they had a *gut feeling* that something just *wasn't right*. There's a way that *seems* right to *us*. There's a way, but there's a *more excellent* way.

Are we slaves to our memories? Can we choose which memories will consume us either for pain or for joy? Evidently, my first memory came from a place of deep joy when I was approximately one year old. A scene flashes in my mind of me standing on the couch behind my grandpa combing his beautiful white hair. I loved smelling his scent. Some grandpas ooze a fragrance that makes a grandchild feel safe and happy.

My very first precious memory didn't include my family's struggles during that time. Zooming out, this photo tells the story. A tiny dilapidated camper hobbled in the woods of a newly purchased and mostly uncleared piece of land. This was a temporary home for my parents, grandparents, uncle, oldest brother and myself. Yes, seven people living in a tiny camper! "How on earth was there enough room?" you ask!

My grandparents were sick and failing. My uncle had injured his back. Mother met the demands of all of us. I can only imagine how she fretted that my crying at night would keep the family awake. I imagine the stress of her washing my cloth diapers without the luxury of running water, much less a modern clothes dryer. She eventually got a wringer washing machine, which sat outside. The clean clothes squeezed through wringer rollers and she transferred them to the clothesline to air dry. To fill the washer, she carried water in a bucket from a not-so-nearby spring.

By now, Mom was also washing clothes for two more additions to our family, my little sister and our youngest brother. While Mom was getting more water, my young brother got his arm caught in the wringer. Curiosity got the best of him and he teetered on a block of wood to reach this fascinating contraption. He poked his fingers between the rollers and instantly it grabbed his hand! His arm followed through before I could stop it! My shock was broken by Momma's scream. She dropped the water bucket as she ran towards him. That was an exciting day! We were thankful he was okay!

That little scenario should have taught me that fear was not conducive to problem solving. Although I was a very young child, who stood there frozen in fear, I could have simply unplugged the washing machine.

The sting of my family's financial struggles was deflected when Grandpa and Dad played their music. They seemed to know that if we only look at the problems, we miss the truth of a *higher* hope. Dad was, no doubt, full of hope as he drove the borrowed tractor and backed that small camper onto his new land. He was starting a new life. My life was going places also!

As I grew older, I watched my parents overcome some huge obstacles. This inherently taught me that circumstances are not necessarily truth. Although exposed to the poverty spirit at a very young age, I knew deep down that God did not want anyone to suffer lack. I learned to read and His word tells us that He takes pleasure in our prosperity. By the end of this story, you will see what I mean.

My Mother did her best with what she knew. She taught us about love and how to treat people: Do unto others as you would have done unto you. Respect other people's property. Two wrongs don't make a right. She knew the Lord. She could not read or write, but she could read the needs of others and she knew some of the Bible. My siblings and I were astonished that she quoted a lot of scripture. Did she know everything? Of course not, who does? However, she knew what really matters.

While we lived in the little camper, Dad built a small house for us. A two-room living quarters sat atop the basement. While he nailed the subfloor to the upstairs, I teetered around watching his every move. Afraid I would fall off the building, he nailed the bottom of my dress to the subfloor! Ingenious Dad! Thanks for keeping me safe while you worked! In those days, who could afford a playpen for baby when a ten penny nail worked just fine! Likewise, I was kept in place in the previously pictured baby walker that hung from a tree by a rope. Hang in there baby, better days are coming!

My memory from around age four is of riding in our old family car with my face pressed against the window. Absorbing the forest-lined dirt road, I scanned upward above the treetops and stared at the big full moon.

In those moments, I was oblivious to the yucky, thick and choking tobacco smoke. Gazing through the car window, my mind drifted from the noise of my parents and my oldest brother. In that secret place it was just me, the moon and someone bigger than all of us. He was calling my name. I knew, without a doubt, that the one who created that big beautiful moon and peaceful forest could also see *me*!

I grew, but my physical world remained small as if in a snow globe. The rusty disheveled swing frame pulled out of the ground with my every swing. I looked around in this microcosm and wondered what else was out there in the world. Swinging carefully so as not to overturn the swingset, I was content singing loudly to the Lord. With joy in my heart, it never really occurred to me that one day I would actually have a passport. After all, some of my neighbors never traveled beyond the county (*county*, not coun*try*). They died inside their snow globe. Nothing wrong with that, *per se*, because there are rich people who are poor in spirit and there are poor people who are rich in spirit.

Life continued in our little house that Dad built. It was situated remotely from the watchful eyes of building inspectors, the codes and such. The upstairs was divided in half. One half was a bedroom for the entire family. A full-size bed sat on each end of the long room. One bed was for my parents and the other was for all four of us kids. We hung our clothes on nails. (Another good use of ten penny nails.) Without drywall, or insulation between the exposed two-by-fours, it was cold at night. My brother stuffed newspaper between the cracks. Paper was not entirely sufficient to keep out the cold, but it did keep out the snow.

The other half of the upstairs was a living room and kitchen combination. There was no indoor plumbing. Later, Dad allowed Mom to temporarily work in a poultry plant. She saved enough money to lay pipe to our house from the neighbor's spring water supply. This brought cold water into the kitchen sink, but there was not enough money for a hot water tank. At least she didn't have to carry buckets of water up the long hill anymore. We never had an inside bathroom.

Mom heated water on a wood burning cook stove and we took sponge baths from a large galvanized pan. Dad warmed the house by stoking the fire in the pot-belly heater. The most difficult part of sponge bathing was washing my long hair. I got a chill waiting for Mom to change out the soapy pan water. Clinging to one of only three towels that the family shared, I peeped through watching her lift the water kettle and pour yet another round of hot water into the pan. Each time, she carefully tested the rinse water so as not to burn me. This process was shortened if soap was in low supply.

The basement was a fascinating place where I watched Dad bring broken-down furniture back to life. I can still see him wearing his tack apron while bent over a stripped-down chair frame. He rebuilt each piece from the frame up until he had resurrected the masterpiece. His finished work was better than the new!

In Dad's shop were beautiful rolls of fabric. "Knee high to a grasshopper," Dad would say as I climbed up on the cutting table to *help* him. He let me make the buttons! Oh how I loved doing it! This was the best part because it was the finishing touch! "Dad, my fingers are *not* too tiny! I can do it!" I was proud that I could wrap the beautiful fabric onto the two-part metal discs and place them in the button maker. With a clunk, the wrought iron handle caught the fabric and squeezed the parts together! See, I told you fascinating things happened in the shop!

Yes, Dad was self-employed in his own basement re-upholstery shop! After working fourteen years on assembly lines at a furniture factory, he figured out how to do it on his own. He left the factory in the first year of my birth and set out to our new homestead. Unfortunately, there wasn't always enough work. Not many people in our socioeconomic area could afford to have their furniture recovered. I noticed that it was when work was scarce, he seemed to argue with Mom. He originally had thirty acres at our new home. Sadly, he eventually sold all but two in order to have money to pay bills.

During lean times, Dad worked for other employers and our family stayed in nearby rental homes. This pattern repeated, which meant that my two brothers, one sister and me attended a total of seven different elementary schools. Much of the time, we didn't attend school at all. Dad actually got into a little bit of trouble for that. Poor attendance was stressful for me as a student. It was difficult to keep up with the lessons, especially with math.

Chapter 2

TWO KINGDOMS

AT ABOUT AGE SEVEN, I BEGAN TO EXPERI-
ence two strong forces: *Love* and *Fear*. These two
influences were competing for my life. Also, my true
identity came under attack. In other words, I allowed
various circumstances to deceive me into thinking that
I was less valuable than other people. I recognized at a
very early age that there are two paths. One kingdom
is dark, but the other is light.

My most treasured childhood activities were reading
and spending time with my elderly neighbor, Nannie.
Not very long after I learned to read with *Dick and
Jane* school books, I developed a hunger to read more
about God. I just had to know everything I could find
out about Him! I sat in the neighbor's plush grass
and read the Bible. Reading opened up a whole new
world for me! Sometimes it got me into trouble if I were
reading too many books when Mom needed my help.
She would say, "If you have time to read, you have time

to sweep the floor." I don't blame Mom for that. She meant no harm.

Sitting in that grass, I found my refuge in God's Word. Like any child with any book, I started on page one and kept on reading. To me, the Bible was a *love letter* from God. Love got brighter. Hope developed.

"IT WAS MY VERY OWN TREASURE BOX!"

Many adventures took place! God parted the Red Sea! Oh my! With awe and wonder, I could only imagine that scene!

My young eyes searched for the deeper meaning of when Abraham took Isaac up on the mountain. I didn't yet understand what God was asking Abraham at that time or why He was asking it, but I knew that God was unquestionably a *very good God*. He deserved my trust, gratitude and loyal love. Don't we all like to be trusted if we have shown ourselves trustworthy? I knew there had to be a deeper meaning to that scenario. Deeper indeed.

Also reading about Solomon, I started putting two and two together! God does not want His children to be poor!

IF THERE IS A LACK, THERE IS A LIE.

Solomon had great provision. He was the richest in the land and the most wise. Hey, this was a different philosophy that I knew about up to this point. So far, I had only heard some adults say, "The poorer you are, the closer you are to God." However, that statement is nowhere in the Bible! Abraham was also very prosperous and he was definitely close to God! (We should not place our trust in nor *value* riches *more* than we value God, but God values us. He wants to bless *His* kids!) We place God above everything and He gives us all things richly to enjoy. Also see 2 Peter 1:3 God does not want His children to lack any good thing.

> Charge them that are rich in this world, that they be not *high minded*, nor t*rust in uncertain riches*, but in the living God, who giveth us richly all things to enjoy. (I Timothy 6:*17*)

For the Lord God is a sun and shield: the Lord will give grace and glory; no good thing will he withhold from them that walk uprightly. (Psalms 84:11,KJV)

I clung to every promise of God as life went on. As you can see there were good times and bad times. I was seeking the Lord and the enemy seemed to be making efforts to steal my worship and my peace. Sometimes after reading, I felt as though evil itself chased me around my neighbor's home. I loved that one-hundred-year-old home with the beautiful hand-laid flat rock chimney and I was not going to stop spending time in the secret place with the Lord.

I was continuously attacked with fear. A mentally challenged neighbor frightened me. A a child, I didn't understand it. In reality, he was a dear man who would not hurt a flea. No matter what people told me about his gentleness, I was still afraid. I don't know why. Perhaps it was something in his eyes.

We had a long school bus ride through the country. Although I loved that social time with the kids, I spent much of the time praying that man would not be at the bus stop. One day, he was there. I hid in the johnny house until he left. I thought he would never leave! It was a stinky place to hide!

No one understood why I had so much fear in my life and when they talked about it I wondered why I wasn't brave like other people. However, I did find bravery in only one place and only when I applied it to my life. For example, Mom taught me to sing the scriptures and that gave me true relief. She sang with me after night-mares. In fact, she sang the following and I learned to sing it to myself.

> Fear thou not; for I am with thee: be not dis-mayed; for I am thy God:I will strengthen thee; yea, I will help thee; yea, I will uphold thee with the right hand of my righteous-ness. (Isaiah 41:10)

I cannot thank her enough for teaching me to sing of God's protection. This song powerfully chased away fear. It became my lifelong friend. I loved Mom's stories about her own childhood, especially her teenage years. She told me about going to a Church camp meeting with Aunt Mildred. The service was held in a large tent with a sawdust floor. I wanted to hear every detail! She described the congregation praying in other languages. "I want to do that! Tell me more!" I said to Mom. My favorite photo of mother is of her getting baptized in the local river. We must have coping skills that are solid and sure. My journey has been filled with victories and problems, but the victories always came.

Our family enjoyed singing hymns, especially in the car. There was no radio. Dad and my uncles played banjo, guitar, and fiddle. Their music was a central part of our visits with extended family and neighbors.

Ups and downs continued. My family reported many stories about me walking in my sleep. They told me all the things I said and did while sleeping. One night Dad found me fully dressed and standing in the middle of the yard. When asked what was I doing, he said I replied, "I'm ready for school."

I was frightened by a neighbor-lady. The local children thought she looked like a witch. She is difficult to describe, but you can imagine pictures in a story book. No matter how hot the weather, she wore layers upon layers of raggedy black clothes. She had a wrinkled face and a large nose. She walked with a tall stick and continuously muttered to herself. Her speech was difficult to understand. It was a bizarre manner of speaking in short chanting phrases. I've never heard anyone speak the way she spoke. She lived nearby in a dark old house with boarded up windows. A kerosene lamp was her only lighting. The only food I ever saw her eat was cornmeal mush.

We never saw any of her family other than her mentally delayed son. Nobody seemed to know who his father might be. I developed empathy for her after I became an adult. I imagined her delivering her son, all alone, in that dark old house. I never knew her to go to a doctor and there were no midwives in our area.

Some neighbors suspected that her son received a disability check and she had money hidden in the house and buried in the yard. She never purchased anything. I never knew her to work at a job. She never left the area.

Our goat disappeared. A few days later, she came walking up the dirt road with it and gave it back to Dad. My brother said she didn't have luxuries like an ax or sickle. He guessed that she *borrowed* the goat to eat the tall vines that were growing up the side of her house.

The neighbor kids said she was indeed a witch. I avoided her, although she took a special interest towards me. I hid each time she came to visit, but I heard her tell mom that she would like to have me. She always asked Mom where I *was* although my three siblings were in plain view all around her. (Years later, while I was pregnant with my first child, she looked at me and quite assuredly said, "You will have a boy." The eerie way she looked at me and *said* it gave me chills. Later, I had a boy.)

As previously mentioned, my happy days were spent with Nannie. She and her husband lived on the other side of our dirt road and were only two of our few and far apart neighbors. They sold some of their land to Dad. I know that I was planted there so they could be an important part of my life.

Nannie never raised her voice or spoke unkindly about anyone. Sometimes, I stayed overnight and snuggled close to her soft cotton gown. She let me *help* her churn butter. Oh, what I would give this moment for a taste of her butter! She also did a lot of needlework. When her eyes became dim, I threaded her needles for her. She taught me how to knit! She was my safe place. If Mom and Dad were arguing, I ran to Nannie's house and curled up on her bed.

On her wall was an outdated calendar with a photo of a guardian angel helping two small children cross a precarious footbridge.

That scene gave me great comfort. I knew in my heart that God was taking care of me.

He knew that I needed those precious souls in my life. I was extremely attached to Nannie, that dear white-haired, example of a godly woman. I loved going to the little white country Church with her. I proudly wore the pair of shiny black shoes that she gave me. Her grandchild had outgrown them, but they fit me perfectly! Nannie's eyes sparkled also, but especially when the minister spoke about God. I knew that I wanted what I saw in her eyes!

I loved the way she touched my face with her soft elderly hands. After I was grown with a family of my own, I awoke one morning and wanted to go visit Nannie, but I was told, "No, maybe you can go on Friday." My dear precious Nannie died the next day before I could see her one last time! Grief overtook me! She will live forever in my heart.

While growing up, she gave me a sense of value and belonging. However, other parts of my life were harsh. I was not so valued by my classmates. My siblings and I attended many different schools and we often missed classes. Self-esteem began to deteriorate. I felt inferior to my classmates as they made fun of me. My clothes were different than their clothes. Mine were old, ill-fitting and reeked of cigarette smoke.

What's wrong with hand-me-down clothes? My family and I were thankful and were just as excited about them as if they had been new. Socks were a scarce commodity. We each had only two pair. Mine were too long and probably belonged to Mom. I placed the heel of the socks on my heels and folded the front half way back underneath my foot. That was not very comfortable, but as long as I kept my shoes on, no one could tell my socks were too big. At age ten, I received my first pair of *new* shoes during my first visit to a department store! I was beyond thrilled to pick out my own new shoes! The pair I loved most were too tight, but I wanted them so badly that I didn't tell Dad that they were too small.

At elementary school, I tried out for the cheerleading team. A strong point in my favor was being the smallest, which easily put me on top of the pyramid. I remember feeling so exhilarated on top! However, I overheard some girls say, "Don't pick her. She has too many bobby pins in her hair!" It's okay that I didn't make the team. I wouldn't have been able to participate anyway because we lived too far from school. Dad had no gas money for such nonsense as cheerleading.

I didn't actually realize we were poor until a *nice* classmate invited me to spend the night at her home. I couldn't believe my eyes! Her house had drywall and an indoor bathroom! She had her own bedroom. I can still see her toy box. A toy box! Who ever heard of such a thing? Who has so many toys that it takes a big box to contain them? I remember thinking that she must be rich! I never invited her, or any other children, to spend the night with me.

My parents didn't seem to take much stock in formal education, but they had plenty of common sense and ingenuity. I learned a lot from them. They were not afraid of manual labor. Daddy had a fifth grade education. No doubt, he also missed a lot of school while working at the family homestead. He could read and write, but his lettering was oddly shaped. In fact, I've never seen lettering like his. Although his spelling was lacking, his trademark letters became an endearment to me. He expressed his heart and I treasured every word he ever wrote in a card or letter to me.

Mom could not read or write. Instead, her father needed her time to be spent on the other end of a cross-cut-saw. Apparently, the family's need for firewood was deemed more important than her education. He died when she was only nine. He was reported to be mean-spirited. He beat mom, her mother, her siblings and the dog.

My Grandmother was a tender and godly woman whom I loved very much. When I was a child, she occasionally brought me little packets of jelly. You've seen those individual jellies commonly found on restaurant tables. However, I had never been to a restaurant. Somehow, I thought those little treasures were made especially for me! This memory has grown *sweeter* than jelly with each passing year. Later, I understood that going to a restaurant was a rare treat for Grandma. When she could afford to go, her thoughts were on us who didn't have the same opportunity.

Mom spoke these words to me, "Your grandpa beat my mom, your dad has beaten me, and you could end up with a husband that beats you." It's also noteworthy, that while *playing house as a kid,* my pretend husband's name turned out to be *the same* name of my real life adult husband. Spoken declarations have power. Mother, unaware and unintentionally, *spoke* a decree into my life. "You will also declare a thing *and* it will be established for you." (Job 22:28a). "Death and life are in the power of the tongue and they that love it shall eat the fruit thereof." (Proverbs 18:2)

I turned twelve and received my first store-bought dress. The orange and brown stripes of that polyester dress remain clear in my mind's eye. The joy of that moment was crushed when I learned that the new dress was to wear to my parents' divorce hearing.

Of course, I loved Mom, but I was also a Daddy's girl. After the divorce, they shared custody of us kids. Dad tended to keep me longer than our allotted visit time. Perhaps he did that because he didn't want me to leave or maybe it was because he wanted to harass Mom. Maybe both? Then, I was asked to go to the Judge's chambers and state which parent I wanted to live with as my primary residence. I decided to live with Mom. No child should have to make that choice. However, if you are a parent or child who fell under those circumstances, move on under forgiveness and grace.

Mom was accustomed to having lack, but after the divorce it was even more difficult. Sometimes, my oldest brother provided our Christmas presents. Speaking of Christmas, my favorite early childhood memory was when my brother and I heard a ruckus on the back porch and ran to see what was the clatter! And what to our wondering eyes did we see? My brother's red wagon and a toy piano for me! We were out of our minds with excitement thinking we had caught Santa delivering our gifts! Oddly, Dad appeared through the *front* door completely out of breath. I laugh now, as I imagine Dad running around the house so we wouldn't see that it was him!

Christmas was a very special occasion when we got candy and fruit. We didn't have stockings hung over the fireplace. Our parents filled small paper bags with nuts, fresh oranges and hard candy. The nuts were in their shells. The orange slice candy was pretty, but I sorted through the bag for a piece of chocolate. We received only one gift all year and that was on Christmas morning. My siblings and I were very thankful and took care of our toys. We eagerly crossed the days off the calendar until next December! Unfortunately, the holiday became less exciting as I grew older and noticed the pain on Mom's face that revealed she couldn't afford Christmas. Later, Mom secured a steady job in a sewing factory. She earned only minimum wage, but managed to move us from a small apartment into a larger rental house. I was fifteen years old.

Chapter 3

LIFE AS I KNEW IT, WAS ABOUT TO CHANGE

MY OLDEST BROTHER PLAYED BASS GUITAR and would have jam sessions with his friend who played the drums. I had my first teenage crush on his friend. Mom agreed to let us go on a double date with my brother, who was to keep a strict watch on me. My *date* was cute and nice, but he paid more attention to my brother's date than me. She was more willing to do the things that I wouldn't.

One evening, this young drummer boy was visiting my brother. Mom was home with us. The boys were talking about forming a band. Suddenly, the phone rang. The caller had met a man in town. He described him as a very talented lead vocalist who also knew his way around a guitar. The caller asked if he could bring him over to audition.

Oh, how I wish that phone had never rung! It's peculiar to me how our lives can turn on a dime. In

23

an instant, things can change for better or for worse. Looking back through my life, many pivotal moments occurred with the ringing of the phone.

The boys were eager to meet this mystery person and get an actual band together. Quite oddly, the drummer boy took a serious tone and asked me to go into another room because nobody *really* knew anything about this guy. Now, I realize that was an incredibly prophetic thing to say!

I went into the other room to read. I could hear the boys scuffling around setting up instruments. Suddenly, I heard a perfect voice that sounded exactly like Elvis Presley! Without thinking, I ran out to see the show! I mean seriously, in the seventies, what fifteen year old girl didn't love the music of Elvis Presley? The three of them played songs throughout the evening. I sat quietly on the couch, listening. Although I was young, I could appreciate really good music compared to *not so good* music. He was talented, no doubt about it.

During a break, the new guy suddenly sat down beside me on the couch. He was too close for my comfort. His eyes were demanding and he seemed to be *in charge.* He instantly declared, "You're going to be mine. Say that you love me."

Who does that? He was fairly handsome, yes, but not overly so. I was not romantically attracted to him. After all, he was ten years older than me. At his first words, there seemed to be a vacuum in the atmosphere, but I didn't understand it at that time. I was in a trance under his control. It was as if my mind went blank and I had become under his will. I would not fully understand this until thirty-four years later. Why, why, why of all the living rooms in the entire world, did he have to show up in mine?

They continued playing music that night and he often stared at me. He occasionally walked back and forth as if he were on a mission. I noticed he periodically went into the kitchen and spoke to my mother as if he were demanding something of her. It all seemed so surreal. That night, my life changed.

The next thing I knew, he appeared at our home every day. At various times, he demanded, "Say that you love me! Let me hear you say it!" He asked me what had I always wanted but never received and would I like to have a pony. Why did he ask me those things? He acted as if he had the money; in reality he did not.

I saw him talking to Mom again. He followed her down the wooden steps to our back yard, towering over the back of her head. She came back inside with him on her heels. As they approached me, I heard Mom telling him that she would only sign for him to marry me if he promised he would let me finish school. (What?!)

My next memory was wearing a meager white dress riding in the car on our way to South Carolina. It was legal in that state to marry a minor with a parent's consent. No, I was not pregnant. We had known him for less than two weeks. However, there we stood in the home of the Justice of the Peace. Ironically and unknowingly, my own peace was about to be stolen.

My mother married my father when she was only fourteen. In the days of antiquity, girls married at very young ages. I guess my getting married at fifteen didn't seem outlandish to Mom. She also seemed to be under this guy's spell.

Chapter 4

REALITY BEGINS FOR THE CHILD BRIDE

WE WERE LIVING WITH MOM AND MY brother. They left the house to start their work day. Fall had quickly arrived and it was the first day of high school. I got dressed and had just finished putting my long hair up in a ponytail. Suddenly from behind, *husband* grabbed my ponytail and slung me across the floor while shouting, "Where do you think you're going?" I scrambled up from the floor, stunned. I just couldn't believe it! This must be a mistake, I thought. Looking into his eyes of rage, I trembled. "To school," I meekly replied. He growled, "Like hell you are!" That was that!

That evening, Mom learned that he had not kept the promise he made to her. He would not allow me to finish high school. We were all in a state of shock. Like flipping a switch, his demeanor suddenly changed back to his Mr. Nice storefront character. He acted as if we all should be grateful for his very existence. We would soon come to know that this was his pattern: violence followed by false kindness.

After a couple of months, he took me out of Mom's house. I was living in the unknown, but one thing I knew for sure: not to do anything to make him angry! I still couldn't believe what had happened. I felt like a cat that shakes its head after falling off the window sill having just been asleep. Perhaps the slinging me across the floor was just a one-time fluke.

My life seemed to be in a different time warp and my mind felt numb. I wondered how it was all going to pan out for me. It seemed so weird not to go to school. One day simply turned into the next. When would the other shoe drop?

I began to discover more about him. Not only was he musically gifted, he was curiously intelligent. Without any training, he could tear down a car engine and quickly put it back together. However, I never saw him work a steady job. I still don't know where he occasionally got money, except for the few times he played music at bars and hustled pool. Yes, he knew his way around a pool table. The problem was that he loved violence more than peace, and he instigated chaos. A bar room brawl would break out between him and the infuriated guys who had just lost all their money.

One night the drummer didn't show, so I sat down at the drums and from that point became a band member. The violence became particularly terrifying when a bar fight was carried outside. I jumped in the car and locked the doors. Like a deer in the headlights, I watched in horrifying disbelief as he simultaneously and single handedly fought and beat up all four of the strong men that were larger than he. They were left sprawled out on the parking lot! He laughed eerily as we sped away in our car!

That scene rooted fear deep into my young mind. It was a demonstration beyond normal *human* strength. I was convinced that if four strong men couldn't get away from him, neither could I.

He was fearless, strong, cunning, intelligent, handsome and seductive. He furiously fought anything, anywhere, anytime! Going forward, I would intermittently see the unnatural strength and what it meant.

NEEDLESS TO SAY, FEAR HAD SEIZED ME AND I BELIEVED THAT I WAS TRAPPED FOREVER.

Furthermore, I was about to discover that he was leading a secret life.

He loaded his guitar in the 1957 Chevy and told Mom that he was going up north for a visit. Mom replied, "Okay, we'll see you when you get back." Oh no! That was not going to be how that went down! He quickly set Mom straight! I would be going with him! He threw a few loose items of clothing in the back seat and commanded me to get in the car. (Most people would have used a suitcase. I guess we would have also had we owned one.) I will never forget the look on Mom's face while she watched our car pull out of the driveway. I knew she felt as though she would never see me again.

I learned that his mother and other family members lived in a northern state. His parents were divorced. He told me that his Dad had been a violent man because of being stressed in the Navy. We visited all of them. However, in my wildest dreams, I could not have anticipated that our first stop would be at his *girlfriend's* apartment! His girlfriend? Shocked, I discovered that she had been pregnant with his child and had just delivered! Hello!

He was so smug as he introduced me to her. "This is my new wife," he announced, as if she was were supposed to accept that as a *good* thing. At first, she seemed to be in shock. Then she quickly glanced at me with pity. It was as if she wanted to help me in some way, but her expression clearly stated that she had no clue how. I knew she wanted to warn me of the type of man he was. Obviously, she was also afraid of him and was trying to *only* say whatever she had to say to keep him from exploding.

My shell of a mind had been solely occupied with avoiding his rages and wondering what might be coming next, but this new discovery was a different kind of curve ball. Not only had this stranger of a *husband* suddenly taken me as his child bride property, he also simultaneously had a girlfriend and a baby!

I realized I had never asked him any questions. How dare I question him! He didn't answer to anybody! I was afraid to talk to him, never sure what might set off one of his rampages. I spent most of my time placating him and trying to keep him busy singing. He thrived on receiving praises for his talent and I liked having his hands around the guitar neck instead of around my neck.

Back in the car, he acted as though nothing had happened. To him, it was no big deal that we had just left his girlfriend's house! Stunned, I sat quietly in the car like a statue. He bragged on and on about how there was a lot of Mafia there and that he had gotten away with fighting someone and had put out his eye. I don't know if all that was true, but knowing his true character, I didn't doubt it.

Sitting there trying to tune him out, I reflected on the prior drive to his girlfriend's apartment. I recalled how he had given me my marching orders to stay in *my place* and be nice to her. I remembered him telling me that I should be grateful just to be with him. He told me that I should be happy to meet her and his new baby and that I could never hold a candle to her. "She is smart and beautiful."

My replay of recent events was interrupted as I realized that he was still rambling on about various things. As usual, much of what he said was for the sole purpose of putting me down. He said, "My girlfriend is smarter than you. See why I couldn't let you stay in school. You're not smart enough to attend school here in the north either. You're a stupid southerner."

I tried to block out his cruel words. I wanted to block out everything, but my mind wandered back again to the visit. I had politely obeyed his instructions. He seemed quite content to simultaneously have a girlfriend and a wife living far apart in different states. At least I *hoped* we would be living in different states! Oh, how I wanted to go home! How I yearned for my Mom that day!

We drove on around his old hometown and visited the remainder of his family. We mostly stayed at his mother's apartment. He sternly impressed upon me how she was the perfect housekeeper and there was no dirt anywhere in *her* home. In his mind, she was the only person who knew how to *properly* cook and clean. Of course, I was perfectly capable of doing the same things when he would allow me out of his clutches long enough to do them.

I got little glimpses of joy during the short walks to the local deli. There, I had the best Philly Steak sandwich that I had ever eaten! Northerners really do know how to make a great Philly steak sandwich and amazing pizza.

I can still see that old store. I liked the hefty guy wearing a white apron. He talked with a strange accent. I liked his laughter. He seemed happy while cutting the gorgeous deli meats! I can still smell that atmosphere. It was a wonderful place. I wanted to hide in the store, but I knew *husband* would find me. My daydreaming was interrupted by the thought that I better get back soon so I wouldn't be in trouble. After all, it was a *privilege* for me to carry the gallon of milk back to his Mom. I was supposed to be *making myself useful.*

Surprise again! After another short drive, I was introduced to yet another woman who was approximately his age. He described her as the only woman he ever truly loved or ever would truly love. (Nice to hear.) I discovered that he was the father of her school age daughter. He had lived with this woman before he met his other girlfriend.

The next day, he suddenly decided to drive us back to our southern home. He muttered something about dirty cops up north. I had no idea what that meant. All I cared about was getting back home to see my Mom! The whole time we were away, I couldn't call home. Cell phones were not yet commonplace. Her landline phone service had been disconnected due to lack of funds. If she had owned a working telephone, I don't think he would have allowed me to call. I was distressed because I knew that Mom worried about me the entire time I was gone. I had never been that far from home. To make matters worse, I was with an unpredictable husband while feeling like a stranger to everyone else.

By the way, here's a quick funny story. Many years later, Mom got a cell phone. She called it a *celephone*. So funny! You must agree that *celephone* sounds like telephone. This is such a sweet memory. I love that she called it that. I wonder how she would pronounce an iPhone? i-lephone? It makes perfect sense to me! No matter how we pronounce it, Mom and I had no phone communication. I couldn't tell her that I was on my way home. Maybe it was for the best that she didn't know that I was traveling in bad weather. She would have worried all the more.

Indeed, we got caught in a severe snowstorm on the interstate. The visibility was less than one car length. The bumper to bumper traffic slowed to a standstill. We were stuck most of the night on the snow and sleet covered road, but I was thankful we had not slid off the road or worse.

The car engine was turned off to conserve gas. Of course, without the heater and only wearing a thin coat, I was freezing. Why did I bother to look in the back seat? I already knew there were no luxuries like snacks. I could see my cold breath, but no blankets! My freezing hands grabbed the clothes that were piled in the back and I piled them on myself. I buried my face and silently prayed. He finally started the car again. The engine was on only long enough to break the ice forming on the windshield and what felt like my bones. He didn't seem bothered at all that I was freezing. In fact, he seemed to enjoy watching me suffer.

Amazingly, the car did not run out of gas before the road cleared. In fact, I don't remember ever pulling into a gas station. I smile as I recall my prayer! After an endless night on our long journey, we finally arrived home! The car door slammed. The window curtain opened. I saw my Mother's sweet face again!

Chapter 5

FIRST GLIMPSES OF THE DEEPER EVIL

AFTER SEEING MOM'S BREATH OF RELIEF, I FELL into bed under many blankets. While waiting to get warm enough to fall asleep, I reflected on how worried Mom must have been and all that had transpired on our journey.

Late morning light was warm and welcomed. Almost awake, I wondered if I should open my eyes. Had it all been a dream? Did he actually have a dual life in the northern state? Did I actually meet his other women, new baby and other child? If I keep my eyes closed, will it all go away?

IF I OPEN MY EYES, CAN I HAVE A DIFFERENT LIFE?

Fully awake now, I was glad to be home. Unfortunately, this would be a *brief* moment of relief. He seemed eerily and eagerly anticipating something. That afternoon he said, "Get in the car. We're going to see a movie." This was a new happening. Where did he get the money for a movie? Obviously, we had no money for food or hotel along the treacherous journey back home last night. Anyway, the popular movie at the time was "The Exorcist". He could not wait to go see it! I had never seen him so excited.

I meekly told him that I preferred not to see the movie, but for him to go without me. He became enraged and reminded me that I am always to do exactly as told! He grabbed me and forced me into the car and off to the theater we went.

Unlike many people, I never found it *entertaining* to watch horror movies, much less ones dealing with spiritual darkness. Some people think that feeding our minds with such material is harmless, but we should take notice what the eye sees and the ear hears. We become what we eat. You don't have to take my word for it. Observe the lifestyles of those living in chaos versus the lifestyles of those who steward their environment. Light has no fellowship with darkness. Violence feeds on violence. Pretty soon, the hunger for it becomes stronger. Evil is not a topic to glorify, take lightly or to be entertained. Certainly, of all the movies ever made, I absolutely did not want to see *that* one!

Our car screeched to a halt in front of the theater. He jerked open the car door and jerked me out, squeezing my arm while pushing me inside the theater.

I figured my only escape from the movie would be to sit there with my eyes closed and my fingers in my ears. It was no use! The theater's sound system seemed to be at its max volume. The sound attached to the unknown seemed worse than not seeing it. Still, I did everything I could not to see or hear.

I was so traumatized by that movie that I didn't sleep at all for three nights. The third night we were lying in bed in the dim light of the kerosene lamp. Of course, our electricity had been turned off since the bill was not paid. The lamp light suddenly blew out, without a breeze and for no reason. Simultaneously, similar to the scene in the movie, a noise came from the attic sounding like rats scratching the floor. Sensing my fear, *husband* began laughing a maniacal laugh! I had never heard laughing exactly like that before, not even from him! (I knew what the Bible said about such things, but I would not fully understand this until thirty-four years later.)

The voices coming out of him were non-human and evil. I couldn't take it anymore. Some inner strength rose up from deep inside me and I screamed, "Who are you??!!" At that, his evil laughter continued even louder. He was full of glee that he had struck such terror in me. He replied, "Legions."

Chapter 6

BRIEF ESCAPE

WOULD PEACEFUL SLEEP EVER COME TO ME again? Can humans go this long without sleeping? For many years that movie and his reaction haunted me. One day, then another went by; simply existing. There were the strangers that he beat up in the bars. There were those whose homes he broke into just for fun. He broke in to terrorize someone he apparently knew from his mysterious past. They were indeed so afraid of him that they never pressed charges.

His friends were seduced by his charm. That reminds me of going to a swimming party at the pond. He threw his wedding ring in and bragged about his ability to stay under the water for long periods of time and find things. In his usual *ring leader* style, he took charge of the crowd and told them all to place their bets. I knew that he was not accustomed to losing and that he would make sure he won. After showing off by staying under the water, for what seemed like forever, he popped up. He proudly held up his closed fist and *claimed* that he had found the ring. Then he whispered to me that he did not find it. He collected his money by deceit and they all continued drinking alcohol and swimming. However, I had never learned to swim. My parents were afraid of water and never let us near the river.

The next thing I knew, he threw *me* in the pond as he said, "Sink or swim!" The last thing I remembered was sheer terror, then darkness, then lying in the mud spitting, sputtering and gasping for breath. I knew he dragged me out for only one reason. There were witnesses to what he did to me.

My worst night, so far, came following a series of rampages. We were visiting the young drummer boy, whose dad was not at home. We sat up late in his living room watching the Johnny Carson Show. I was sitting on the couch barefoot. *Husband* reached over and began bending my toes backwards. At first he bent them slowly, but then kept going!

I tried to ignore that this was actually happening. I realized that it had been unusually peaceful so far this night.

IT SEEMED AS IF HIS CRAVING TO WREAK HAVOC WAS BUILDING, AND HIS NEED TO INDUCE TORTURE MUST BE FED.

With all that was within me, I tried to rise above the pain as if nothing was happening. My toes were screaming, but I dared not scream! I tried my best to *sound* cheerful through my clenched teeth. I squeaked, "Please play the guitar and sing for us." This survival tactic to distract him didn't work.

He kept on bending my toes backward until I felt they would completely break. I wept silently in severe pain! There it was! My display of tears gave him an *excuse* to completely explode and unleash his fury on me! After all, I had called attention to his behavior. I surely thought that he was going to kill me!

Across the room the boy looked horrified. He jumped up and ran out of the house. *Husband* was occupied beating me with his fists and dragging me by my hair all around the large living room. He periodically choked me during this violent rage. (During that time I was unaware that the boy had fled next door and called the police.)

Suddenly, *husband* realized the boy had left the room, but not wanting to be interrupted, he dragged me outside and continued the merciless beating in the driveway! All the while, wild eyed, he frantically looked around the yard for the boy.

Through my already swollen eyes, I could see two police cars slide sideways into the driveway. Four strong cops sprang out of their cars and ran toward us. They shouted, "Let her go! You're under arrest!" For a split second hope sparked in me, but he threw me down hard on the concrete drive. Then with all his force and fury, he ran *toward* the policemen! He fought all of them simultaneously! He took the gun away from one of the cops and threw it in the bushes! Somehow another cop got loose from him, ran to his squad car and called for more backup.

Then, out of nowhere, the boy's dad appeared. He grabbed me and ran with me through the tree line across to his neighbor's yard. One of the back up cops quickly pushed us both inside his police car. I don't remember actually riding in the car. I don't know if I was in total shock or if I fainted. I don't recall entering the hospital emergency room, but I have a fleeting memory of the doctor examining my bruised neck and face and taking photos.

The next thing I remember was waking up at my Dad's house. Dad gently handed me a plate of fried eggs and a cup of coffee. He said, "You're safe now. Just rest." His face reflected all the emotions a father would have looking at his daughter's battered body. My face let him know that I was still in a daze. He gave me some time, and later explained that he and the boy's dad had pressed charges and my abuser was in jail. Soon, he was prosecuted and sent to prison.

Chapter 7

ANOTHER PHONE CALL

I DIDN'T KNOW HOW MUCH TIME HAD PASSED. I had lost sense of reality and was just a shell of a person. The memory lapses were a reprieve following the concussion and emotional trauma. Dad handing me that plate of fried eggs was also a gift. That sweet taste of *normal* life took me back to the days of childhood when Dad often made us breakfast. Could this really be happening now? Was I really in my Dad's house feeling safe like his kid again? In that moment, I wished that I could just start over. In reality, it *was* my chance. Too bad I didn't take it!

The phone rang. I jumped with a startle! It was like something shifted in the atmosphere. Oh how I wish I had never answered the phone! What would my life have been like had I just let that phone keep on ringing?

Husband was calling from prison. It was *him!* Right away, without pausing, he began a litany of saying how sorry he was...that he didn't know what he was doing that night he hurt me so badly...that he'd had a lot of time to think about it since being in prison almost three months. He said, "I've changed."

My mind could hardly comprehend what was happening. *I felt like the person that I used to be was far away and in a nonexistent place.* I felt insignificant and without a choice.

Did he just say that he had been away almost three months? I had been in a prison of my own, but without bars. Time and normalcy were foreign to me. I never looked at a calendar back then. Time was marked by each new sunrise; I survived another day.

Anyway, *husband* continued speaking in rapid fire. I've had time to realize how awful I was and how badly I hurt you. I'm so so sorry." He began to cry profusely and explained that he had been in the prison's counseling programs and that he had learned to control his anger.

HE SAID, "I'LL NEVER HURT YOU AGAIN."

Never happen again. How many times would I hear that? If only I had been older and wiser! If only I had been in my right mind! If only I had *not pitied* him! If only I had not been under his spell. If only I had NOT ANSWERED THE PHONE! I hung up the phone and the look on my Dad's face *should* have been all I needed to know. I should have known what dad knew, that a snake does not change its stripes. Snakes never do! I fell under the seduction of the deceiver's cunning

43

words. I believed the lie and what *sounded* like a repentant heart. He would be released from his prison and my prison would continue.

Chapter 8

ANOTHER THREE MONTHS

NEXT THING I KNEW, HE CAME TO **GET** ME. Dad didn't know what to do. I regret with all my heart worrying him by leaving that day. I knew one thing; husband's asking me to come with him was not really a *request*. It was a *command*. Had I not gone, I don't know what would've happened. I didn't want him to hurt my Dad. You might be thinking that if he had hurt my father he would've been slammed right back into prison. However, both Dad and I would've been dead before the police could have gotten to us. Dad's home was far from town so we never saw a police car pass by our area.

Obviously, at age sixteen, I was not sound minded. *I remained under the influence of the con artist's inner evil.* You may be thinking that *husband* was a sick man who could not help his behavior and that he needed psychiatric care. There are many psychiatric diagnoses for his behavior as I am also somewhat formally educated in that arena. However, many people witnessed his skilled ability to control his manipulative behavior in order to keep himself out of trouble. He could turn it on and off at the drop of a dime. Depending on the circumstance, he could be anything he needed to be. At any time, he could navigate the system and influence other people. There are human definitions for lots of things, but God has definitions for things as well.

After his short prison stay, I found myself back under his strong grip and ever watchful eye. He plopped me down in a field that was grown up with underbrush. This property was only a few miles down the road from Dad's house. As we walked through the field, I noticed that the *sweet repentant voice* I had heard from the prison phone was no longer present! He was no longer *pleading*. Nothing had really changed.

At the bottom of the field, sat an isolated one room shack. Apparently, this was home and we were squatters. I don't remember taking any supplies from the old car that he had somehow obtained. Of course not! We didn't have any earthly belongings. We had no jobs and no means to an end.

I stepped up through the spiderwebs onto the dilapidated wooden step and creaked open the slab door. At the moment, it didn't matter about the gaps between its rough boards. The weather was warm *that* day. I liked the sunlight streaking through the door. It didn't matter that the door had no lock. After all, the enemy had just stepped inside with me. My least concern was for *outside* threats.

Once inside, I carefully walked across the creaky floor and noticed the weeds growing up between the planks. The only furniture was an old moldy mattress on the floor and a sawed-off tree stump for a stool. Looking up, I saw a large beam of sunlight shining through the gap between the exposed rusty tin roof and the timber frame. The rough boards were loosely connected and served as the shack's walls.

Just then, a bird flew into the room through the gap in the roof! Startled by us, the bird flew around wildly then flew out through the already open back door. Beyond the bird's escape door was the forest that was thickly twisted with underbrush.

Years later while watching the movie, *Forrest Gump*, I was reminded of this scenario. I identified with what Jenny said, "Dear God, make me a bird. So I can fly far. Far, far away from here."

The woods would prove to be a goldmine of resources for me. From time to time, I crouched down and hid within its thick hiding places. Soon, I would search through it for huckleberries. Mmm, huckleberries! Those were a great delight after two weeks of not having any other food.

One day, I discovered a two-pack of saltine crackers that had fallen through the wide crack between the planks of the floor. No doubt the crackers had been there for years or perhaps an angel had just left them for me. I carefully fished out the packet up through the crack taking care not to crumble the crackers. Just as I took a bite of one cracker, *husband* suddenly appeared out of nowhere, grabbed the other cracker, ate it and slapped me!

Inside the old abandoned shack was a wood burning fireplace made of old hand-stacked stone. It was full of old ashes and spiderwebs as if someone had suddenly fled, never to return. The fireplace proved to be an important resource, as well as a source of pain.

Winter had arrived. Lying on the old musty floor mattress, my sleep was interrupted by his shouting, "Wake up and go get some firewood!" He rolled over in bed and I stumbled out in the moonlight to find dead sticks and pieces of logs from my beloved forest. Back inside, the fireplace provided warmth and light.

Of course, there was no electricity. Not a big deal. I had grown up learning to manage without it from time to time. There was no indoor plumbing in the shack, but neither had there been in my childhood home. I was already accustomed to going into the woods, which provided privacy for elimination and leaves for sanitation. There was no indoor water for bathing and no luxuries such as a washing machine. No problem, I found a creek of water that ran through *my* woods.

There was no cook-stove, but there wasn't any food to cook anyway. Oh wait a minute! One day a bag of dried pinto beans appeared. I do not know from whence they came! I excitedly found an old bucket by the back door which was perfect for bringing water from the creek to the house. I poured the water in the old cast iron pot that I found sitting in the corner of the fire-place. In no time at all those beans were boiling! Soon, the house smelled of real food!

However, that dear old fireplace betrayed me because the fire could not be regulated. Flames were high and hot. In my haste to eat, I failed to move the pot to the edge of the flames for the beans to cook more slowly. I couldn't stay close by to constantly stir the beans because he kept yelling for me to go fetch more firewood.

Needless to say, when I walked back in the shack with my arms full of wood, I was met with the smell of burnt beans and fist blows to my face. This beating continued until he threw me across the house, landing me almost in the fireplace. He shouted all the while about how stupid I was that I couldn't cook beans without burning them and now we would starve again!

Surprisingly, a few days later, Dad came in the door! I had not had a visitor since the bird and I had not seen Dad since leaving his house. I was so happy to see him, but hurt to see his pain upon finding me *yet again* in such a bind. How it must have tormented him, but his hands were tied the day I walked away from the refuge of his shelter. I imagine our heavenly Father feeling the same way when His kids walk away from His shelter.

One day, my oldest brother appeared unexpectedly. When he staggered out of the car that had just slid side-ways at the top of the field, I knew he was drunk. This was not going to go well. He had come to rescue me. Yes, he had a very tender heart, especially toward me.

He staggered down the field to where we were standing. There was an ax wedged atop the wood-splitting stump. He began cursing at *husband* calling him a "wife beater" and that he should pick on someone his own size. In horror, I ran between them as *husband* reached for the ax handle. Crying and screaming, I begged my brother to go home! I worried that he could be killed at any moment.

It's amazing how one can scream and silently pray at the same time! The screaming didn't help anything, but the prayer worked great! Suddenly, *husband's* face and posture changed and he curiously started laughing and making fun of my brother! I was in disbelief as he let go of the ax handle and rolled on the ground laughing. I convinced my brother that I was okay, thanked him profusely for trying to save me, and urged him to quickly go home. Thankfully, that prayer was also answered. He reluctantly went home.

Normally, I was not allowed to leave the shack. Dad came by just long enough to miraculously drop off a wood cookstove! I didn't know how this would actually help me since we had no actual food. However, I was thrilled to have the stove and hopefully I could manage it better than the fireplace! This was no *ordinary* stove. *This* was a gift from my beloved friend, Nannie.

As a very young child, I had watched her cook many meals on that stove. Her elderly arms brushed by her vintage apron as she pulled biscuits from the oven. She put wood into the other side to keep the fire burning. I can still see her wipe the sweat from her brow. Although she was hot and tired, her kind brown eyes sparkled. The corners of her mouth always seemed to be smiling. I wanted to be just like her. She was kind and peaceful no matter what.

When I was sick, she prepared an onion and sulfa home remedy in that stove's oven. She split the onion in half and placed a snuff spoon of sulfa powder in the center of one half. The halves were placed back together and wrapped with a wet cheesecloth. Then, she baked it until the onion softened and absorbed the sulfa. Next, she squeezed its juice into a clean snuff glass and wiped her hands on her apron. She turned her tender face to me and handed me the *medicine* to drink. Perfect for bronchitis! No doubt, you can see why that cook stove was a treasured gift from her. That was a fine day when Dad brought it to me at the shack.

The sloped field of underbrush between the front of the shack and the road seemed to separate me from the outside world. On this day, it was aglow with fire. In the distance, through the smoke, I detected my Mother walking towards me. I didn't know how she knew where to find me or how she knew we needed help at that moment. *Husband* kept me in isolation and we had no phone. Although my parents were divorced, I guess Dad told Mom and my brother where I was living. I was just so happy she came!

The only other recent visitors were his friends that occasionally brought him beer. *Husband* had decided that we were going to clear the field and plant a garden.

How? I wasn't sure because we had no seeds. Although beer was a sustaining nutrient for *him*, I was pretty sure that we could not plant that in the ground and have beans and potatoes sprout! Anyway, he had found a rusty hoe with a broken handle. With the hoe in one hand and a match in the other, he set fire to the field to clear the brush.

As Mom came walking down the field, she could see me falling and spilling my buckets of water. The fire was getting out of hand. I thought I was dizzy and fainting because I was weak from being malnourished. As Mom got closer, she could see him kicking me! He was yelling for me to get up and keep the water coming! Although less physically capable of fighting than my brother, Mom rounded her little shoulders like a banty rooster and ran toward him! She screamed, "Leave her alone! Can't you see she's sick?"

Her intervention frightened me. I figured this would make matters worse. Normally, if anyone challenged him, he would beat me all the more. On this occasion, I was too weak to pray in my mind or with my mouth, but God heard the prayer of my heart! Suddenly, *husband* backed off as if some unseen force had pushed him!

He jerked up the empty water buckets that were lying sideways on the ground and stomped off to get more water. He realized that the whole mountain was about to catch fire unless he got control of it. I realized that God had intervened on my behalf. The power inside my Mom screamed louder than the power inside my abuser!

Mom poured water on my face and made me drink some. I tried to walk again, but was too weak and dizzy. She lifted my chin, looked into my eyes and said, "You're pregnant!" I was stunned by what she said and all that had just happened.

Getting pregnant was never on my radar. My daily focus had been to please him in order to survive. Mom took me into the house and told me to stay there. Feverishly working, they got the brush fire under control. Clearly, my life was out of control.

Having seen smoke, a passersby stopped his car at the top of the field. They handed *husband* a cold beer and tarried to shoot the breeze. While he was distracted by them, Mom put me in her car and took me to the County Health Department.

I already felt better, just riding in the car with her. She told me we could go to the Health Department without money or insurance. Oh yes, even if birth control had crossed my almost sixteen year old mind, I had no access to it. There was no gas money to go anywhere and if there was, he certainly would not waste it on my needs.

Indeed, it had been a long time since I scrounged for old rags to use in lieu of the nice store-purchased sanitary napkins. This may sound blunt and foreign to the modern mind. However, it was a reality for me. Mom and Grandma sometimes had to resort to the same available resources. So did a lot women before modern conveniences were invented or afforded.

This reminds me that Jesus washed away our sins and made us clean. In antiquity, women were considered unclean during their menstrual cycles. Prior to Jesus sanctifying us, this scripture referenced the state of mankind before redemption: "But we are all as an unclean thing and all **our** righteousnesses are as **filthy rags** and we all do fade as a leaf and our iniquities, like the wind, have taken us away" (Isaiah 64:6, bold emphasis mine). Thankfully, in this current age of grace, we understand that it is not *our* righteousness that makes us clean, but it is the *Lord's* righteousness!

Mom and I arrived at the Health Department. The nurse asked me to provide a urine sample. This took a while because I was dehydrated. Finally the doctor walked in with a judgmental look on his face, as the nurse rolled a framed white curtain screen between Mom and me. He examined me, which was altogether a new experience! It turned out that Mom was correct. I was three months pregnant!

I placed my hands on my belly and smiled. I'm going to have a baby! The world stood still as I imagined little baby fingers and little baby toes. For a moment, I felt like a normal person. I had purpose. I would have a baby to love who would also love me. Love was coming! Being an expectant mother is such a privilege and responsibility. My happiness quickly turned into concern as I realized the struggles my baby might endure. I remembered my situation. Why had I answered that phone three months ago? What next?

Chapter 9

WHERE ARE WE GOING?

BACK HOME, HE CURSED ME FOR GETTING pregnant. He shouted, "Now what are we gonna do? How could you have been so stupid?" After beating me and kicking me in the stomach, he fell across the musty old floor mattress that I blamed for my predicament. He miraculously fell asleep, thereby ending the beating.

Months went by. Life in the shack had not changed, but a *new life* was growing inside me. I continued to carry wood and water and scrounge for food in the woods. One night, *husband* disappeared. He returned late the next afternoon saying he had gone to play music at a bar and had fun with a woman that was much prettier than me.

Apparently, he earned some gas money by singing at the bar. "Get in the car!" he said. Just like that! Late in the last month of my pregnancy, away we drove. Where, why, or for how long, I did not know.

We drove for awhile, then ran out of gas and started walking. The September night was cool and dark. It was difficult for me to walk long distances during the late stage of my pregnancy. I finally asked him how far he thought we had walked. He said, "Almost ten miles, I guess." A tobacco barn came into view. We went inside and slept on the dirt floor until daylight.

We walked a little farther, and a farmhouse came into view. Surprisingly, the folks invited us inside their home. I have no idea what story he told them and I don't remember their names, but they were nice and they had food!

That night, I enjoyed sleeping in a real bed. Suddenly, I awoke in pain and it was not from being beaten. This time, the pain came from my belly and the surges of cramps wrapped my midsection. Fully awake now, I wondered if this meant my baby was coming! Back then, I didn't know anything about pregnancy, labor, or delivery. I didn't know what to expect or what to do.

Apparently the woman who had allowed us to stay in her home the previous night had realized I was actually in labor. She told her husband to take a can of gas out to our stranded car so *husband* could take me to the hospital. It was a good thing she knew what to do.

Seemingly annoyed, *husband* drove me to the hospital without exchanging any words. Focused on what was happening to my body and trying not to *bother him*, I remained as quiet as possible. After a long drive, he pulled up to the front of the hospital and told me to get out of the car. He drove away.

Someone saw me just standing there outside the hospital door and took me to the Labor and Delivery Department. I'm sure a clerk asked me for insurance information and our address. We certainly didn't have health insurance, but I was much too focused on labor to be embarrassed. I didn't know how to explain to her that we had lived as squatters in a shack that didn't have a mailbox. Agh! And now we really didn't live anywhere!

My next memory was the nurse asking me if I would weigh a hundred pounds soaking wet! She instructed me to step up on the hospital scales, which rattled as she slid the silver weights across the black metal bar. Through eyes of pity, she peered toward the numbers. It turned out that I weighed *exactly that*!

"Nine months pregnant, weighing in at
one hundred pounds!"

At that point, I became frightened because she obviously thought my weight was a bad thing, and I wondered if my baby would be okay. I realized that we had starved for most of my pregnancy. Here I was at the hospital for the first time ever. They wouldn't let me drink anything. Hour after hour I begged the nurses for water, but they always refused. After I vomited, they handed me a little red cup. Without looking, I gulped it down with glee! The nurse squealed, "That was mouthwash!" With joy I replied,"It was wet!"

Labor was very long. The sun went up and came down and went up and came down again. The hands on the clock seemed to go around and around forever as I lay there alone. I didn't know how long normal labors should take. I was in a teaching hospital so a lot of students examined me. They asked me tons of questions. Apparently because of my age, weight and apparent social situation, I was a *person of interest.*

They formed a huddle across the room and discussed my case. I could hear their concerns. They decided to put a needle in my back with medicine to *help me.* However, by that time I was almost finished with the transition stage and it was time to push. That medicine was placed too late and was of no use to me.

I pushed for a long time, but I liked pushing better than the part that came before it! I got tired and the next thing I remember was the *salad tongs* and a shout, "It's a boy!" They handed him to me with a bruise on his forehead. I thought he was the most beautiful thick black haired precious baby I had ever seen! My heart melted into a place that only a mother understands.

Despite my being malnourished, my son came out weighing six pounds and healthy! He had a common condition they called yellow jaundice, but the nurse told me not to worry; he would simply be kept under a bilirubin light for a few days.

Now what? I was still alone. I didn't know how Mother found out I was in the hospital with a new baby, but she called me. She didn't have money for gas to come see me and grandson. She said that Dad had been informed, but he couldn't come. My heart was broken. I felt so alone, yet I was glad that *husband* was not there. Labor had been intense, but not as intense as all the things he had put me through. Where was he anyway? I didn't know. I hoped I would never see him again.

The nurse brought my bundle of joy back in my room after giving him his first sponge bath. I was not alone! I had my very own beautiful Son! Before my smile could fully form, *husband* suddenly stormed through the door and barked, "Time to go!" He grabbed himself some of my water and without looking at me asked, "Does he have yellow jaundice? If he doesn't, I'll know he's not *my* kid. All my kids were born with it!" Before he could get all those words out, the nurse marched in behind him! She gave him a hard glare and sternly said, "Fine! She can be released, but the baby has to stay three days under the bilirubin light!"

So there! Confirmed! He had *yellow jaundice* and *husband* was smug about that. I was devastated. Devastated that I was given no choice, but to leave the hospital without my baby! The nurse assured me that my son would be fine, but I didn't want to leave at all. Was there any other way? So much uncertainty! Would *husband* bring me back to get him?

Chapter 10

MOTHERHOOD, WOMANHOOD

WATCHING THE HOSPITAL DISAPPEAR IN THE rear view mirror was the hardest thing I had endured so far. I silently begged God to watch over my baby and get me back there to get him. I rode silently in the car while *husband* bragged about sleeping with some woman while I was in the hospital having his baby. He muttered something about finding us a place to live. I tuned out his ramblings. My only thoughts were about my son and how much I already missed holding him in my arms!

My thoughts were interrupted by the jerking of the car brakes. I realized we were back at that farmhouse where the folks had let us sleep the night that I went into labor. The lady let me call the hospital every day to see how my son was doing. I was thankful to be able to call, but I really wanted to hold him every day. The fact that I wasn't allowed to stay hospitalized with my baby was gut wrenching.

Finally! The three days ended and the nurse said that I could come get my son! (A lot can happen in three days: Can you imagine the torment Mary endured watching her Son be crucified!? Then imagine her elation as she learned her Son had risen from the dead three days later! I also think about our heavenly Father *waiting* until His Son rose to life!) I was thankful on so many levels!

My son was back in my arms! My breast milk had come in and both of us were *relieved.* Breastfeeding is a rewarding privilege and a brilliant design. I'm glad I was born a woman. Watching the contentment on the face of a nursing baby is priceless. It truly is *priceless* and I was thankful that I didn't have to rely on purchasing milk from a store. We had no money for that.

Breast milk is the perfect temperature and always ready! God is an amazing provider! It saddens me how certain periods of culture have robbed women's ease and confidence in a perfectly natural way of life. The absence of woman-to-woman teachings regarding this practice has left many new moms feeling like failures. Within a few days, many moms have given up. Sure, like anything in life, some issues can happen. Mastitis is one challenge, but women have dealt with that since Eve. Nowadays, there's a wealth of resources and support from fellow moms and professionals to help overcome problems, but many new moms give up immediately.

Breastfeeding is designed to be successful as well as ultimately enjoyable. Words of failure are not helpful. For example, many new mothers have been tricked into thinking they didn't produce enough milk. Nipple soreness is indeed a *tough* experience, but hang in there because the nipples *will* toughen after a few weeks. Smooth sailing may seem far-fetched, but trust me, it will come.

Many women have never had anyone properly explain the *let down* reflex. This is a *mind-body* phenomenon where the milk drops down through the milk ducts to the baby. This process is hindered if the mom has not been shown *how* to relax and *have her mind tell her breasts* to release the milk. Sometimes this happens naturally on its own, especially if mom is relaxed. Other times, it can seem like an impossible task if we make it more difficult than it truly is. Not everyone struggles with it, but some do. In this modern age, *instincts* have been unused and replaced with artificial alternatives and societal misconceptions.

IT SADDENS ME WHEN THE *BRIDGE OF KNOWLEDGE* FROM GENERATION TO GENERATION IS LOST.

A disconnect occurs when young ladies resist the wisdom and experience of our foremothers.

I was thankful that my mom taught me by example that breastfeeding is simply what women do. It was as common as breathing and there were never any discussions between the women I knew. They simply did it. In my situation, I couldn't accept failure. My baby had to survive.

Our minds can tell our bodies to slow down our breathing. Our minds tell our legs to walk. Likewise, our minds can tell us to relax, focus on visualizing and imagining a sensation of milk coming down toward the spout (nipple), just like pouring milk out of a jug. It's not an arduous feat. Simply look at your tiny baby and realize how beautiful you are as you supply life-giving nourishment. The let-down-reflex happens as you do that. Decide not to allow your baby's impatient crying make you anxious. Think of the crying as simply *signaling* the milk to come.

Another challenge is helping the baby latch on. Moms and babies can be taught how to properly place the nipple in the baby's mouth so baby can obtain the milk and not have the nipple in painful positions. Sometimes this is as natural as falling off a log backwards. Sometimes this seems impossible, but if we hang in there and don't give up, mother and baby will be successful and rewarded. My first few days breastfeeding were challenging, but survival kicked in and we were off to the races.

God designed females (humans and mammals) to breastfeed. He knows what He's doing. He's not going to create a faulty mechanism. Trust Him. Trust yourself. Trust your baby. God designed peace and joy. Anxiety is our enemy.

Bottle feeding is not being judged here. Whatever is chosen should be exactly tha*t, your choice.* There is no right or wrong method. I'm only saying, "Feed your baby however you choose, but don't give up on your preference simply because your joy *was stolen* by lies of inabilities. Words of failure are our enemy. What lies have we believed? You are beautifully created and fully equipped. We live and we learn. Keep moving. No regrets! Live free. Enjoy being a Mom. Do it your way, but also don't be afraid to accept help.

While we were guests at the farmhouse, I placed a box beside the bed where I could touch tiny baby while we slept. I put lots of blankets on him. Sleeping very lightly to protect him, I could hear the floor squeak. It was the lady of the house coming in, once again, to take some blankets off. Apparently, she thought he was too hot. I pretended to be asleep until she left the room, then covered him up again. My eyes closed gently.

Moments later, *husband* shouted, "Time to go!" Off we went! Where to, I did not know. After a bit we arrived back at the shack. He looked around for something. The shack was empty except for a few changes of clothing. I noticed that my wood cookstove from Nannie was gone! My only prized earthly possession was gone! It was really gone! He sold it while I was alone in the hospital having his child! No doubt it was sold for beer money for him and the other woman! He seemed different lately, as though he had some kind of plan in mind. "Get back in the car!" he growled. We would never come back to the shack.

Chapter 11

TO THE CITY

WE DROVE TO A SMALL CITY AND PARKED IN the driveway of a modest home. Looking out my car window, I was fixated on the beautiful tree to my right. Daydreaming for a moment, I wondered who lived there and why we had come.

My *happy-place-moment* was disturbed by the slamming of his car door. He shouted, "Come on!" I pulled my infant son higher into my arms and got out of the car. I noticed him fumbling with a key at the front door. That seemed odd. I wondered why he had a key to someone's home. Then he motioned for me to come inside and said, "We're living here now."

Inside, I saw a scene very different from the old shack. I couldn't believe my eyes! Although modest, it was nice and it was furnished. The mattresses were not on the floor! One bedroom actually had a crib! To this day, I've never heard of a *crib* being included in a rental home! The kitchen had a refrigerator and best of all, an *electric* stove! Guess what? There was electricity when I flipped on the light! However, there was no telephone. I couldn't let my Dad know where I was living.

I had no idea how *husband* had found the money to rent this place. Of course, I never dared to ask him questions. I kept my head down and stayed quiet. We settled in and I was beyond thankful for this house! It seemed he was more interested in the girls at the bars, and I got to rest while he went there.

At approximately two in the morning, he came home from the bar. The dreaded sound of his car engine woke me. I looked through the curtains just in time to see the two wheels hop the curb as the car screeched to a halt in front of the house. He slumped over in the front seat. I ran out to see what was going on and he croaked, "I've been shot!" He limped inside and told me to go to the neighbor's house and call an ambulance.

Back in the house, I saw the bullet hole at the top of his leg and the exit wound on his lower leg. I remember thinking that the shooter was a poor shot and should have aimed higher! I assumed the gun went off in a downward fashion during a scuffle. The wounds didn't look so bad from the outside, although they were bleeding. That was the first time I had ever seen *him* in pain. It was a different experience altogether.

When the ambulance arrived, they told me to get up front and off to the bigger city hospital we went. The bullet created more damage than suspected. During surgery hardware was placed in one of the lower leg bones. I'm sure there were issues of him *explaining* why he had a bullet in his leg. I have no idea what story he told them. I assumed that since he knew he was at fault that he feared things could get messy. No doubt, he told them some interesting tale. There was no legal follow-up. He was highly agitated while in the hospital. As usual, I was a target of his frustrations.

After getting back home from the hospital, he beat me up because I had ridden in the front of the ambulance the night they transported him to the hospital. He said that I should have ridden in the back with him and that he didn't like how the driver was *looking* at me. What? I had only followed official instructions. After all, I was accustomed to doing as I was told.

Later, a significant infection developed in his leg and the hardware had to be removed. His leg was slow to heal. Bone infections, indeed, often recur and can become chronic. He required crutches for a while and walked with a limp thereafter. He filed for disability and was approved. Although I'm not proud of that, it was a miracle blessing of provision for me and the family.

Chapter 12

SPEAKING OF FAMILY

A S MENTIONED EARLIER, HE HAD TAKEN ME to a northern state soon after we were married and introduced me to the surprise girlfriend and their baby. Little did I know that I was about to receive another surprise. "Get in the car!" he said. We drove across our town to someone's home. He got out and seemed to know the place. I saw a woman peep through the window and quickly jerk the curtain closed. He ran forward and banged on the door for a long time. Finally, the door creaked open with the chain still intact. He yelled for her to open the door and he yelled for me to come! Bewildered and frightened, I scrambled out of the car with my baby in my arms and teetered quickly toward the house. She saw me approaching and reluctantly opened her door. We stepped inside and found a four year old hiding behind her leg. *Husband* seemed to know the mother. By the look of fear in her eyes, she knew him also. She was his ex-wife.

He asked her, "Where are my other children?" Her eyes darted around as if she were hoping for some form of escape. She reluctantly replied, "The school bus will be here any minute." I quietly sat down trying to look invisible. Feeling like an imposter, I was in total shock—again! What would happen next? What would happen to her? What would happen to them? What would happen to me and my own baby?

My thoughts were interrupted by the sound of the squeaky school bus brakes. The kids filed into the house. They obviously didn't know what to say or do. Everyone was on eggshells—everyone *but him*.

He acted as if hanging out with them was supposed to be a normal thing, but his *attempts to interact* with the children were awkward. They obviously had not seen him in a long time and were very cautious around him. He made no show of violence, but their mom stared at her telephone as if everything within her wanted to call the police. Then, I saw him whisper something to her. She quickly sat down in submission with a forlorn look on her face that seemed to say, "It's over now." At that time, I could not foresee what would come.

He *told* her that we would visit again soon. I caught the piercing look in his eyes and the stance of his body as she leaned back away from him. He was not *requesting* an invitation! Then he told me to get in the car. We drove home in silence as if nothing had ever happened. As expected, I did not question him about anything. I quietly obeyed his commands and followed him around, catering to his every whim. We did go back for one more visit.

One day very soon after the second visit, I was out in the yard with my baby when his ex-wife drove up to the curb in an old station wagon. He seemed to be expecting her. He burst out of the house with purpose. With a commanding demeanor, he ran up and leaned into her car window. Simultaneously, all four of the children got out of the car and scurried across the yard toward the house. I looked back and husband's head was still in her car window. Then suddenly, she drove away!

Looking smug, he walked past the children and me, and went back into our house. The children looked on in horror as they watched their mother's car fade out of sight! Obviously shocked that their mother had not gotten out of the car with them, they soon realized that this was not just a *little visit.*

Chapter 13

SUDDENLY A MOTHER OF FIVE

I WAS BARELY PAST AGE SIXTEEN. I STOOD IN THE yard with my own baby on my hip and four children staring back at me. Tears began to flow, yet they seemed afraid to cry. We were all afraid to cry. Somehow, we all knew that we had to figure this out together. I crumbled to the ground and they all clung to me for dear life. As quickly as we could, we pulled ourselves together and sheepishly went inside.

In a moment of time their world had turned upside down, but his world seemed just fine. He just sat there and watched television ignoring all of us as if nothing had happened. I led the children into the kitchen to find them something to eat.

Over the next two years, the children and I developed a pattern of sticking together and staying out of his way. It broke my heart when they asked for their mother. I believed that wherever she was, if still alive, their Mom's heart was also breaking. Surely she had been given some sort of an ultimatum. We all had to survive.

He had short periods of time when he demonstrated affection and entertained us with his music. He could be nice when *he wanted* to be. The children and I tried to enjoy any pleasure we could find, although we never knew how long it would last. Without warning, his pattern always returned to violence.

One day he came home with a friend behind him pulling a horse trailer. He was in a good mood that day. Looking out the window, I could see him smiling as he sprang out of his car, quickly ran to the back of the trailer, and opened its door. Now mind you, we lived within city limits with a small fenced in backyard, but out popped a pony led by a rope!

Of course, the children were beside themselves with joy! They all ran to the backyard to see it. I was happy as well. I love horses. Unfortunately, this was no horse. Ponies are notorious for being temperamental and obstinate. Cute as it was, it was difficult to ride. Instantly, it bucked me off and really hurt my knee. Once again, brief pleasure turned to fear and pain.

He was mad at me because I *got* hurt. He slapped me around and told me to go inside. Once inside, I didn't know what the children were experiencing outside. Perhaps they were riding without problems or perhaps they were being made to *be tough and rule the pony*!

I had a very painful knee. Quickly, it became tightly swollen and filled with fluid. He came inside and stomped around the house looking for something. He muttered something about not seeking a doctor.

He rambled through the kitchen drawer and found a narrow pointy knife and inserted it into my knee! Blood-tinged fluid gushed out of my knee joint and tears gushed out of my eyes, but my screams of horror could not be released! No, sir! Screams would make him more upset. So I cried silently, hoping that he would do nothing else with that knife!

He wrapped my knee with a kitchen towel and tied it. The towel caught the remaining blood-tinged fluid that continued to drain. As soon as my knee was wrapped, I went back down the steep porch stairs and brought the youngest daughter inside to keep an eye on her while I cooked dinner.

Event after chaotic event was our lifestyle. He went to court for being involved in another episode of public violence. Afterward, he was ordered to see two counselors. The occupational counselor gave him an IQ test and told me that, "He scored high off the charts." He went on to say, "He can be anything he *wants* to be."

His psychologist told him that his children and I should not provoke him so he could stay calm. *Are you kidding me?* Some might say that he had a mental problem. Those who knew him well, understood that he was brutally mean and he enjoyed it. He actually could control his behavior when needed.

IN A COURT OF LAW, HE WAS CUNNING
AND SILVER-TONGUED.

He quoted scripture and made all feel as though he was the greatest man alive. Whatever came out of his mouth, people believed. Other women were also under his spell. At first, it was difficult for me to accept his affairs. However, his nights away became a welcomed relief for the children and me.

Being focused on raising the kids kept me sane, except for the insanity of trying to keep them safe. When he was away at night, I gathered them around the kitchen table and read the Bible to them. Then we talked about what we read. We prayed together and sang hymns. This strengthened and sustained us between and during his rampages.

At times, we heard him stomping through the house looking for us. His oldest daughter and I would crouch down in the kitchen in front of the oven and pray. We held onto each other and prayed the best we knew how. We expected answers and though times were rough and got rougher, God ultimately delivered us from the evil. Although we were very young, we knew deep down that good would overcome evil. However, the evil one wants us to doubt, get tired and give up. She and I never gave up and we never will.

We shared an extraordinary bond because we depended on each other. I was close to all the children, but the oldest daughter and I were not far apart in age and we took on the role of protecting the other children. The outside world had no clue, but we understood what we were up against. Life was fragile and precious and our love for each other was strong and deep. To this day, she calls me early on my birthday, Mother's Day and Christmas. She continues to call me Momma, which I hold as a sacred privilege! Of course, nobody could take the place of her biological mother, we all knew that. I simply did the best I could to care for them and they in turn took care of me. As terrible as our lives were, I'm privileged to have known these children and how they impacted my life forever.

Another night, another struggle. My baby son was sleeping in bed with me on this particular night. I had been very sick during the day with pain and weakness, but I didn't have a clue what was wrong. *Husband* was away at the bar and no doubt had spent the remainder of the night with some woman.

Suddenly, my baby began crying loudly, which awakened me and his oldest sister! She came running barefoot into my room to find me vomiting on the floor by the bed. She touched me and announced, "You're burning up hot!" Apparently, my fever was so high that my hot body had awakened the baby. At that point, I was not able to take care of anyone, including myself. Displaying wisdom beyond her years, daughter ran across the street to the elderly couple's home and called my mother. How did she know Mom's phone number? She was a child! I never gave it to her!

Mom came quickly. I remember her lifting my limp body and forcing me to drink water. Daylight came and as soon as business hours opened, Mom took me to the doctor. We took the baby with us and the oldest daughter watched the other children. *Husband* had not yet come home.

The very painful and expensive tests included a lighted camera inserted into my bladder. The doctor said, "The entire walls of your bladder are coated with infection. Also you have a *severe* kidney infection." The doctor told Mom that I was very sick and should be admitted to the hospital.

I told the doctor that I must go home, that I had no choice. Mom took the little money that she had and purchased my antibiotic. Unfortunately, I was allergic to it and had to stop taking it. Back home, *husband* was very mad and cursed Mother for taking me to the doctor. He yelled, "She's alright! We don't need no doctor!" I was sick for weeks, but received a miraculous healing. Under those circumstances, lacking the proper medical care, recovery otherwise would have been highly unlikely.

Chapter 14

DON'T POKE THE BEAR

HIS VIOLENT OUTBREAKS WERE AGAIN becoming more frequent. His mother had come from up north to visit us. One day, I was sitting on the couch as he snapped at a couple of the kids. His mother cautiously said something to him. Suddenly he swirled around, spread his arms wide and with cupped hands, slapped them together over my ears! For a moment, I couldn't hear anything! Then, through intense pain and loud ringing, I heard his muffled shouting. He yelled at his Mom, "Don't you tell me what I can't do to my kids!"

Then, he told the children to stand on their heads in front of the wall. His mother, the kids and I were horrified. Those poor children were lined up standing on their heads with their hands on the floor. Of course they grew tired and their heels would touch the wall. When they fell to the floor, he slapped them and shouted, "Stay on your heads until I release you!"

He kept glancing back at his Mom and me and laughed. He enjoyed the fact that he was ripping our hearts apart! He screeched, "Is THIS what you wanted?" She and I were mortified and wanted to take their places, but we knew better than to try anything because he would've hurt them more or do the unthinkable. Look what had already happened when she tried to stop him! Clearly, he was setting a precedent.

The sheer evil in his eyes told us never to report him or try going for help, or worse would happen. I sat there not able to hear very well except for the sharp ringing in my ears. I felt my heart was ripping into shreds watching those children and I prayed with all my might for God to help us. Help us he did! In the very next instant, *husband* curiously started yawning and went directly to bed. To our great relief, he stopped the madness, at least for that night.

Chapter 15

CAN'T TAKE IT ANYMORE!

THE RAGES WERE COMING MORE FREQUENTLY now. He was never satisfied. He told us that he could be a famous musician if he only had the chance. We all knew he truly was talented and that he could indeed be famous. We encouraged him to sing and told him that he would go far. Secretly, I hoped that he would go far, far away and stay away.

If he was not busy playing the guitar, he was busy playing the devil. While beating and choking me, his pattern was to command me to kiss him. He liked the tears. While tears streamed down my swollen face and lips, he would say, "I like salty kisses." During my despair and disgust, I secretly wondered if he would like it if I vomited in his mouth!

To complete his pattern, he went on and on about how sorry he was and that he would *never* do it again. Time after time, he cried pitifully. By the end of each of his charades, I ended up feeling sorry for him. *Imagine that!*

How could I fall for that over and over again?

During each new attack, he displayed enjoyment from tormenting and dragging me from one end of the house— and from one end of emotion— to the other.

The evil in his eyes had reached a new height. The beating and taunting this particular night seemed to go on forever. He intermittently straddled me and choked me. The choking sessions brought me near death. *This was his favorite form of torture because it left fewer bruises but instilled more fear.* He alternated that with the fist to the face and kicking me around the room. He screamed hatred and evil things that made no sense at all. At one moment, the oldest daughter peeked around the door, but for her safety, I gave her *the look* to signal her to go back to bed or hide.

He eerily glanced over at his crutches that he had been using since the time he had been shot in the leg. Then suddenly he ripped off all my clothing and knocked me down to the floor again. What he said next sent a fear though my spine worse than I could imagine and the thought of it still blows my mind!

Slammed against the cold living room floor, completely naked, I heard him wretchedly scream, "I'm going to ram this crutch all the way through your vagina up to your head!" Yes, he actually said those very words as he raised the crutch high in the air with a crazed look in his eyes! This was the height of all my fears so far. I knew he would surely do it! *I prayed fast and quick!* I prayed like I had never prayed before and, trust me, I've prayed lots of fervent prayers! Oddly, he threw the crutch down as if doing so surprised even him! He shook his head in confusion and stopped everything for a moment.

Then he dragged me up to a standing position and kept on punching me. As my body swirled around, he kicked me from behind. He kicked me again toward the front door and screamed, "Get out!" Had he actually said, "Get out?" I couldn't believe it!

I desperately *wanted* to go, but I thought this was another of his games. He liked to play games where he would say one thing, but mean another. Then he would beat me saying that I had not listened carefully to his orders. Therefore, I figured him telling me to leave was a *test* to see if I would actually try to escape only for him to drag me back inside and kill me for trying to leave. It's crazy how fast thoughts can fly through your mind during a life and death situation!

As I frantically pulled at the door to open it, I suddenly and ironically asked him for a towel. Normally, I never spoke to him at all during beatings. Even more ironic, a towel was lying across a chair by the door. (Looking back, why would a towel have been there? Towels were *always* in the bathroom. The kids and I dared never to leave anything out of place.) Anyway, even more incredulous, he threw the towel at me and kicked me through the open front door out into the yard. I landed on one ankle and planted it hard to get traction. It was badly sprained in that moment.

This was no time to think about my ankle or being naked in the city with houses all around and cars going by. I had to keep moving! I never ran so fast in my life! I dug my feet into the ground with every painful stride. It was almost as if I could feel his breath on the back of my neck! My heart pounded as I ran. I was convinced that he was on my heels and I wouldn't look behind me! Gripping the towel, I darted around the corner of the block toward a convenience store. Oh Lord! The reality hit me that I was naked in the middle of the night, running toward a brightly lit convenience store where stood a male clerk and two young male customers.

Although the towel was a meager defense between me and them, my biggest concern was to stay alive and get farther away from *husband*! Still running, I crashed into the counter and pleaded with the clerk to call the police. His obvious look of disgust meant he didn't want to get involved. He obviously assumed that I was someone who was always being abused and he had instantly stereotyped me. Funny how much one facial expression can reveal.

The two young boys also saw that the clerk was not going to help me. While still gasping for breath, I heard them say, "We'll help you! Get in our car!" I was afraid of those boys also, but somehow I trusted that those two *angels* would somehow help me. Jerking open the car door, not fast enough to suit me, I scrambled into their backseat. I cried, "Please drive fast!" "Where to?" they asked, as they screeched out of the parking lot. I pleaded, "Just keep going!" I clung to my towel and said, *"Husband* is very mean and strong. He will follow us and try to kill us. Keep going before he catches us!" I had said all that to keep their attention on the road instead of on me. Plus I imagined that he truly was running close behind. Looking back, I have no doubt that, this too, was a divine intervention. It makes no sense that he wasn't close on my heels, because I know he could normally run faster than I could.

After the boys drove a little farther away, they asked me again where I wanted to go. While watching the rear window to see if car lights were following us, I told them where my Mom lived. They dropped me off there and spun away into the distance.

Half asleep, Mom opened the door. By the look on her face, I knew my face looked very banged up and full of desperation. I screamed, "Get your keys! Get your keys! Let's go!" She didn't have time to process any of this. By the time she grabbed her keys and purse, I was already in her car. I begged her to drive fast. "Where?" she asked. I said, "Go anywhere! Head to the mountains!" We did. She drove and drove and drove. I kept looking behind for any sign of headlights following us.

For a while, we were quiet in the car. Then finally in the still of the dark night, she gently said, "You know you can't go back. He's going to end up killing you. You know you could've been killed tonight." The reality of her words pierced through my body. My desperation hurt as much as the many *wounds and* stung as badly as my busted and bleeding lips. I gently agreed, "I know Mom, I know. **I can't take it anymore.** I won't go back. I'm never going back. It's over." Just then, the sun came up shining brightly into my sore eyes along with the harsh glare of another monumental reality. My baby! I had to go back and get my baby!

Mom, in her wisdom, was quiet again for a while. Then she said, "Well, we're going to go get your baby. Then you're going home with me!" We were worried about all of his children, as well. What about them? We drove back to his house. Mom and I cautiously and reluctantly walked in the door. *I couldn't believe I had to walk back in that same door of which I had just escaped!*

Thankfully, my son was sleeping safely in his crib. Looking at him was soothing to my sore eyes. I covered him up and went back into the living room. I sat on the couch for a moment collecting my thoughts of how we were going to get back out of the house. Mom found a brown paper bag and soaked it in vinegar. She touched it lightly to my swollen face and the vinegar stung my busted lips. I winced. She said, "Honey, this is an old home remedy. It will help you." I agreed.

Suddenly, *husband* pushed her out of the way and sat down on the couch beside me. She moved to the nearby chair and kept a watchful eye on us. I was comforted that she was there. He began turning on his charm. Oh how pitiful he was! Oh how he was never ever going to hurt me again! He went on and on and turned the situation around, indicating that we should feel sorry for him. He didn't understand why he did such things for no reason. He forced tears and pretended to be sorry. I had heard this too many times before and finally realized he was a perpetual liar. I was tired of it. I knew it was a miracle that I was still alive and that next time could be my last.

He tried to kiss me with his twisted kiss of fake affection. However, this time, I remembered that he likes *salty* kisses.

THIS ATTEMPT TO DECEIVE ME FAILED.

I caught a *glimpse of joy* in his eyes when I winced as he touched my split and swollen lips. Just then, a newly born strength rose up from deep within. I said, "I have to leave. I can't take this anymore. You never stop. You just keep doing it. I have to go."

I got up to go get my baby out of the crib so Mom could take us out of there forever. He got up also and went into the other room. I was relieved that he didn't follow me. I came back into the living room with my baby in my arms. He came back in with a *rifle on his arm!* He yelled, "You're not going anywhere!" He raised the rifle toward Mom. I raised a prayer! The gun fired, but the bullet narrowly missed her! At that point, I was more afraid for my Mom than for myself.

He commanded her to leave! As much as I didn't want to be left with him, I was relieved to see her walk out of there alive!

Our lives depended on my remaining quiet and still, but my heart silently screamed, "Oh Mom! Oh Mom!" Her eyes connected with mine and she understood my silent words to her, "You're okay Mom! It's ok for you to go. You tried to help me! You're so brave!" Likewise, her heart silently screamed back to me, "Oh daughter! I don't want to leave you! How can I leave you?" We both knew that if she didn't go that one or both of us would be killed. I imagined her hand trembling as she inserted the key into her car and reluctantly drove away. She was probably thinking the same thoughts about me, that I was sitting in the house trembling. What next?

Chapter 16

I WAS DIFFERENT NOW

HE WALKED OUT OF THE ROOM AND PUT AWAY the gun. I sat down on the couch holding my baby. I was afraid to move, but my legs would not stop shaking. I took comfort holding my baby boy close to me for a while. Unbelievably, even though a gun had fired, my baby had not cried! For the remainder of that horrible day and for the next few weeks, *husband* acted as if nothing had happened.

He was the same, but I had changed.

SOMETHING DEEP INSIDE ME WAS EMERGING
AS A FIGHTER.

However, this was no ordinary fight. I knew I had to fight smarter, not harder. Somehow I had to get out for good. How, or when, I didn't know, but I knew I would.

Not knowing what to do, it didn't take long for those thoughts of escape to dissipate. He had made it clear that nobody could help me. I was back into the day-to-day survival mode. The kids and I became adept at walking on eggshells and trying to control the atmosphere. We always spoke kindly to him, taking great care not to provoke him and avoided eye contact. I asked the oldest daughter to please keep the other kids entertained and quiet while I tried to entertain and keep him quiet. We kept the house spotless. We stayed polite and busy. This was our diligent and exhausting state of mind. Where was my strength to make a plan?

I had already seen that I couldn't get help from my parents and keep them safe. Decades later, I took comfort that *husband* could never again threaten or hurt them. Mom fell asleep and flew away, having succumbed to lifelong disappointments and lung cancer. My Dad preceded her with a broken heart, loneliness, alcoholism and emphysema. All my life I begged them not to smoke. What actually took their lives? Had I been part of their demise? I dearly regretted every heartache I ever caused them.

Lies of hopelessness and addiction are strong, but truth is stronger. What lies have you believed? There are many forms of bondage. What choices will you make? No one *on earth* seemed to be able to help me, but I knew from whence my help cometh. "I will lift up my eyes to the hills. From whence comes my help? My help comes from the Lord, who made heaven and earth." (Psalms 121:1,2)

Chapter 17

PREPARATIONS FOR A FUTURE

A SHIFT BEGAN. I REALIZED THAT INSTEAD OF turning *pieces* of it over to the Lord, that the whole thing had to be given to Him. The children and I had not seen all of it yet, but our prayers were being answered. New liberties were miraculously allowed. For example, *husband* surprisingly granted us a rare visit with the children's maternal grandmother. This behavior was definitely out of his character.

Of course, being with her was very good for them. They felt as though they were with a part of their own mother. Grandmother was a prayer answered for me as well. I loved her very much. Ironically, four decades and one day after I wrote this chapter, this dear treasured woman left behind the cares of this world.

Back when we were all kids, our brief visits with her were healing and precious. She looked at me with loving pity. She took me under her wing even though I was not a blood relative. She bought me an electric hand mixer and said, "You can make cream potatoes for the children." I treasured that mixer as much as I had treasured my prized wood burning cookstove.

As mentioned, our release from isolation was highly unusual. Miraculously, he *allowed* me to go to a sewing class! Grandmother had generously given me a sewing machine and arranged a class! Seriously! Who does that? See what I mean? She was not only loving, but very wise about the needs of a human heart. Sewing was a great joy to me and gave me a sense of normalcy. Humans need a purpose both naturally and spiritually.

Normally, I wasn't allowed out of *husband's* sight. Sometimes he waited in the car while I shopped for groceries. My heart pounded as I raced down each aisle grabbing food as fast as I could. If I was gone too long, I was accused of doing who knows what, with who knows whom. I'm not quite sure how I could've done anything wrong during a short grocery store visit. Having said that, you can imagine my shock that he allowed me to take those sewing classes! There was no rhyme or reason to his behavior.

It was more shocking that he allowed me to study and obtain the General Education Diploma, (GED) commonly considered equivalent to a high school diploma. Then as icing on the cake, I attended one community college course.

As a young kid, I briefly worked in the tobacco field. Who knew that fact would help me at a time such as this? The children and I were at one of the visits with a state-mandated counselor that *husband* was required to attend after he got into some trouble with the law. Somehow it came up that I could take a college class. Of course, I didn't have the money. However, I had worked on the tobacco farm as a younger child, which apparently qualified me for some type of small education stipend called a Migrant Worker's grant. I honestly don't remember all the details about that; all I know is this small amount of money paid for my little secretary course and the gas to get to school. This was divine intervention.

Although I was extremely thankful to go to the Medical Secretary Course, it was difficult to concentrate. My mind was filled with what he might do to me when I got back home. Also, I could study only when he was asleep, and he rarely slept. His exaggerated expectation to constantly be catered to demanded all my attention. My continuous efforts to prevent his outrages were useless. *He didn't need a reason to blow up; if it rained, it was evidently my fault.* Still somehow, I got to go to class!

Some years later, I learned that he was preoccupied with girlfriends during that time, but I no longer cared about that stuff. I had school! The children and I had some newly found liberties. Blessings were coming in weird disguises!

As strange as this may sound, it was as if I were in some unseen pocket that allowed me to slip by the evil vacuum! It was evident that more provisions were arriving due to the prayers for the *entire* situation. Provision was coming! (See Jeremiah 29:11.)

God was clearing the path before my feet, although I didn't know the fullness of it *yet*. Also, the evil one continued setting fires. Lord, show me the glory behind the veil. Jesus once said, "I have yet many things to say unto you, but *ye cannot bear them now." (John 16:12, KJV).*

Please bear with my story.

Chapter 18

WINDS OF CHANGE

DING, DING DING, ROUND EIGHT! *HUSBAND'S* usual hunger for chaos was revving up again. He told me to get in the car! Then he raced the car down the highway. This was one of his favorite behavior patterns. He seemed to hope someone would challenge him or that he would be pulled over by the police.

Husband couldn't understand why the car couldn't wreck. He certainly tried to wreck us! He pushed high speeds. We reeled on two wheels. We swerved erratically in and out of the ditches. We barely missed the trees, as some unseen force kept the car from flipping over or crashing into oncoming traffic!

He loved to stop on a bridge, drag me out of the car, lean me over the rail and threaten to throw me off the bridge. For years I had a fear of bridges. He displayed great joy observing the fear on my face. What he couldn't see was my silent and powerful prayers. What neither of us could see were God's angels keeping the car from wrecking as they hearkened to God's words regarding my prayers.

> For he shall give his angels charge over thee to keep thee in all thy ways. They shall bear thee up in their hands, lest thou dash thy foot against a stone" (Psalm 91:11, 12, KJV).

> He that dwells in the secret place of the most High shall abide under the shadow of the Almighty. I will say of the Lord, He is my refuge and my fortress: my God; in him will I trust (Psalm 91:1,2, KJV).

I clung to many such promises. Don't look at the giant, but focus on the redeemer! Never give up, but look up! No matter what happens, keep believing.

In the meantime, the enemy wanted to steal that from me, and on raged the storm. Sometimes, my greatest desire was simply to go to sleep, but *husband* seemed never to sleep! I never understood how he could go so long without it. He did not allow me to sleep as long as he was awake. When I fell asleep in the car, he would slam on the brakes and slam my face into the windshield! He thought that was a clever way to wake me. As my head bounced backward in severe pain, I cupped my hands to catch the blood streaming from my nose. He growled, "I told you to stay awake!"

94

Perhaps you're wondering why the seatbelt didn't keep me from hitting the windshield. Seatbelt! I chuckle. In the mid 1970's there were no seatbelt laws and I don't remember ever seeing a seatbelt in our old car. My ultimate safety required something far greater than a seatbelt! Perhaps a seatbelt could have been placed around his neck! That would have kept me safe! Oops, was that my outside voice?

I tried so hard never to fall asleep in the car. I knew he would hurt me every time, but eventually I couldn't hold my eyes open any longer. Bam! It would happen again! However, once I was fully awake, I fixed my mind on the only place I could find rest. As the Lord said, "Come unto me all ye that labor and are heavy laden and I will give you rest" *(Matthew 11:28)*. I focused on the one who was stronger than the evil. The strongest.

> Be of good courage and he shall strengthen your heart all ye that hope in the Lord (Psalm 31:24). Trust in him at all times ye people, pour out your heart before him. God is a refuge for us. Selah. (Psalms 62:8)

I chanted to myself, "Don't get weary in the waiting. He is faithful. Hold fast to God's promises. Jesus saves." Those words of truth got me through the upcoming times. Aren't there opposing teams in sports and business? Yes! Correct! Do we retreat and sit on the bench or do we hold the line believing in the game plan?

Where was I? Oh yes, I forgot to tell you that we no longer lived in the nice house in the city. I was disappointed to leave it. One day he suddenly threw all of our belongings in the car and muttered that we were leaving (again)! The last to go was a Siamese cat. I thought he would never get that cat in the cardboard box! I don't know who didn't want to leave more, me or the cat! I watched it struggle and claw to keep from going into the box. I understood the protest completely! My body also ached to resist! If only my arms and legs would stretch far enough to keep *me* from being shoved into that car!

Riding again in silence, I didn't know where we were going or why we had to leave. We drove out into the country toward my Dad's home. I was thrilled to *think* we might visit. It had been too long since I had seen him. Sadly, we stopped short of Dad's place. Believe it or not, we stopped barely beyond the old shack we had left before I delivered my baby.

Our car pulled up at a cinder block building. Alongside it sat a rusty single wide trailer. The trailer almost touched the building. It was cattywampus, as if abandoned quickly by the truck that haphazardly left it there. Lots of tall weeds had grown all around and between the structures as well as in the driveway. You guessed it! The small cinder block building would be our home.

Stepping inside, spider webs were seen everywhere. They especially covered the one window and clung to the rough surfaced cinder block inner walls. The floors were bare concrete. There were only two doors.

DOORS ARE IMPORTANT.

There was an old bed in the living area and a separate drafty area containing two old mattresses on the floor. The entire building smelled yucky and required much cleaning. It took some time for the kids and me to remove the dirt, trash and moldy food scraps from years past.

The kitchen included a potbelly wood burning heater. Oddly, there was a ceramic bathtub along the wall. At the other end of the bathtub was the kitchen sink. Such an odd and non-private location for a bathtub, but it was near the warm heater. The location for the ramshackle plumbing was convenient, I presumed.

Beyond the old rusty farm sink, sat an equally rusty cookstove. Although electric, only two burners worked and only the bottom element of the oven provided heat. The cat couldn't adjust to the new (old) place and didn't eat for a week. I couldn't blame it. We didn't eat much either, but for different reasons.

Years ago, the building had been home to an old man who had no living family. He had declined both physically and mentally and was unable to care for the home or himself. How or when I did not know, but evidently *husband* had worked out a deal for us to live in the block building in exchange for *taking care* of the old man who lived in the adjacent single wide trailer.

By this time, *husband's* violent behavior was revving up yet again. It demanded all my attention to appease him and keep him away from the children. While I was doing that, the children assisted the old man with his daily needs. The horrible aspects of our life escalated, and we all became more and more weary. As we looked at each other's faces, we couldn't hold the gaze long. The pain looking back at us was too much.

Unexpectedly, *husband's* mother appeared in the driveway pulling her own single wide house trailer. Apparently, this was *her* new home as well. She had migrated south. She plopped the trailer down on the red clay dirt behind our house. Having her there provided only a minor buffer, minor because she stayed to herself. You may remember what happened the last time she *tried to help.* There's no point in describing *all* the horrifying things that happened. In fact, some periods of time are completely lost from my memory.

Daily life for the children and me was that of slavery. We kept the cinder block building clean, carried firewood and cleared the grounds of brush. We didn't mind working, but it was the atmosphere of expectation that was extreme. *Treated as slaves, we feared the consequences if we failed.*

ABOVE ALL, HIS BOOTS MUST BE PULLED OFF FOR HIM AND HIS BEER SERVED COLD.

It better be cold enough! He acquired a couple of horses. As usual the joy from the horses was followed by painful associations.

Some nights his pot smoking and beer drinking buddies visited. In a little bit, you will see how I truly learned not to judge a book by its cover. Nonetheless, I didn't approve of this behavior. I especially didn't want the children exposed to more of what we already had. The upside to those nights were they offered a welcome reprieve from the stress. If he managed to be in a good mood, music and laughter replaced the violence.

Chapter 19

ESCALATING AGAIN

DURING OTHER LONG AND ISOLATED NIGHTS, horrors reached new heights. *The atmosphere was filled with impending doom.* By now, I was growing weary physically and mentally.

The kids were sleeping, and this evening he was particularly agitated. He began pacing the floor then shouted, "Get in the car!" To keep him from waking the children, *leaving* seemed like a good idea. I should have known that it was not!

He spun out of the dirt driveway as fast as the car would go. He continued this erratic driving intent on killing both of us. Although the car couldn't navigate the hairpin curves at those speeds, it miraculously didn't wrap around a tree. Although control was lost on the loose gravel, the car never flipped over as it fishtailed on and off the road. Seemingly disappointed that we were both still alive, he barreled the car back toward the *house* and dragged me inside!

With my heart still pounding from that car ride, he beat me throughout the night. During the beatings, he decided *he* wanted sex. He insisted that it be in a body part that was very painful to me. I found this a disgusting and terrifying violation. To make this more exciting for him and to create more torment for me, he proceeded while holding a gun to my head. As though this were not horrifying enough, with the gun still pointed at my head, he told me to kneel before him and worship him. By the way, the children were in the next room, sleeping I hoped. I silently told God that I was kneeling only to pray to him. I said, "You are my God and the Father of my Lord Jesus Christ. God you know my heart and you know that I do not worship *husband or his demons.* Please make this stop." Then suddenly *husband* fell asleep. It stopped!

The next evening, he sat in the car again and continuously blew the horn. I reluctantly went outside and slowly walked over to the driver's side. He demanded, "Get in the car!" So soon after the latest worst-ever event, I was nearing my breaking point. In fact, **I had reached my breaking point.** Last night had been unbearable. I couldn't take it anymore.

With the horn still blowing, I reluctantly went out and stood by his car door. In an effort to distract him and calm the beast, I begged him to come back inside and play music for me. He didn't get out of the driver's seat. Instead, he suddenly reached up through his car window and grabbed the back of my head with both his hands and slammed my face into the car door. For a second I was blinded by the pain, but the sight of bright red blood streaming down the side of that yellow car door woke me up! I realized that if I didn't do something I would actually be killed! I ran! I knew I had to either run or fight. At least if he caught me, I may as well go out fighting.

I ran! He plowed toward me with the car. Just in the nick of time, I dodged backwards as the car rammed the outside frame of the carport! He was furious that he had missed me with the car! He jumped out of the car faster than humanly possible. In a full rage, he dragged me back into the house and beat me. He threw me on the floor in front of him, as his perverse desires had driven him to do the previous night. The evil in his eyes seemed to signal that he would kill me at that moment!

I just couldn't take it anymore. I felt that I had truly lost my mind. The fear was too much to handle and I just wanted it to be over for good. Tired of the beatings, tired of the constant fear, tired of it all, something deep inside me snapped! I told him, "Go ahead and kill me. Just go ahead and get it over with!" It shocked even me to hear myself say that out loud, but I had reached the end of my rope. He on the other hand, enjoyed my utter despair so much that he began laughing at me. He laughed for a while in his maniacal way and continued to beat me.

Wakened by the yelling, my toddler son stumbled into the kitchen area. About that time, *husband* grabbed him by the arm and slung him into the other room. Miraculously, he didn't cry. I assume the oldest daughter grabbed him and put him in bed with her to keep him quiet and safe. I couldn't do anything myself at that moment because he turned and knocked me into the hot potbelly stove, which jarred open its door. The back of my thigh was burned. Fire cinders spilled out on the concrete floor and onto my legs. Then he picked me up and threw me into the ceramic tub by the wall. I felt my pelvis crack at that moment about the same time my head hit the cinder block wall above the tub.

Morning found me crawling painfully out of the tub, shocked I was still alive to see the sun come up. I went outside to have a serious talk with God.

Chapter 20

THE PRAYER

I SAT OUTSIDE ON A FLAT ROCK AND BEHELD THE vibrant color of the fall leaves. I had never witnessed leaves so brilliant. Even the air seemed carefree. I could breathe. Although my ribs were painful, life filled my lungs. The atmosphere had shifted. To this day, I cannot tell whether my eyes were simply in awe of the nature of God's gorgeous creation or if it was a true supernatural awakening.

This moment was interrupted by the unsolicited reflection of the previous night. I rather had not thought about that, but my busted pelvis began to hurt while sitting on that hard rock. The sting of my busted lip was also a harsh intrusion. The frequency and level of violence had escalated, which gave me no choice but to take a decisive look. Not only had I reached my breaking point, but up until last night I had been able to protect my young son. We *had* to get out and I knew it! I had to get out so that I could get help for all his kids as well.

Sitting there looking at God's gorgeous creation, I knew what I had always known: God does not want anyone living under bondage, fear and torment.

I PRAYED DIFFERENTLY THAT MORNING.

I told God that I knew He didn't like divorce and that I didn't want to sin against Him. I talked to Him about all the times I prayed that *husband* would change. Obviously he had not changed, but had become worse. Then came the pivotal moment of truth! Suddenly from deep within, the thought came: of course, God didn't answer the prayer for husband to change because God gives everyone a free will! *Husband* had to personally choose to change. Meanwhile, I could be killed waiting around *hoping he might want* to change!

We can continue praying that people will want to change, but we are not expected to subject ourselves to harm *while* praying for that to happen. Would you be married to Charles Manson? You might *pray* for him, but I doubt you would be married to him. I realized that *husband* had to make his own choice and that I could not do that *for* him.

I prayed, "Father I seek your will. I need your help and your instructions. If *you* say it's okay that I go, I will go. If there's no other solution, please literally take me by my hand and lead me out the door. Then, I will know it was of you."

105

That's exactly what happened next! The day crashed in with repeated violence. He woke up continuing his crazed mood and chaos. Suddenly, he whizzed by me riding his horse. I watched as he erratically raced back and forth. In a full gallop, he directed the horse behind our house, across the red dirt clay, through the door and completely inside his mom's trailer!

I knew I had taken a hard hit to my head the night before and that I hadn't slept the last three nights, but I rubbed my swollen eyes to see whether that had actually just happened! Had he *really* ridden that horse into his mother's house trailer? How could a horse that big get in there? How could it get out? What kind of damage might be happening to the house, the horse and his mom? That poor horse! I could only imagine its eyes wide and wild, legs crouched and scrubbing against the narrow back door trying to get out with husband on its back yelling and hitting the poor thing! Seeing this chaotic behavior revving up again, I reached a new level of panic.

The moment I ran into the house, the phone rang. This ring, in particular, came from heaven. Unlike the former pivotal phone calls, I was glad I answered the phone today! I would discover that God was sending help! This was the boy that had lately shown up with his girlfriend for periodic visits to smoke pot, drink beer and listen to *husband's* music. I detested that behavior, but I liked that they kept husband occupied. I would soon learn that love comes in many forms and not to judge a book by its cover. Ring, ring, the phone had dinged!

"Hello." The caller sensed the fear in my voice as I answered the phone and his tone suddenly changed. Although, he had asked to speak to *husband*, I could tell that he was now more concerned about me. Meanwhile, I was preoccupied with the yelling outside as *husband* kept racing around the yard on the horse.

With an excuse, I tried to hide what husband was *really* doing at the moment and why he couldn't come to the phone. However, the caller knew better. He then seriously directed his conversation to *me*. He said, "Listen, my girlfriend told me that you would get out of there if you could." My heart pounded so hard I could hardly speak. I finally said, "No, I never said that!" You see, I didn't trust him or anybody else. I thought this might be a set up. I never told people about my life. I knew better. I had always been told to keep my mouth shut. The caller insisted, "Look, you have to get away from him! We have seen all your bruises and how you cower around him! Now listen, we can help you get out of there!" ...silent pause...I knew he was right. Last night was the first time husband had grabbed my little son. Thank God he wasn't hurt! Thinking of that during the pause on the phone reminded me of our desperation. *Husband* raced by on the horse again, yelling angrily into the air for no apparent reason. Looking back, it was as if the Lord was saying to me, "Do you see that? Do you see what is happening? I'm showing *you* that I heard your prayer and *you* must run like the horse." I knew I had to get off the phone quickly before he came inside and caught me on the phone. Time, so precious yet so demanding! I could barely breathe! I clung to the phone like a lifeline yet afraid I would be caught! "Hurry and listen to me," said the voice on the phone again. "You gotta be strong now!"

I knew I couldn't bear another night of fighting for my life. I knew if I didn't get out that I would be leaving in a casket. Some snakes are poisonous. Would you live in a den of poisonous vipers or would you get out of that pit? Sometimes we endure certain things, but ask the Lord if endurance is the temporary plan or if He has a different plan. When the redeemer calls, please say yes. Listen closely. We can hear the redeemer's voice above the voice of the deceiver. **We can choose freedom over bondage, and life over death!**

Quickly the caller laid out the plan. I could barely hear it over my racing and fearful thoughts. He instructed me, "My girlfriend won't come with me this time. I will bring my Dad instead. We will use the excuse that Dad wants to hear your husband play music. In return we will have bottles of liquor to *share*." He told me that he and his girlfriend had noticed that *husband* manages large quantities of beer, but that he can't manage hard liquor. "Once he passes out from the liquor, we'll get you out of there," he said.

I exclaimed, "No! I can't go. I'm afraid!" I told the boy that *husband* always warned me never try to escape.

"You'll never get out of the driveway alive!" he would say. The caller compassionately, but impatiently and firmly replied, "Die now or die later, but we can get you out of there tonight! We're coming! Be ready!" He hung up the phone with a quick slam!

Sometimes, we have to hear the gospel preached like that! Sometimes we have to be *snapped out of it*! Awakened! Sometimes someone has to scream, "Get out! The house is on fire!" Otherwise, we perish.

Chapter 21

THE GREAT ESCAPE

EVENING APPROACHED, AND IT WAS GETTING dark. The afternoon had been more than tense to say the least. My focus was to act *normal* so he wouldn't be suspicious. I had no idea what *normal* actually looked like, but I didn't want him to notice anything different about me. My fearful aim was twofold: try to stay alive until help arrived and find the courage to go through with the plan.

Help finally arrived! Seeing the van in the driveway caused my heart to flip! I was relieved yet paralyzed with uncertainty. Could this plan actually work? The guys got out of the van and carried on a jovial conversation with husband. Ignoring me, they walked through the door and handed him a beer. Soon, they sat around acting as if they were already drunk. Talking in their rough man-to-man manner, they shared some more beer. Then they requested he play guitar and sing. As this was happening, the dad slipped a bottle of liquor out of his pocket, pretended to take a big gulp of it.

He then passed the bottle to husband. I had just put all the kids to bed so they would not be around the drinking and rowdiness.

Watching all this from a short distance across the room, I gave the guys a look that said, "I'm afraid. I can't do this!" The boy discreetly got up and pretended to go to the bathroom. He sternly whispered to me, "Make sure you're ready!" Then he rejoined the other guys. They continued pretending to drink the liquor and then passed the bottle to husband who proudly gulped it down every time! The plan was going as hoped. I could tell that he was losing his ability to stay awake. Still, somehow, he continued to sluggishly strum the guitar and slur his songs. How long must this take, I wondered! With each passing moment, I was losing my nerve, but I remembered the instructions, "Be ready!"

Ever so quietly, I slipped into the room where all the children were sleeping. Quietly yet frantically, I shoved a few clothes in a paper grocery bag. I cringed as the paper made a noise. Trembling, I hid it out of view. Then carefully and slowly, I slipped my toddler son's coat on him. All the while, I prayed he wouldn't wake up and cry. He didn't! I gingerly covered him up again; hiding the fact he was now sleeping while wearing a coat and shoes! I left the bedroom, hoping my son wouldn't get too hot and start crying. I noticed that I was hot from the adrenaline surge of this whole scenario!

The liquor had done its job! *Husband* wasn't capable of getting up off the couch. He halfway noticed me and issued his usual command, "Take my boots off." I pulled his boots off while the guys watched. I made sure to keep my face to the floor so he would not see anything in my eyes that might alert him that something was unusual. He directed his attention back to the men as he drifted in and out of consciousness. I walked out of his sight and sat at the table. While keeping an ear out for him, my trembling hands discreetly wrote a note.

> **The Note:** I took your boots off for the last time. I'm going far away and won't be back again. No need to look for me at any of our friends' or families' homes. I won't be at any of those places. I didn't tell anyone I was leaving or where I would go. I won't be anywhere that I know you will come looking.

Just as I finished writing, I heard footsteps. Quickly, I covered up the note. Whew! It wasn't him! My rescuer said, "He's out cold, let's go!" Recognizing I was paralyzed in fear, the boy grabbed my arm and stood me up. "Come on!" he said. I quickly propped the note up between the salt and pepper shakers. Then as quietly as I could, I ran to scoop up my sleeping son and grabbed the paper bag.

It's amazing how much one can pray in only a few short seconds. "God please don't let my son wake up.

Please don't let him cry. Please keep the paper bag quiet. Please don't let *husband* wake up. Please let this plan work." Without looking back, afraid of what I might see, I ran to the van as fast and as quietly as I could go!

The van door pulled partially closed behind me to avoid any noise. Without turning on any lights or the engine, the emergency brake was released and we coasted down the curvy gravel road. "Emergency brakes," I chuckled. This was an *emergency!* Prayer is my emergency brake against danger. Why did the gravel have to make so much noise? The van could not coast down that hill fast enough for me. However, we got away unnoticed! I made it out of the driveway alive!

We couldn't coast any further and the engine had to be started. I cringed with the noise and begged them to drive as fast as they could without stopping. I had absolutely no idea where we were going and I really didn't care at that moment. Suddenly as though they had read my mind, the driver said, "I have family far south from here."

Things *were* happening fast, but it didn't seem fast enough to me. Having made it through the past week and through this night, my mind seemed to say that none of this was real. Suddenly, my heart was ripping into shreds because I couldn't get *all* the kids out with me! We couldn't take them across state lines because they were not legally my children. (*Husband* had told me many times in the past to never try taking his kids across state lines if I didn't want to end up in jail!) At this time, I figured once I got out, I could get them help. I prayed that *husband* would sleep at least until late morning and not bother the children until help arrived.

We drove on until after sunrise while I pleaded for them not to stop. They reminded me that we really must stop for gas. I asked if we had enough gas to make it until eight o'clock. I wanted to put as much distance between us and home as possible.

While they pumped gas, I asked for change to use the pay phone. At that moment, I realized that I had no money at all. All my toddler and I had in this world were the few clothes in a paper bag. I was on the road with two men that I didn't really know, going somewhere I didn't know. Was this more dangerous than what I had left behind? I wondered.

The voice on the phone broke my thoughts, I quickly asked the operator to connect me to an agency in our home county. Hurriedly tapping my foot, I kept a close eye on the van. I hoped my son would remain asleep while I was on the phone. The van had no windows in the back so I couldn't see what he might be doing and I didn't want him to awake and be frightened.

I scanned my surroundings the whole time. I couldn't wait for the office to answer. Finally she answered, "How can I help you?" I replied, "I'm out! I'm out! Please go to the home and get the other children! Please get them out!" I told them the address and reported that they would be in danger now that I was not there to keep him busy. I persisted, "Please, please go get those children to safety! Go see for yourself!"

I hung up the phone as the guys hung up the gas nozzle. I was back in the van by the time they closed their doors.

Chapter 22

FROM THE FRYING PAN INTO THE FIRE

I RODE IN THE BACK OF A PANEL VAN WITHOUT windows and remained focused on my young son. I was in a surreal state of mind, unrealistically sensing that husband was following us and would catch us any minute. Although I insisted we keep driving without stopping, I began to get hungry. Soon, my son would need to eat. We eventually went through a fast food drive through and I was thankful that the driver bought our food. The drive was long and thankfully my son napped. However, being hyper-vigilant, I closed my eyes only for brief periods. The next thing I knew, the van slowed, pulled onto a long driveway and came to a stop.

We arrived at the home of a middle aged man and his wife. Without much conversation, my rescuers dropped me quickly so they could get back to their home hopefully before anyone realized they were gone. Certainly they wanted to be home in case husband came there looking for me. I was later told that he did just that. In a rage, he went everywhere looking for me. He broke into my Dad's house, even though I left the note telling him I wouldn't be there. He went to my Mom's doing the same thing, which really scared my little sister.

I was now as far south as I could go on land. That night, I slept in a deep sleep from sheer exhaustion and woke the next morning in this strange place. I discovered I had been left in a home that was remote, but along a well-traveled road.

On the wife's way out the door, she told me that there were bacon and eggs in the refrigerator that I could cook for my child and her husband. I cooked the bacon with my son wrapped around my leg. Stealthily, her husband slipped behind me, rubbing up against me and stated, "You and I are going to be friends." I was sickened by this additional invasion. My heart was pounding, but I kept flipping the bacon and searching my brain for what to do!

Knowing I must pretend to be going along with him, I managed to say, "Oh that's good...will you please go to the store for me while I finish cooking your breakfast? We don't have any milk." Sickened by the falsely seductive tone I had to use, I barely managed to get out those words! Praise God, he fell for it and left!

In a panic, I had to figure out how to escape from him! I had no idea how far away the store was or how soon he would return. Just at that moment, the television displayed an 800 number on its screen and announced, "Call this number for the Battered Women's Shelter." Frantically, I looked for pen and paper and rapidly dialed the number. I begged for help. They asked me where I was. I told her I didn't know, but she calmly instructed me to look around the house for mail and find the address on an envelope. I quickly did that. Next she said, "Go stand by the road. A Greyhound bus will be coming by there soon." I let her know that I had no money. She said, "Tell the driver that the Battered Women's Shelter will pay when you arrive. We have a contract with them. I'll be waiting for you at the bus station."

I slammed down the phone and quickly grabbed my son and our paper bag. As fast as his little legs could keep up, we ran to the main road. All the while I scanned the scene for the man's truck to reappear. I whispered to the unseen bus, "Please hurry, please hurry." Praise God, the bus came right away and we were gone!

When we got to the station, I gripped my son's hand as his little legs barely managed the tall bus steps.

Chapter 23

THE SHELTER

WE ENTERED THE LARGE BUSY BUS STATION. I didn't know what to do. I scanned the room looking for the woman I had spoken with on the phone. How would I recognize her? She, of course, had done this many times. No doubt, my son and I were quite obvious to her, probably looking like a pair of frightened refugees. She came to us and quickly said, "Follow me." I didn't know where we were headed, but I was thankful to be farther away from *both* abusers. I was still in disbelief of what had just happened at the home of the family member that was supposed to have been my safe place of temporary refuge.

My son and I arrived at the shelter on the outskirts of a large city. The lady that ran the shelter stopped by the door to write our names on her clipboard list. Of course, I gave her fake names. She showed us to a room upstairs that was bare except for a mattress on the floor. (Why are so many mattresses on the floor?) It's okay. I was grateful for sure! She gave my toddler and me some time alone and said we would have supper later.

That evening I met another girl who was also staying there. She had a baby daughter. She befriended me and wanted to exchange stories. Then, in the fashion of an older sister, she protectively warned me that the lady who ran the shelter was a lesbian and that she might approach me. "What is that?" I asked.

I know you may be wondering how I could ask such a question, but you must remember I was raised in an isolated area in the 1960's to early 70's. My parents, at that time in their culture, didn't speak about matters of sex. Any type of sex talk was never discussed with children. We didn't have a television until I was almost twelve years old. At around age fourteen, my sex talk from Mom was, "Don't let anyone touch you down there." (Whatever that was supposed to mean.) You can see, I really didn't know the definition of a lesbian. Neither did I understand anything else, emotionally or otherwise, regarding sexual matters. During that conversation with my new friend, I didn't know what any of that had to do with me.

The next morning, my new friend told me that she and her baby were moving out of the shelter. On her way out, she told me the electricity was out and there was no food. She went on to say that the lady shelter owner had gone out to get the electricity restored. The screen door slammed behind her. It was hot in the deep south without electricity for an air conditioner. I went downstairs just as the sunlight began to stream across the kitchen floor.

Near the end of the day, the woman returned with some food. My young son and I sat at the table with her as we all ate. She spoke slowly and seemed to be a depressed person. Suddenly, she slid her table chair too close to mine and in a tone that I did not like, she said, "Now that you don't have a husband, what are you going to do for sex?" (What!?) I remembered how my friend had told me that all the other battered women had gotten out of her house as fast as they could and for me to be careful. I was frightened and tired of being under abuse or the threat of abuse. I quickly replied, "Sex is the *last* thing I want at this time! I'm trying to survive!" She got up from the table and I wasn't sure what would happen next. As she left the dining room, she informed me that she would be stepping out the following morning to go get me signed up for food stamps and other helpful programs.

I remember hearing her voice fade off as I wondered what I was going to do about this situation. I took my son upstairs to our assigned room. I was shaking like a scared rabbit. The bedroom door didn't have a lock! I stayed awake all night watching the door and hoping she wouldn't come into the room. Keep in mind my upbringing. I had never been exposed to the outside world. This was definitely a different realm for me. I was afraid. Patterns of abuse were all I knew at that time.

This was forty years ago, so please don't judge all battered women's shelters by my one isolated experience. My gratitude is beyond description that truly awesome shelters exist today. They are safe places to go and often the *only* place to go. Therefore, I cannot stress enough that everyone needs to become well informed about these places of refuge. Please know all the options for your own safety or for the safety of others.

Chapter 24

NOW WHAT?

THE SUN WAS UP AND SO WAS I. CAUTIOUSLY, I went downstairs. The house facilitator was preoccupied. She grabbed her purse and announced, "Money just came in the mail so I'm going downtown to pay bills." I was overjoyed that she was leaving.

No one was supposed to leave without her knowing it or without her knowing where. However, as soon as she left, we left! I ran upstairs and grabbed our paper bag and my son. Out the door we went, not stopping to *sign out!*

We walked briskly down the sidewalk, opposite of the way she went. I had no idea where we would go or what we would do. I did not know the area at all. Only a couple of days ago, we had ridden in her car from the bus station to the shelter. Not taking any notice of my surroundings, I had focused only on my son in the back seat instead of looking out the car window to see where we were being taken.

I rounded the street corner with my son and we simply continued walking. Ahead on the right, I noticed a large brick Baptist Church. As if on autopilot, I walked inside holding my son's hand. It was a week day, but the front doors were open. A man was sitting on the front bench doing something. He looked up and asked if he could help us.

Next, I heard myself say, "We have no place to live." Then I asked him, "Do you have a wife and children?" He seemed kind and compassionate as he replied that he did. I asked him if my son and I could come to his house only briefly until I could find work. I explained that I would cook, clean and babysit for his children. I remember his look of disbelief as I spoke. He excused himself for a moment and went to call his wife.

He returned and said, "You and your son can go home with me and meet my wife. We will see how we can help you." For the first time, I felt safe. He asked only a few questions, as if he understood that we first needed to be loved and fed.

The car eased into his garage. His home looked like a mansion to me. His wife was so pleasant and inviting. She led us to a spare room that had real beds (not a mattress on the floor). Everything smelled so clean. She told us we could take a bath and rest while she cooked lunch. I repeatedly told her thank you and kept asking her to let me help her cook. She graciously said, "Tomorrow you can help. For now, just relax and get settled." She left for a moment and returned with clean clothes for me from her closet. She also brought an outfit for my son from her son's closet. She nodded as if to say, "Those are for you. You'll both be okay." She smiled and softly closed the door. She took my paper bag with her and I heard her washing machine start up before she walked down the long hallway to her kitchen.

After I gave my son a bath, he napped while I took a shower. Then I went into their kitchen where she and her husband sat quietly talking. When they saw me approaching, they suddenly stopped talking and smiled graciously. They made me feel welcome. "Lunch is almost ready!" she announced. They said that my son and I could stay with them and that they would help us. They asked only a few more questions about my situation. Assuming I had not slept much lately, they allowed me to go early to bed after an awesome dinner.

The next morning, the woman went to work. I told her I would clean and cook dinner. That evening we had more discussion about how I got there and why. They were very compassionate and nonjudgmental. I stayed with them for a few weeks. Once they trusted me, I occasionally baby sat while they went out for the evening. I expressed to him how much I really wanted to find a job and a place of my own. I found out that he was a deacon at the Church and an editor for a major newspaper in the large city. When he was able to get away from the office, he drove me around to apply for jobs. I suspect that he secretly made some calls on my behalf after I placed applications.

Chapter 25

NEW LIFE IN THE DEEP SOUTH

THE PHONE RANG AT THE DEACON'S HOME. I answered. The lady asked for me. Once I realized that she was calling to set up a job interview, I replied, "I am she! Thank you for calling. I will be there!"

I could barely wait for Deacon to get home so I could tell him about this and ask him for a ride to the interview! This would be my first professional job. Previous to my escape, God had prepared me for this job by giving me miraculous access to a pertinent college course.

For the first month, Deacon drove me to my new job at the Outpatient Lab, X-ray, and EKG Clinic attached to the nearby hospital. My son attended the Church Daycare Center.

THIS CRITICAL PROVISION LAUNCHED ME INTO SUCCESS!

Sometimes, all we need is a boost so we can take it from there.

Deacon and his wife let me stay with them until I received a couple of paychecks and began to earn my own way. Anyone can see that this provision was poured out to me from God by the hands of his faithful servants. May God abundantly bless Deacon and his family. *They freely gave, knowing I could give them nothing in return except gratitude.*

I loved my new job as a medical receptionist for the outpatient department. With the help of the lab and x-ray techs, I learned the basic job duties. I was thankful for their kindnesses and acceptance! I decided to check out a medical dictionary from the library and taught myself to transcribe the x-ray reports. As I learned, I gathered valuable experience, which really came in handy later.

Make no mistake, this job and the divine intervention of the deacon were all blessings from God the Blesser. Abundance comes from Jesus, who came that we might have life more abundantly! Only months prior, I had no access to a job or the simple privilege of sleeping in peace and safety. No, I cannot take credit for these accomplishments. They were gifts from God.

One of the fun things that happened while working at the clinic was the opportunity to meet the St. Louis Cardinals baseball team! They came for spring training, and our outpatient diagnostic center did their physical exams and laboratory testing. The team invited my son and me to be their guests at one of their games. During the game, they gave my son a baseball signed by a Hall of Fame member, Lou Brock, along with Keith Hernandez and others from the late 1970's roster. We still have that ball!

With the next paycheck, I had enough money to rent an apartment. Deacon drove me to look at it. That was a glorious day! I now realize that he and his wife secretly paid the first month deposit as well as the first deposit for the electricity to be turned on and he signed his name for both accounts. I would not put my name on anything official. You see, I was afraid that *husband* would find me. He had always warned me that if I ever did get away from him that he could always find me because I have a Social Security Number. Therefore, I chose not to put anything in my own name.

The evil one wants to bind our minds and make everything seem worse than it really is. In fact, if things seem really bad, we should take a much deeper look.

WE WILL FIND A LIE AT THE ROOT OF IT.

There appears to be two obvious mentalities in this world: 1) Some people think the world owes them a living regardless of their laziness. They usually have a long list of *perceived* reasons why they are not working. 2) Others are embarrassed not to be able to help themselves. They have obvious barriers and hardships, many of which can be overcome. They usually overcome them. Their embarrassment is genuine and not based on pride. These dear ones *want* to work and they often praise God for their provisions.

Praise the Lord for placing in the hearts of Deacon and his wife the gracious desire to help me get on my feet. *You see, people need just enough help to get on their feet.* **People need help until they can see the truth for themselves.** It's no shame if we get knocked down. However, we are not meant to *stay* down. Helping is not the same thing as enabling repetitive unfruitful behaviors.

> But thou shalt remember the Lord thy God: for it is he that giveth thee **power to get wealth**, that he may establish his covenant which he swore unto thy fathers, as it is this day. (Deuteronomy 8:18, KJV, bold emphasis, mine)

I received that promise then and many times since. This is just the beginning. God honored my mustard seed faith. I pursued Him with great determination. Along the way, you'll see where the thief was involved with his intent to cause doubt and weariness. However, we must never give up during those times. We wait upon the Lord.

Every month, I gave Deacon my payment for the rent and electricity. Looking back, I think the Church slightly subsidized the price for my son's daycare. My job was better than most, yet there was not enough money between paychecks. After packing my son's lunch, I often ran out of food for myself. To supplement and to earn money for a lawyer to pay for the divorce, I picked up a part-time job in the evenings working at a fast food chain. I still have the pay stub from that year, when hourly wages were $1.50.

At closing time, there were burgers remaining on the rack that were to be discarded. During my closing duties, I picked up a burger to take home with me. The manager saw this and said, "We're not supposed to do that." She must have seen a sad and embarrassed expression on my face because she then softened, smiled and restated, "But if I don't see you take it, it doesn't matter, because it will go into the trash anyway." God also provided extra daycare for the evening job. My fellow former resident of the battered women's shelter and I traded babysitting services for each other's toddlers.

Moving into the apartment was easy. After all, we only had that brown paper bag containing a few of our clothes. Part of me felt sad when I threw away that old torn bag. I wonder why we hold onto things that are symbols of sadness? Actually, it wasn't all bad. It reminded me that we escaped and I was thankful that we had a change of clothing, which was far more than some people had.

With our clothes put away, I took my son's hand and we walked to the nearest grocery store for eggs, bread and peanut butter. The apartment kitchen was bare except for an aluminum pie pan found in the metal drawer under the electric stove. A single bent fork lay in the cabinet drawer. Yay! I scrambled some eggs with the fork while cooking them in the thin aluminum pie pan on the stovetop. You can bet that I didn't let those eggs burn. I remembered the horrors from the shack when I burned the pot of pinto beans.

You may think this situation was sadly lacking. I thought so, too, for a second, but I was thankful that I had a stovetop that could be regulated instead of cooking on the fireplace. We had food and electricity! I was thrilled with the apartment kitchen because it was *my* kitchen. The apartment was a place of our own; a place of safety for my son and me.

During the day, I blocked the bad memories. I pretended that I was born in that southernmost state and that none of the past had happened. This worked well most of the time, but not while sleeping. The nightmares were vicious. Living in the lightning capital of the United States was stressful for me when the loud thunder claps coincided with my nightmares. Some nights, when I was frightened, I got in bed with my toddler. How crazy is that? Usually, it's the toddler that jumps in bed with the parent!

My son *seemed* to be doing better than me. He was about two and a half years old when we escaped and I didn't think he remembered our past. However, one day on our walk, he noticed a man working underneath his car and my toddler said, "Momma, be quiet. That man might hurt us." I didn't expect him to say that! I reassured my son and then I prayed for him. My goal was for him to have a normal life filled with joy. We walked farther down the cobblestone road to the bay area and the nearby park where we played together and had good times.

Someone gave us a beautiful Irish Setter. I named her Brandy. She loved the water! She would jump in the channel and swim until she was too tired to keep swimming! Back at our garage apartment, she tried to sit on my lap as if she were a tiny puppy. She was a sweet companion for my son as well. Sadly, one day she disappeared.

Life goes on and we put one foot in front of the other. My son and I were walking from the grocery store when the paper bag that I was carrying tore. Cans of food fell onto the street and rolled in all different directions! I quickly tried to catch them while keeping my son from running into the street! Funny how one can manage life threatening situations, and yet a little incident like that can push one over the edge! I remember sitting there on the sidewalk sobbing. I finally got myself together and gathered as many cans as I could carry in my arms while managing to hold onto my son's hand. (No baby stroller, no bag for groceries and no car.) Keep moving. Find a better way. Walking home like that, I had a light bulb moment. The next time I went to the grocery store, I "borrowed" one of the store's shopping carts and pushed it all the way to my apartment. Since I had the cart on grocery day, I figured I may as well use it to haul clothes to the laundromat! Not only was this safer, but it also provided a fun ride for my son. It was during those walks that I missed the dog most. Somehow, I felt safer when the dog was with us.

Our small apartment was built over a detached garage and was within walking distance of my job! This was a huge blessing because I had no car. Although I was thankful, I complained that I was soaked in sweat by the time I arrived at work. Even though I took a shower prior to walking out the door, I was not accustomed to the humid eighty degree weather that greeted me. How could it possibly be that hot before eight o'clock in the morning?!

My son had childhood asthma that was aggravated by the climate. Deacon paid my son's doctor bills until I saved up enough money to repay him. I was reminded, again, of the Lord's provision. "...my God shall supply all your need according to his riches in glory by Christ Jesus" (Philippians 4:19). The higher kingdom comes into view and hope is born! I held onto God's promises and you will see that He is faithful.

My son's asthma went away. We were on our way to a new life. A lady from the Church gave me a set of mixing bowls for a housewarming gift. Forty years later, I still have that nest of bowls. I will always keep them. Today, my kitchen is fully stocked to the point of over-flow. As I sit in our current home, with a lovely interior

I designed myself, with all our needs met and exceeded, I have no doubt how I got it. The Lord is my provider!

> Let them shout for joy, and be glad, that favor my righteous cause: yea, let them say continually, Let the Lord be magnified, which **hath pleasure in the prosperity** of his servant. (Psalms 35:27, KJV, bold emphasis mine)

God takes pleasure in our prosperity. He is a good Father! "Let the beauty of the Lord our God be upon us, and establish the work of our hands for us" (Psalm 90:17).

Chapter 26

TRANSITION

THE SPIRIT OF FEAR MUST BE THE NEXT TO GO. Fear found me no matter how far I roamed. **We cannot run from fear, but fear should run from us.** Hold that thought; this will make more sense later.

I didn't have any communication with my family after I escaped. I was deceived into thinking that if I told anyone where I was that *husband* would skillfully force them to reveal my whereabouts. My dear mother thought *husband* had killed me and buried me in the woods behind our house. I felt terrible for causing her such anguish. Had I been thinking clearly, I would have reasoned that she would have died before giving him that information. In fact, she had put herself in harm's way several times in the past on my behalf.

I finally called my Dad and told him where I was. I can still hear the relief in his voice. We devised a plan to help disguise my whereabouts. I wrote a short note to *husband that* only stated, "Your son is okay and doing well." The note was placed in a stamped envelope addressed to *husband's* address; which was then placed in a larger envelope and mailed to my Dad. Dad removed *husband's* letter, drove to a neighboring county's post office and dropped the letter in the mail to husband. That gave the letter a local postmark. We did this about every six months. Dad mailed each of the subsequent letters from a different county's post office. It appeared as though I was moving from place to place around the local area and thus kept *husband* diverted as to where to look for me. The whole time I was in a state twelve hours from home. Also, the Lord provided a unique way for me to obtain the divorce without *husband* finding out my location!

One grand time, Dad drove the long distance to visit me! He suddenly walked in my office door at work! Surprise! I was overjoyed to see his face! Only those who knew him would understand what a big deal it was for him to drive that far! His finances were limited and he was not familiar with driving in a big city. His lifestyle was one of a bygone era. He visited me for only two days, but I treasured our time together more than words can say.

I could see the sadness in Dad's eyes as he drove away knowing I had nothing to drive. (Drive. This reminds me how thankful I was that I had obtained a driver's license before my escape. It so happened that a few days following my sixteenth birthday, *husband* was in a rare good mood and he took me to the Division of Motor Vehicles to test for a license. On that day, I had no idea the importance of that opportunity.) Since I already had a license, I didn't bother to obtain one in the new state of which I was in hiding. After Dad's visit, he sent a letter asking me to come home and pick up a 1963 Ford that he had obtained for me. I remember that it cost three hundred dollars, but I don't remember Dad expecting me to repay the full amount.

When my son and I stepped off the Greyhound bus, Dad was waiting at the bus station. He was so happy to see us, but his expression changed when he noticed that my toddler wasn't wearing a belt to hold up his pants. Saddened by that sight, he drove us to a nearby store and bought his grandson a belt. Shopping for anything was a rare exception for my Dad. Most of the time his own needs were not met.

I asked him to drive me to the nearby forest. I had missed the mountains and the smell of damp fallen leaves. You might think a forest would bring back bad memories of the time when I was starving and hiding therein, but the woods also took me back to *early* childhood where I had many adventures with my siblings. The forest provided toys like sticks for fortresses and for playing Robin Hood. The moss made a lovely carpet for my imaginary playhouse!

During the short visit with Dad to pick up a car, I couldn't remember all the different back roads that led to his house. Pieces of my mind seemed to be missing. I constantly looked over my shoulder. I was very uncomfortable being near the places the abuser had been. It was really difficult to leave Dad again, but I couldn't rest until I started driving back to my refuge. The farther away, the better.

Chapter 27

MIGRATING

I WAS RELIEVED TO BE BACK AT MY PLACE OF hiding in the deep south. Altogether, I had been there about eighteen months. Ironically, a neighbor from back home incidentally learned from Dad what had become of me. Dad, knowing that he could trust him, gave him my phone number. Incredibly surprised to receive the call, I was excited to hear from an acquaintance.

After a chat on the phone, he persisted and followed up with many other phone calls. He wrote kind letters. After some time passed, he ultimately asked me to move to the mountains. This appealed to me. I would be close (but not too close) to *home* and my family.

However, as time drew near for me to go, I got cold feet. I didn't trust myself or anyone else. I finally decided not to go. Two days later, the phone rang and he asked, "Can you come pick me up at the airport? I'm here for a visit." (Surprise! He was in my town!)

Oh well, what could I do? I got in the car and went to get him. When I arrived, a bit of humor broke some of my anxiety. I pulled up to the front door of the big city airport, jumped out of my car and left the engine running. My old car didn't have an actual key. Dad had given me a pen knife to start it. At that moment, I didn't want to deal with all that, so I didn't turn the car off. Suddenly, a security guard grabbed my arm and asked, "Don't you realize it's against the law to leave a car engine running here?" No, I guess I didn't know. Getting back in the car, I laughed at my own inexperience. It felt good to laugh. I quickly parked the car, turned off the engine and ran back inside to find my surprise visitor.

He didn't notice me and I couldn't see him behind the newspaper. (I've since noticed how a thin piece of paper can separate people.) Anyway, after searching through the large airport lobby, I finally noticed him from the side opening of the paper. "Oh, there you are!" I said. We awkwardly greeted each other and drove back to my apartment.

Throughout the visit he was very kind and spent time playing with my son at the beach. He convinced me that he wanted to take care of us. He assured me that if it didn't work out, we could peacefully part ways with no hard feelings. After he left to return to his home. I thought about it for the next few weeks and I decided to pack up and move.

Clunk! The old heavy car door closed. My hands lingered on the door handle. Standing there, I took a long last look at the apartment that had been my first taste of independent freedom. I closed my eyes to interrupt the memories and took a deep breath. A rare breeze broke the moment as my long brown hair stuck to my face. I wiped the doubts away along with the sweat from my forehead. Not gonna miss this humid climate, I thought.

Turning my attention back to the car door, there sat my little son smiling up at me through the glass. I winked at him and playfully ran to the other side and got in the car. Sitting in the driver's seat, my hands seemed small as they tightly gripped the steering wheel. I felt stuck for a moment. Then a memory flashed of *husband* commanding me to "get in the car!" I instantly realized that, this time, I was the one in charge. I would be driving and I was in control of the car now. Through thankful tears, I put the car in gear. With a jerk forward, my highlighted *paper* map slid off the cracked dashboard. As I reached to grab it, I wondered if I had enough gas money for the twelve hour trip.

Before turning onto the main road, I looked around inside the car. Everything we owned was packed in the front and back seat. My toddler and I drove away on that hot spring day of 1978. I recalled the emotional goodbye to Deacon and his family. Through many tears, I expressed the gratitude in my heart for all he had done for us.

As I drove down the street, I remembered the struggles and the good times we had there. My life was fluctuating between the rear view mirror and the front window. What am I doing? What's next? Should I turn around and stay? Then, from the back seat, a little voice asked, "Are we at 'Virginja' yet?" Thank God for the joy of a child to remind us of our hopes, dreams and adventure. Yes, I like that! It sounds like a magical place. Let's stop by "*Virginja*" on our way! There we will find forest, mountains and *cool breezes*.

Chapter 28

LIFE IN THE MOUNTAINS, PART 1

THE DRIVE HAD BEEN LONG. I SHOULD'VE stopped to rest, but hotel fees were not in my budget back in those days. At two in the morning, I was weary from the last fifty foggy miles on the dark curvy mountain roads! Finally, the lighted building came into view! Let me tell you, that was a grand sight for sore eyes! I rolled the car to a stop and with a breath of relief, shifted the gear stick into park. I quietly opened the car door so as not to wake my son, but the mountain air was more than a *cool breeze*. It was downright cold! My son was awake now and so was I!

About that time, my friend came out and wrapped my sleepy son in a blanket and carried him inside where it was warm. That truly warmed my heart, but when the room door closed, I felt an awkwardness of uncertainty. My eyes dropped, feeling like a burden in this one room rental and unsure of what to do next. I let out a nervous cough. *Now* was not the time for doubts.

I was cold and exhausted. Silently, I fell across the spare bed beside my son, cuddled him and fell asleep.

The next morning it didn't take long to unpack the back seat of the car. However, it took many years to unpack the baggage in my mind. Although I was closer to my family, I would rarely see them. The lack of gas money and decent tires for their cars hindered them from visiting. The few times I was brave enough to visit them, anxiety shortened my stay. They lived too close to the place I had originally escaped. By this time, my abuser had been sentenced to prison for forty years, but in my mind I could see him around every curve.

I felt slightly safer in the mountain curves, but the memories swerved through my dreams—nightmares, actually. One night as I slept, a pie pan slid in the kitchen and fell on the floor making a loud noise. I suddenly jumped to my feet in the middle of the bed. Half asleep and screaming, my next realization was being grabbed around my legs by my new friend who yelled, "It's ok! it's ok! It was just a pan in the kitchen!" It took forever for my heart rate to drop and for me to go back to sleep. Sleep. I never really slept soundly and the nightmares continued for the next twenty-five years.

Meanwhile, I was beginning to build my life again. Within a couple of weeks after arriving, my toddler son and our new friend rented an old, but quaint farmhouse. It was the largest home I had ever lived in and I loved it! It had a Victorian feel to it with a beautiful wooden staircase and windows from floor to ceiling.

There was a fireplace in most of the rooms, but I didn't have to depend on them for cooking as I had in the old shack of the past. Having come from small furnished rentals, neither of us had furniture or basic household items. Until a couple of paychecks arrived, a cooler doubled as a chair and a refrigerator. We didn't mind. We were just getting started. He had been a bachelor for years. He worked hard and lived a simple, quiet and peaceful life. I liked that.

I was quickly blessed with a job doing medical transcription at a hospital an hour away. Yes, in those beautiful mountains, most everything was an hour away. My little son seemed quite happy in the new large rental home. He had lots of room to play hide and seek. We all were trying to find our way.

Moving ahead through life, I continued to feel as though I was on the outside looking in. It seemed that I was different from everyone else. I heard about the Vietnam vets with post-traumatic stress disorder and I could relate to that. If the phone rang, I jumped. If someone at work raised their voice, my heart pounded. If a car backfired, I ducked. In general, I could not relate to most people. It seemed to me that some people were shallow, smug and ungrateful. I felt many were unaware of how precious and fragile life really is.

For years, I had a victim mentality. I don't sit with my back to a door, especially in public places. I continued to live like a refugee, constantly looking over my shoulder. Other times, I would laugh and dance around the house simply because I was safe.

After dancing around each other for a year and silently trying to decide if we should marry, we did. Life resumed unchanged immediately after the customary ceremony with a few of his family, an elderly neighbor couple and my Dad present.

Simple and sweet as this was, I remember my groom paying more attention to his sisters that day than he did to me. He and most of his family didn't carry much emotion. It was *their nature*. We had a piece of cake at the back of the Church and walked out to the gravel parking lot without a celebratory reception. We got in our cars, left the tiny Church and all went home as if nothing had happened.

I didn't want to acknowledge my lonely sinking feeling. I quickly ignored that little pinch. Certainly, all should be perfect so soon after the ceremony! At least this wedding was better than the prior child-bride wedding, which I later viewed as similar to standing on an auction block!

Thankfulness quickly overrode my comparison. As mentioned, I was now free from the former abuser. God arranged things so I could get the divorce without the abuser finding me. He never found us! Now, my new life was beginning. My hope was that this new marriage would easily be better than the old.

I quickly swallowed my concerns that my new husband didn't seem very *present*. I couldn't face that reality. What was I going to do? I couldn't run back into the Church and say that I had changed my mind! Did he marry me simply because it was the next convenient thing to do or did he simply pity me? I wanted to think it was because he passionately loved me.

Of course when you're almost twenty and grasping for an unsung dream, you *want* to believe what every young woman wants to believe. You want a happy ending with a knight in shining armor. After all, my new husband was exactly the opposite of my abuser. The new man was stable. My basic needs were met. We had food and shelter. He did not yell or beat me and I was not afraid of him. He was very quiet. (Too quiet, I later learned.) He worked hard and rested without conversation. I was thankful for the peacefulness. I began to wonder if he would like me more as time went by or if he had only married me to protect my honor. For the following fifteen years, I ignored my loneliness.

Both of us had lived through tough childhoods. Trauma or neglect on any level can leave people with a skewed view of life. Some have never learned how to behave in a healthy relationship. Ideally, individuals need to heal from past traumas, or the pattern can repeat. Things can work out well— or not.

Where was I? Oh yes, back to the beginning of our marriage. The farmhouse rental that I loved so much sold, and we had to move. I was highly disappointed, but strived to grow stronger with each disappointment.

We found a smaller rental house nearby. It had a peach and an apple tree, as well as space for a vegetable garden. This served the family well and I discovered that I was expecting my second child! We were all thrilled! The latter end of the pregnancy was difficult as I had toxemia and labor had to be induced due my dangerously high blood pressure. Thankfully, my new son was born in the nick of time without having to resort to a C-section. His older, five-year-old-brother was lonely until this little baby arrived! Big brother was overjoyed to have a companion while I was busy with chores after a full day of work. There was always much to be done after the long drive home: cooking, cleaning, laundry, weeding the garden, and canning the vegetables. The fruit trees were awesome for making home-canned baby food.

Although both of us were working, money was tight. Buying bread *and* milk was a squeeze. Upset that he was working so hard without proper compensation, I called a different employer who paid better and more consistently. He was, indeed, hiring!

Thankful for that, I stopped working and thought I could stay home with the baby and his brother. However, after only a couple months, we realized that two incomes were absolutely necessary. Health insurance must be provided. The boys had their bare basic needs met, but I had their future on my mind.

I found a job working for orthopedic surgeons. The clinic was an hour from home in the opposite direction from my last job. The morning drive was quiet and gave me time to think and pray. The evening drive was exhausting. I got sleepy as I thought about all the things that had to be done when I got home. Back in that culture, at least in our house, the woman did *all* the domestic work and child rearing. The husbands worked at their jobs— and that was all. They stuck to "man's work", as they would say! That's how they were raised. That was all they knew.

One of the surgeons I worked for recognized my work ethic. He noticed that I was the first to arrive at work and the last to leave, although I lived farther than any other employee. After dropping the children off at our neighbor's house and no matter how treacherous the snowy roads were, I managed to arrive at work early. He also noticed my old-fashioned family values and was amazed to hear about the home-cooked meals. It was nice to have complimentary words spoken to me.

After only one month, he and the other surgeon came into my office and closed the door. My heart sank. My first thought was that I had done something wrong or had not done something well enough. Instead, they said they were giving me a raise! They were pleased to tell me that no one else had stuck it out as long as I had! You see, one of the surgeons was terrible at dictating his clinic notes. He was impossible to understand over the dictaphone. He spoke ridiculously fast and barely enunciated the words. He didn't like to dictate so he flew through it as fast as he could, barely hitting the highlights before he clicked off the recorder! The first dictation I tried to transcribe, was impossible. Desperate for help, I found previous patient records from the filing cabinet and pulled his previous notes. They were horribly inaccurate and had missing sections. However, I gleaned what I could from them. Typing what little I could hear, I simply did the best I could, but I also left a few blanks. What separated my work from the previous transcriptionists' was that I would not *leave* the blanks. Instead, I went to him when he wasn't busy and asked him what he had said. I penciled in the few missing words then retyped the note completely and accurately. After a few times of doing that, I learned that he basically said the same things all the time and I figured out the rest by my knowledge of medical terminology, anatomy, and his usual practice. The surgeons were impressed and gave me a raise! I loved working for them.

I remember a question that was on the job application asking for the applicant's one and five year goals. I wrote that I wanted to be a surgical Nurse Practitioner.

One of the surgeons became my lifelong friend. He took me for a ride in his Maserati. My car broke down in their office parking lot and he came out and fixed it. Seriously, an orthopedic surgeon who also designed jet parts for the Blue Angels' aircrafts, rolled up his sleeves and popped the hood of my old car!

I loved his wife also. One day, she sat on the corner of my desk and confided in me that she had been trying for ten years to get pregnant. I remember this like it was yesterday. I simply looked her in the eyes and matter of factly said, "That's not a problem at all, God makes the barren to have children." I believed the scriptures with all my heart. There was not a trace of doubt in my mind. It was a childlike faith moment! I declared it as a true absolute fact—as true as the chair I was sitting in and within a few months she was pregnant! Not only that, she had another son right away.

Ironically, a week or so later, my bladder frequently interrupted my office duties. My workmate noticed my constant running to the restroom. She said, "You should go get a pregnancy test." I replied, "Get outta here. No way! I'm using birth control. I have an I.U.D. Plus, I have a baby still in diapers. She rolled her eyes in response and did not stop talking about her suspicion. Tired of hearing her nag me, I said, "Fine!" Then I walked to the nearby pharmacy and bought a pregnancy test. A few minutes later, I came out of the restroom crying. I was in shock! How could this be possible? About that time the surgeon walked by, saw my emotional state, handed my workmate a twenty dollar bill and told her to take me to lunch and not bring me back until I was calm.

I loved working there. To this day, that surgeon remains my friend. I can call him or his wife at any time for anything. They were good people who were placed in my path to help me. They made my life brighter!

Chapter 29

A NEW SEASON

STRUGGLES FADE AWAY IN THE LIGHT OF HOPE and faith. We decide. If all we see are the struggles, we must look deeper. At first look, the pregnancy test seemed to reveal my limited finances and the demands of my other two sons. My mind flooded with fear about how to continue working and take proper care of three children.

Once I calmed down from the shock of being pregnant, I remembered that God would provide as he always had. I became excited about the coming baby! I continued working and was thankful.

While enjoying being an expectant mother and not minding the frequent restroom visits, I sat happily on the commode before sudden fear struck again. I saw bleeding! At first, I was devastated. Then I grabbed my mind and remembered not to look at what I could see with my natural eyes. Looking at the problem would not fix anything. God was my hope. I prayed, "God! I want this baby so much. Please save my baby!" He did! Thomas was born twenty-two months after my second son!

When my baby was born, the doctor announced, "It's a boy and he came with a toy!"

He had a souvenir, the IUD. A healthy full-term baby! I pictured Thomas coming out with his little fist holding up the IUD, crying triumphantly, "I made it in spite of you!" The Copper T intrauterine device was actually clutched in the afterbirth and not in his tiny fist. It delivered into the metal pan, clink!

Nine months previously, the *souvenir* had slipped out of place allowing his conception. It was a miracle that it did not prevent his survival. Medical statistics show a high risk to baby and mother with a foreign body like that in the womb.

Enjoying my baby and his two brothers, I resigned from my job. I didn't make enough money to pay a babysitter for three children. I stretched every dollar the best I could. I breastfed and used cloth diapers. Our vegetable garden and fruit trees were great resources. However, after only a few months, it became necessary that I return to work in spite of the high cost of a babysitter. **Although I didn't fully understand it yet, God had a plan.** He was preparing my path for the future, a path that would ultimately help all of us.

An ad for a nursing job appeared in the local newspaper. Finally...a local job! I thought I could do it, so I applied. This family practice clinic was seated remotely in the mountains and served our entire large county.

In reality, it also served as an emergency staging area until folks could get to the hospital an hour from there.

During the interview, Dr. K. asked me if I was a nurse. I replied, "No, but I can do anything anyone else can, given the chance." I remember the expression on his face. I know now that he was another person that was placed in my path for favor and purpose.

The year was 1983. As promised, the doctor taught me some of the duties of a *nurse*. Because he was the physician overseeing his office, I could perform the simple duties under his supervision and licensure. He taught me how to place a catheter into the bladders of men and women. (I will spare you the funny stories of overcoming my own embarrassment in those first performances!) The doctor also taught me how to draw blood samples from his own arm. Of course, I was not nervous! Ha ha ha! The Comforter is with me, especially when I'm out of my comfort zone!

Dr. K was a perfectionist. So was I. Striving for perfection had been one of my survival skills while with the abusive husband. Although Dr. K's strict behavior and high expectations sparked fear inside me, I was able to manage it and I learned a lot from him.

GOD HELPED ME RISE TO EACH OCCASION!

Navigating those new demands served me well later in my career.

Not only did I gain professional experience, but I was placed there to meet two of my very best friends. They were key players in shaping the person I would become. One was an LPN (licensed practical nurse) who encouraged me and helped me learn clinical skills. Her friendship filled my loneliness. She was the adult I could talk to when no one else was listening. We raised our children together. My other new friend stepped into my life and my life changed forever!

Chapter 30

LIFE IN THE MOUNTAINS, PART II

S HE SAT IN THE CLINIC LOBBY WITH THREE BOYS around her and a new baby girl in her arms. I called, "Wendy, we're ready for you now." She gently smiled and gracefully stood. In one smooth motion, one arm cradled her daughter as she brushed a strand of hair from her own face and gently grabbed the hand of her youngest son. Her other boys followed quietly and obediently.

As soon as I placed them in the exam room, I looked at Wendy and exclaimed, "If you can do it, I can do it!" She quizzically looked surprised. I explained that I also had three boys and would like to have a girl someday. I complimented her on how well-mannered her boys were.

Wendy and I instantly bonded. There was *something* about her. That moment in the clinic was another *shift in the atmosphere*. I didn't yet know why, but it was as if time stood still in the importance of that moment. She repeatedly invited me to her house, but I couldn't be excused from my home duties. So far, my social life had been limited to phone conversations with Mrs. L, my LPN friend. Later, all three of our families bonded and managed to visit each other frequently.

On rare occasions Mrs. L and I had enough money to take all the kids to a movie. The car was filled with extremely excited children! We slipped grape Kool-Aid and peanut butter sandwiches into the theater.

Occasionally, we drove the long distance to the public swimming pool. I wanted the children to have swimming lessons, but my kids taught themselves to swim with the help of their oldest brother. That was easy!

Each time my other friend, Wendy, brought her baby girl to clinic for vaccinations, she asked me to visit her. She mentioned that they held a *fellowship* in their home and studied God's word. She never pressured me at all, not one bit. She patiently and simply repeated the invitation. I'm so glad she persisted. The invitation sat gently in the back of my mind, like a *seed* growing. I could *see* she had something inside her that others did not display.

In the meantime, I had visited many different Churches. Each time, I excitedly and expectantly sat through entire services waiting to hear the *deep* things of God. Instead, I suddenly heard, "Amen. Dismissed." What? I was surprised that it was time to leave so soon! Where was the detailed *meat* of God's word? I wanted to hear more about Him and His Son! It seemed that each *denomination* went through all their structured *formalities,* and abruptly finished for the day. Sure, they meant well. They were loving and sincere, but many times I left more confused than when I arrived. Sometimes they contradicted themselves in the same sentence. Sometimes I left feeling more hopeless and condemned than empowered.

I'm not being critical. I was disappointed. Somehow these good-hearted people with a desire to speak for God fell into man-made traditions somewhere along the way. I love and admire anyone who speaks for God or does anything at all for God. I am thankful for my brothers and sisters in Christ in ministry.

Deep down in my heart, I knew there was *more*.

THE GOD I KNOW, SURELY GIVES US *POWER* OVER THE ENEMY.

The God I know, is forever a miracle working God! Many Churches intensely minister salvation. Hallelujah! However, salvation starts *now* **and** continues throughout eternity. Children of the most high God don't have to wait until the afterlife to live a full life.

We profess with our mouths the Lord Jesus. We must truly mean it from our hearts that Christ Jesus is the Son of God who was raised from the dead and we receive His lordship over our lives (Romans 10:9-10 paraphrased).

> That the God of our Lord Jesus Christ, the Father of glory, may give unto you the spirit of wisdom and revelation in the knowledge

of him: The eyes of your understanding being enlightened; that ye may know what is the hope of his calling, and what the riches of the glory of his inheritance in the saints, And what is the exceeding greatness of **his power to us-ward who believe**, according to the working of his mighty power, Which he wrought in **Christ**, when he raised him from the dead, and set him at his own right hand in the heavenly places,

Far above all principality, and power, and might, and dominion, and every name that is named, not only in this world, but also in that which is to come: And hath put all things under his feet, and gave him to be the head over all things to the Church, Which is his body, the fullness of him that filleth all in all. (Ephesians 1:17-22, KJV, bold emphasis, mine)

We need power now in order to stand against the evil one and fully live out God's purpose until Christ reappears. In those early years of searching, I didn't yet know how to express my disappointments and I also had much growing to do. I did know, however, that the *heart* that truly searches will absolutely find the fullness of God. I needed all *the stuff* and not the fluff. <Begin pullquote>If we are flying to the moon, our tanks can't be half full of rocket fuel. **\<End pullquote\>** We've got to go all the way! We can't leave pages out of the playbook. Confusion is not from God.

> Beware lest anyone cheat you through philosophy and empty deceit, according to the **tradition of men**, according to the basic principles of the world, and not according to **Christ**. For in Him dwells all the fullness of the Godhead bodily; and you are complete in Him, who is the head of all principality and power. (Colossians 2:8-10, NKJV, bold emphasis, mine)

Deceiving words can sometimes come from the pulpit. The enemy is tricky and will stoop to anything to catch us in the very place we let down our guard. I say this not to create fear, but to encourage us to be vigilant. We must continue to gather together to hear the word of God, but be careful how we are feeding.

One doctrine that is often taken too far out of context is that of sin consciousness. Constantly beating us over the head about our sins does not empower us, but it pushes us down farther. Most people already know that they are sinners. What we really need to know is *how* to be free. We can see the other side of the lake, but how do we get there? When we *really* see Jesus, we actually *want* to stop sinful behaviors. **It's a heart**

change. *Sin consciousness does not remove sin. Jesus removes sin.*

Intermittently, by God's grace, light broke through. I remembered all the times He intervened in my life. God is loving and forgiving. His mercies are new every morning! After all, He gave us His son who paid the full price for our freedom.

Some of the Churches I visited read the prayer list, but seemingly didn't always expect the sick to actually get healed. Many people say, "Well, if it's God's will to heal, why isn't everyone healed?" Instead, *I pray for everyone to receive the grace of God for a bigger revelation of the finished work of Jesus Christ.* Jesus paid for our healing! He already did His part! The ball is now in our court. It is up to us to *receive* the healing that Jesus already gave us. Receiving is our job. If a quarterback threw a ball, but someone didn't catch it, would we say that he did not throw the ball? We were healed when our Lord's body was broken for us. Every rip and tear in His flesh was for our healing! Would we expect Him to be tied to that post and beaten over and over again every time we get sick? No!

I do not know all the answers, but I know that the word of God plainly says that by Jesus' stripes we were healed. This is my confession no matter what does or does not happen! If sometimes healing does not *manifest,* it is certainly not Jesus' fault and it does not change the truth of God's word!

My heart is to have us awaken to all the promises of God and take Him at His word. Believing is fully expecting that God is who He says He is and that He does what He says He will do. I believe we will *see* many more healings once more people actually believe it. Not many miracles were seen in Jesus' hometown due to an atmosphere of unbelief. Let that not be so for us. Let us be like the multitudes that were healed. We must confess healing with our mouths in Jesus' name and partner with the words of truth. Let's foster a community of belief. Healing is in God's nature and in His heart. He gave us His very own precious Son who bore our sicknesses and our diseases (See Matthew 8:17, ESV). Can you imagine giving a gift as big as your very own Son? Do you think God is serious about what His Son came to accomplish?

Jesus is much more than some *nice* name. It means Savior and it carries p*ower* to change. He is a powerful game changer! Let us get a higher image of who Jesus really is. He is ever present. He is not simply someone of long ago. He is much more than a goody-two-shoes in whose presence you would stiffen and stop telling a dirty joke should He suddenly walk into the room. He's someone whom you really would want to know! Trust me; you *want* to hang out with Him! This Jesus has the power to break every chain! He is whom we should seek more than any other you could ever dream of or envision! He is mighty and awesome!

My heart breaks when I hear false messages spoken that say God makes us sick to teach us lessons. That statement is yet another slap on Jesus' face! How dare we say that! Jesus was already slapped, tortured and broken to pay for our healing. Please don't insult Him again. Did Jesus suffer and die for us or didn't He? Of course He absolutely did! Did He die to save us? Most everyone easily believes that is true.

Why then, do some doubt that He was also beaten for our healing? His sacrifice was for **both**! He is a complete Savior! He made us whole, healed and delivered!

YOU WOULD NOT ACCEPT HALF YOUR PAYCHECK.
WHY WOULD YOU ACCEPT HALF OF THE
GREATEST GIFT TO MANKIND?

Jesus' blood washed away our sins. That is where we place our focus. Sin is not our focus. Teachings focused only on sin have not eradicated sinful acts. However, preaching Jesus is the answer to everything. *His grace empowers us not to allow sin to take dominion.* It's His grace, not our own physical strength. **We must not allow a spirit of unworthiness to rob us of our healing.** Don't look at sin. Look at Jesus. See John 7:19 and 1st Corinthians 15:56,57 that explain sin's strength is in the law, but grace and truth is by Christ Jesus.

There is therefore now **no condemnation** to them which are in Christ Jesus, who walk not after the flesh, but after the Spirit.

For the law of the **Spirit of life in Christ Jesus** hath made me free from the law of sin and death. (Romans 8: 1 and 2, KJV, bold emphasis, mine)

Why are miracles rarely mentioned in some Churches, but are clearly described in the book of Acts? Jesus is the same yesterday, today and forever. (See Hebrews 13:8 and John 14:12.) Why do some people water down the power of God by saying all of that passed away when the apostles died? What sense would it make to stop doing miracles when Jesus spent His ministry teaching us how to do them? Life on earth is tough. We need to use the power that Christ gave us to rise above the enemy *now* and until Christ reappears! (See Ephesians 6:10-18 to learn how to quench *all* the fiery darts of the enemy.)

As I looked around some people in the congregation, seemed to simply be checking the box and warming the Church pews. The looks on some of their faces expressed defeat instead of empowerment. I believe many know there is more, but don't know where to look. I say all of this not to judge or be sarcastic, but to pray for a hunger in God's people so that we don't settle for the status quo. There is always more with

God. If we're looking, we will find Him. All my life I had been looking to go deeper with the Lord. He says if we seek, we will find. What were the chances of my coming from the life I had lived and the places I had ended up in the remote mountains where I would meet Wendy and her family who were on fire for God and His truth?

Phone rang. Wendy asked, "How are you?" Something in her voice gave me peace. She invited me, yet again, to her home. This time, I said yes! My life then changed in a dramatic way. Jesus is *the way*!

After l left her home that night, I ran back into my house shouting, "I found it! I finally found it!" I was asked, "Found what?" I could barely breathe to explain. "God! God is in her house! It's the Church that I have been looking for all my life! They talk about the deep things of God and details of His word. They don't interpret it. They show how His word interprets itself! Not what man *thinks* God says, but what God Himself is actually saying!"

There has to be an absolute truth. Otherwise, if two man-made denominations are saying exactly the opposite, one of them has to be wrong. Truth cannot be divided as opposite or altered to suit different people. There are many opinions but only one truth. Jesus is the truth. (See John 14:6.) I chuckle when someone asks me what Church I attend. I ask them, "Is there more than one?" You see, the Church is the body of Christ. Christ is the head of His Church. I pray we unite in Him and let go of man-made doctrines.

Wendy and her husband Mark, along with Mark's parents, held the Word of God high in their homes. They provided a gathering in Jesus' name to come together as a church. Love was magnified above all! Mark planted the early seeds to help me see grace. I appreciated how he carried both gentleness and strength. The power of God was taught. There was an atmosphere of seeking God's face instead of going through formalities. Wow! I could hardly sleep, so I grabbed my Bible and read and read and read some more! I could hardly contain my renewed hunger.

Of course, people who have only been exposed to the *traditions of men* are

sometimes suspicious of something new. This is no surprise. The religious leaders of Jesus' day did the same thing. The Pharisees and Sadducees resisted Jesus and the freedom He brought.

The good news was that I was hungry for the good news! I would not let go until I learned all that God had for me!

> And ye shall seek me, and find me, when
> ye shall search for me with all your heart
> (Jeremiah 29:13, KJV).

I awoke one morning somehow knowing it would be a significant day for pivotal power. By the way, there was going to be a solar eclipse. In those days, however, my focus was more narrow: getting through the day meeting the demands of a family, a job and praying the washing machine wouldn't overflow. I focused on getting all that God had for me and my children. After my kids grew up, I began to think and pray more globally.

I had been studying the books of Luke and Acts in the Bible. That morning as I sat on my bed, I was crying out for the gift of speaking in tongues. Finally, frustrated that nothing was happening, I called my friend Wendy. Patiently she listened to me whine, then gently said, "Get over here."

She gave me her full attention. In her quiet, shy and gentle way, she sat on the couch with me and listened to my desires. I lamented about how I knew, without a doubt, that all of God's people can manifest the gift of holy spirit by praying, praising, worshipping, singing and speaking in tongues. Scriptures declare it! I knew it was also for me.

Unfortunately, some incomplete teachings have falsely taught that such things passed away with the apostles others have taught that it isn't for everybody.

Again, it was another area for me to dig deeper into what God really says about it. Paul was very adamant about the importance of it for everyone.

Don't be deceived from receiving this power from on high that enables us to walk by the spirit of God. The enemy does not want us to speak in tongues. He does not want us to worship in spirit and in truth. He knows how powerful it is for Christians.

Anyway, Wendy simply agreed that all born-again people can speak in tongues, but many don't know they can or how to do it. She showed me this scripture: "and they were all filled with the Holy Ghost, and began to speak with other tongues, as the Spirit gave them utterance." (Acts 2:4, KJV).

Did you catch that? It says, "began to speak." Wendy explained that in order to speak at all, we have to move our mouths. We move our tongues, we form our cheeks and our lips and we project a sound from our voice box. That is how we speak English or whatever our native tongue happens to be. That is how we speak.

Wendy said, "It is our job to speak, but it is God's job to put the words there." The scripture said, "...as the Spirit gave them utterance." The manifestation of holy spirit is the spirit speaking. Those who are in Christ are no longer only flesh. We are born again of God's spirit. Now, hear this. God gave us free will. He is a giver. He provides things for our benefit, but it's up to us to receive and exercise his gifts.

I wanted it! I want all the promises and gifts! It is critical for us to have His kingdom come in order to stand against the dark and opposing kingdom. For one example, if during a sudden crisis, my physical mind is overwhelmed, I can pray in the spirit.

> Praying always with all prayer and suppli-
> cation in the Spirit, and watching thereunto
> with all perseverance and supplication for

all saints. (Ephesians 6:18) God is a Spirit:
and they that worship him must worship
him in spirit and in truth. (John 4:24)

Wendy reminded me that with our actions we walk
out on God's promises, like walking off the end of a high
dive, knowing He will catch us. Those were inspired
words that specifically meant something personal to
me. I took action by making sounds come out of my
mouth and holy spirit manifested a beautiful heavenly
language. I spoke, but God put the words there! My gift
from Him! For further reading, see Benefits of Speaking
in Tongues (Appendices pp 220-221).

Many Bible study courses have been and more will
continue to be greatly beneficial to me over the course
of my lifetime. However, hearing God's word must be
mixed with believing (see Hebrews 4:2). Knowledge
alone without a relationship with Jesus is not enough
(see 2 Timothy 3:7). The important thing about studying
is to really get to know the one we are studying. God's
word is alive, and it instructs us along our paths. Jesus
is the living word and He gives us understanding (see
Luke 24:45). We have the greatest resource of all,
the Son of the living God. We have someone to go to.
Someone powerful. Someone we can trust!

In order to receive the amazingness of God toward
me, I had to receive the righteousness of Christ Jesus.
If we feel unworthy, we hide and have crazy thoughts of
being less than, and we erroneously assume that God

doesn't want to give particular things to us. We must not believe that lie.

All of God's promises are for us. For no matter how many promises God has made, they are "Yes" in Christ; and so through him the "Amen" (so be it) is spoken by us to the glory of God. (2 Corinthians 1:20, NIV, Parenthetical definition added).

"... the Lord will give grace and glory: no good thing will he withhold from them that walk uprightly." (Psalms 84:11b, KJV bold for emphasis, added).

The next visit with Wendy was the beginning of a true lifetime friendship which has continued since 1983. She interrupted her bread making that day to sit and talk with me. She delved into my life. She genuinely wanted to get to know me. For every short answer I gave her, she asked another question and on and on it went. I told her, "The details are sad and negative and no one wants to hear about that." She replied, "I do."

Wendy continued to probe further into my life for the purpose of my healing. She uncovered the story of my past abusive marriage and began to give me biblical insight about why it happened and what I could do about it. Healing began. You see, talking about the negative stuff is not edifying, but once the darkness is exposed, the light can shine forth brightly. This was a pivotal event for me. Before Wendy befriended me, I avoided mentioning the past to anyone. Previously, talking about the abuse had resulted in an increase of extremely heightened fear. Therefore, I normally buried those memories and they surfaced only through my nightmares or other triggers. *You see, hiding the evil did not get rid of it.* However, honesty, transparency and humility brings healing through Christ. True healing and deliverance must come through Christ.

Somehow, with Wendy, I felt safe. She did not judge me. She gave me powerful scriptures to counteract the damage. I gained strength from understanding why things were the way they were.

Everyday life began to change. I had asked God for a daughter and promised that I would teach her about Him. I became pregnant with my fourth child and this was to be our last pregnancy. Back in 1985, ultrasounds were not provided as frequently as today. They were mainly performed if there was a medical indication. The day came for the ultrasound and can you believe that little stinker kept her body turned in such a way that we could not see her private parts! I would not know until she was born that I was indeed blessed with a daughter! I was so excited, you may have heard me shout with joy at the sight of her! Her Dad was very proud as well, which showed in his face as he held her. Wendy was also at the birth!

Little miracles became commonplace. The following is a series of testimonies that took place when all my children were young. When Thomas was not yet two years old, he went to use his little potty and accidentally locked himself in the bathroom. He was much too young to understand what he had done and didn't

171

have the skills to unlock it. No amount of pleading or instruction was going to help him. The only other entrance was a tiny window above the tub, but it was permanently sealed. Through tears, I stopped looking at the problem and turned my focus to the Lord. I prayed specifically and with authority, I commanded the door to open in Jesus' name! Suddenly the door unlocked!

A few years later, he developed a fever of 105. I gave him a fever reducer, placed him in a room temperature bath, but the fever didn't budge. I put him in the car and prayed on the way to the doctor. When we got there, his fever was completely normal and he had no symptoms of any sickness!

The biggest miracle happened when my daughter who was a toddler by now, fell eight feet onto the concrete basement floor. I was in the basement doing laundry when I heard her come to the top of the steps. I didn't think she could reach the basement door handle, but she did! There she stood! She put her little foot on the front edge of the top step. Not to startle her, I calmly said, "Honey, don't come. Wait. I'm coming to get you." Of course, she kept sliding her foot forward. In an instant, her foot slid off the top step and she toppled sideways, landing head-first onto the concrete floor! There was a handrail, but no wall along the staircase. She slid under the handrail and through the open space!

The second she hit the floor she looked dead. She did not move at all and wasn't breathing! I panicked! I didn't want to move her in case her back or neck was broken, but she definitely appeared dead. Simultaneously, my oldest son saw this from the other corner of the basement. I will never forget how he threw his arms wide open, took a stance and loudly declared, "Mom! She's okay *in Jesus' name!*" Oh God, thank you for my son's declaration of faith! Thank you for the power in the name of your Jesus!

As soon as he *said* that, she took a breath and lifted her head! I grabbed her up, carefully, holding my arm under her back and neck to keep her in a flat position. As soon as my hand touched the back of her head, I felt a significantly depressed skull fracture! As many horrors as I had previously endured in my life, I don't think I had ever trembled as severely as I did in those moments.

I prayed constantly. We called the ambulance, but drove to meet them because we lived far away from the Rescue Station and the major hospital. In the car, she went in and out of consciousness. I know you may not believe this, but at times, her face appeared to me as the face of an angel. She looked as if, spiritually, she were no longer of this world. Oh, how I prayed all the more!

We connected up with the ambulance on the winding country road. The ambulance ride seemed to take forever! At the hospital, an x-ray confirmed the depressed skull fracture. However, no one needed an x-ray to determine the obvious! The neurosurgeon admitted her to the hospital and a CT scan showed no active bleeding. Praise God!

I lay in bed with her all night and prayed. The neurosurgeon informed us that she would probably have seizures the rest of her life.

After the accident, I went into her bedroom night after night to be with her and watch her sleep. I picked her up and held her close to my chest to feel her breathing against my skin. With tears, I would hold and rock her, *thanking God for bringing her back to life!* Praise the Lord! At this writing, she is thirty-two years old and has never had a seizure!

A few years later, her Dad and I drove to town. We were not to be gone longer than twenty minutes. This was the first time leaving the younger kids alone with the oldest sibling. We quickly did our business and jumped back in the car, but the engine wouldn't start! Two well-known and highly skilled mechanics could not discover the problem. Too much time was passing by and I needed to get back home to the children. At first, I panicked, but then I prayed. The car instantly started!

One night, I was driving home with all my children. My car started dinging. The gas gauge displayed empty. We were a long way from the gas station traveling on remote country roads with no houses in sight. No cell phones were available back in those days. I was about to cry, when this little voice from the back seat said, "Mommy remember in the Bible when the lamps didn't run out of oil?"

MY FOCUS SNAPPED TO THE WORD OF GOD FROM THE MOUTH OF A CHILD!

Thomas was much too young to understand that that concept— wasn't he? What is it with little boy voices from the back seat of my car?! Once again, a child jolted me into thinking on *things above* instead of the things on the earth. Childlike faith plus kingdom thinking equals results!

Jolted out of fear, I stopped looking at the gas gauge and looked to the Lord. He can do the impossible! It seemed like the car was running on air. After what seemed like forever, I saw a gas station in the distance! We coasted for a few feet on the parking lot. Next, it felt like I needed to get out and push the car up to the tanks. I wondered if I could do it even if I poured out all of my strength. Instead, I poured out all of my praises at the clunk of the gas nozzle and the sound of gas flowing. The gas spilled over onto my shoes. My cup runneth over! My lamp did not run out of oil.

Chapter 31

SCHOOL, PART I

ALTHOUGH EACH NEW JOB WAS BETTER THAN the last, I needed better pay to make ends meet. Wanting to give my children a better life than I had, I sought higher education. God opened a door for me to work, performing basic nursing duties though I was not officially a nurse. Therefore, I began chipping away, one class at a time, to become a Registered Nurse.

How do you eat an elephant? One bite at a time! Juggling school and family seemed impossible, but many other parents have done the same. Every financial, emotional and logistical barrier screamed that school was out of my reach. **I've come to learn that most apparent barriers are simply lies that prevent us from reaching our God-given potential.** Allow me to make these four statements. If I can do it, anyone can do it. I could not have done it without the Lord's provision. I was determined, and failure was not an option. Sometimes we have to be comfortable with delayed gratification.

Please avoid dropping out of high school or giving up on any level. It's easier to go to school when you have no other responsibilities. When we're young, we want more time for play, but play-time is better attained throughout all stages of life if unnecessary challenges are addressed early and smartly. Wise investment of time will pay dividends over time.

Lack of a solid early educational background and having cultural disadvantages proved challenging for me. As previously mentioned, there had been a pattern of missing classes. Therefore, understanding college math was extremely difficult. It seemed that every math teacher performed speed writing on the chalkboard, as if every student already knew math. Through many tears in the college restroom, I persisted. I clung to the fact that God promised that I can do all things through Christ who strengthens me.

I also received help from my oldest son. He did his school work and helped me with mine! He worked part time at the grocery store and helped me with the household chores. He grew up too fast. I owe a huge debt of gratitude to him! He entertained his younger siblings and entertained me while I studied and worked. I taught him G, C, and D chords and he played the guitar as I washed the dishes. We sang together in the kitchen as well as in the car. Thereafter, he became a self-taught lead guitarist and currently performs publicly as a lead vocalist. He has his own entertainment business.

He grew up and married a beautiful wife who also has an amazing singing voice, positive attitude and a beautiful heart. She lights up a room and the lives of her children. They are blessed with five musically talented children. My oldest trio of grandsons harmonize nicely. His fourth son will complete the quartet, once he is a little older. His second son is an amazing dancer! The third son is the little genius. All five excel academically. The entire family has taken lead roles in live plays. My oldest granddaughter is a talented vocalist. I'm thankful they are successful in school and that my oldest son has a legacy of his own.

He is the musician and teacher in all of our eyes. He probably doesn't see himself as a teacher, but he was the only one who could teach his young sister how to tie her shoes. He has taught me many different things, especially with computer technology. When he applies himself in any of those moments, he has a way about him that is effective. When he is in that zone, he is patient. Like all of us, we have to remember to be patient with ourselves and others. Sometimes we do. Sometimes we don't. The Lord can help us in that area because He is the most patient of all.

You can see why I had to recognize my son for helping me through school and through other tough times. We essentially grew up together. A couple of years ago, he wrote a tribute about me and my life to give me honor. I was deeply touched. It was a great relief to know that he did not think I had failed him.

Back to my early college days. One night after math class, I remained until all the other students had left. The professor, in his rush to leave, suddenly noticed me sitting there. He asked me what I was doing, and I replied, "I'm sitting here until you teach me math. Perhaps you and the other students already know this stuff, but I do not. And that is why I am in school, for the purpose of learning. Now that class is over and my questions won't slow you or the other students down, please sit here and teach me. If you prefer, we can make an appointment." He then, graciously and effectively, taught me and I was thankful.

The speech professor walked into the classroom without looking at us students. On this first night of class, her opening statement was, "You're all going to make C's. Your southern accent exudes ignorance, and I *will* get that out of you by the end of the semester!"

Her statement struck a memory of what *husband* used to say to me. He often told me that being a southerner made me too stupid to go to school in a northern state. I was no stranger to being talked down to and looked down upon, yet those words stung. Had I been stronger, I would have reported that speech professor. Instead, I was determined to rise above it. Ultimately, I was the only student who made an *A* in her class. For twenty-eight years, I had spoken with a southern accent, so I didn't know how she was supposed to get that out of me in one semester!

Regardless of my self-conscious embarrassment, with vigor I practiced delivering the speeches I wrote. We were assigned informational, persuasive, and demonstrative speeches.

For my demonstration speech, I brought my six-year-old son to class and demonstrated a haircut. I explained how I learned the hair cutting techniques from the diagrams in a library book. I ended the speech by telling the student audience that after lots of mistakes and practice, I had improved. Thankfully, my son was too young to care about perfection and he forgave me for the time I snipped his ear! During that ending remark, I laughed, snipped the last lock of hair and removed his cape! He smiled at the students with his toothless grin, and the entire class erupted in laughter. Apparently, I had them eating out of my hand, southern accent or not! However, I think it was my son's cuteness that really won their hearts and my A-grade!

The persuasive speech was not as lighthearted but important. I wrote and delivered it with visceral passion and cited statistics that showed which states at that time, twenty-five years ago, had passed laws treating domestic violence as seriously as other violent crimes. Unfortunately, these laws were not uniformly *enforced.*

I earned my first degree at age thirty-two, Associate in Applied Science in Nursing. All four of my children gathered around me in the graduation photo. little daughter wore her pretty white dress of which she later vomited on that very hot day. That reminds me of the time when she was riding with me to school and suddenly leaned over my seat and vomited over my shoulder. Although with the speed of light, I grabbed a sandwich baggie, dumped the sandwich and caught some of the mess, I failed to catch *all* that came upon me! We arrived to my class and to her on-campus day care, smelling not so fresh and feeling not so relaxed! It's funny now, but not so much then!

After graduation, came further study for the state board exam. Back in those days, the boards were taken on paper instead of a computer. We had to wait *six weeks* for the results. We didn't have the luxury of an email. When the letter finally came, I was outside, con-ducting a yard sale. I grabbed the envelope from the mailbox. With trembling hands, I could barely open it! Breathing fast and afraid to look, I saw it stamped: *Passed!* I had passed the boards!

The old man at the yard sale was as thrilled as I was when I grabbed him! He had no idea why I was jumping up and down, but he appreciated the hug and the excitement! There was less excitement at the clinic, as they were not budgeted for an R.N. salary.

Chapter 32

HOSPITAL WORK

MOVING ON FROM THE CLINIC WITH A PRO-
fessional degree, the path had been cleared for
me to grow in a new area. Although I didn't yet know it,
that new adventure would prepare me for the distant
future. I was hired at the hospital. Their Emergency
Department had no openings, so they put me in the
Operating Room. I absolutely loved it! This specialty
was definitely for me! Intimidating? Yes! Out of my
comfort zone? Yes!

I got busy reading everything I could find about
surgery. Clinical rotations during nursing school does
not focus on surgery. Surgery is a specialty different
from everything else. Those skills are developed with
hands-on learning and wisdom comes within that environment. I borrowed the surgeon's old textbooks and
studied every procedure. I began making index cards
for each surgeon. I meticulously wrote all of their pref-
erences and idiosyncrasies and stored the cards in my
locker. Every morning, I arrived to work extra early and

reviewed my notes. The most difficult-to-please surgeons began requesting me to assist on their cases. A few other surgical nurses were jealous. They also made fun of me for making notes on everything. Ironically, I arrived one night for an emergency surgery and found a couple of those nurses ransacking my locker looking for my notes! You should've seen their faces when I asked them what they were looking for!

There are three distinct roles in the operating room. The *Circulator* (Circulating RN) is in charge of the room to which she or he is assigned. They do all the documentation of the surgical procedure. They are not dressed in sterile attire and can go in and out of the room for supplies, instruments and manage specimens. They communicate with the surgeon, families, the team and the recovery room or nowadays called the Post Anesthesia Care Unit.

The *Scrub Nurse* can be an RN, LPN or Surgical Tech. (Funny, I didn't know until a few years later that my middle son thought that I scrubbed the operating room floors. Ha Ha. Many times I did, but that is not what the term *Scrub Nurse* means.) They "Run the table", as we say. They are also knowledgeable of the procedures and handling of specimens. They and all the team keep up with safety, policy and technology. They remain sterile, organize the surgical instruments, anticipate and pass the instruments, suture and implants to the assistant and the surgeon.

183

The surgical *Assistant* actually assists the surgeon in performing the surgery. The extent of the *helping* depends on the level of expertise and credentials needed to do so.

At the beginning of my career, in a small hospital, I floated between all three roles depending on the need at any given hour. There were not any Physician Assistants or Nurse Practitioners at that facility. Therefore, only the very few of us who had met all the requirements and had sufficient training were surgical assistants.

I took this responsibility seriously and wanted to be as skilled and fully educated as possible. This was the starting point of an arduous journey that took years to accomplish. I will briefly introduce you to some of the aspects of it and more will be discussed later. I pursued the role by beginning the qualification process for two additional specialty board certifications. These proved to be time consuming, challenging and costly, but I loved it. There were many obstacles along the way regarding my timeline, but I wouldn't let go. Mostly, the obstacles appeared in the form of jealousy. Unfortunately, that continues today in many settings.

It saddens me that too often women do not promote other women.

Two thousand surgical assisting practice hours were required to sit for the board exam. This had to be accomplished within a specified time frame. However, influenced by jealous opposition, I was often assigned a different role for the day, which delayed this goal. Ultimately, I relocated to a hospital that *promised* I would get all my assisting hours in time to sit for the certification. That promise was broken and in order to reach my goal, I saw no choice but to resign. Several independent surgeons agreed for me to assist them, but the volume was low. Therefore, I worked as a medical transcriptionist at night to pay the bills so I would be more readily available during the day, Still, there was not enough hours and time was running out. Thankfully, the neighboring hospital was more accommodating and I was able to complete all the hours on time! I appreciate the nurses who supported me and I should pray for the nurses who did not. It was a glorious day when I passed the certification exam!

The certification opened doors. However, I had limited marketability in regard to financial reimbursements. Some payors didn't recognize the services of a CRNFA (Certified Registered Nurse First Assistant). Some insurances did, but others did not. Therefore, I embarked on a long journey as the Operating Room Nurses' Legislative Liaison for my state. I fought to keep the R.N. role in all operating rooms and I fought for equality in reimbursement for the CRNFA. This included leading legislative efforts that involved relentless letters, phone calls, beating on legislators' doors and trying to rally support from my colleagues in order to help our profession. Finally, a bill was written and it passed in the House of Representatives! The health insurance lobbyists were shocked that it passed! I will never forget standing in the House of Representatives that day! Unfortunately, the bill was killed in the Senate but, I was excited that it got through the House! It feels good to be an agent of change!

The fight continued on a national level and I spoke at a conference in Washington D.C. The persuasion efforts continued during individual appointments with U.S. Senators and Congressmen. Some states passed the reimbursement legislation. Others did not. The battle was too long and too fierce, so I finally changed tactics. I decided to apply to graduate school and get my Master's degree to be a provider. I could then function in the role as Nurse Practitioner and remedy the financial and political barriers.

I injected the legislative scenario that was unfolding in order to set the stage for later in my story. I brought you there at this time because those events were being birthed during those early years. Major things have happened simultaneously during most of my life. There has never been a dull moment!

Meanwhile, my job as a registered nurse in the surgery department paid better than my previous jobs. I enjoyed the work and praying for the patients. Although I was advancing, I wanted to go farther and faster to be the very best I could be for my patients and my team. Monthly, there wasn't any extra money left over after buying groceries, clothing and paying the health insurance premiums for our family of six. We kept things simple and excluded recreation and other frills.

It was an exciting day when I paid the last payment on my shiny new electric kitchen stove and my red 1976 Ford Mustang! Oh how elated I was as I carefully detached the final check after writing that last car payment! That was a big deal for me. I had chosen that car and paid for it all by myself! Well, I didn't pick it out *entirely* by myself. While standing alone at the car lot, I asked God if it was the best car to buy. Indeed, it was a good and long lasting car!

I was sad the day I sold it. Through the kitchen window, I watched as my little Mustang faded out of sight. About that time, my second husband drove up with an old Oldsmobile that *he* chose for the family. I didn't like that car, but it was big enough to fit all four children. Then I smiled. I was thankful that I had a car at all and that I had four beautiful children.

Chapter 33

A MOTHER'S HEART

AS MENTIONED, GOD GRANTED ME A daughter after my three boys. I kept my promise that I would teach her all about Him and I prayed that she would do the same for her children. She is fulfilling that prayer now on both accounts. She has two beautiful girls of her own. Her three year old already talks about Jesus. She is quick to pray for a boo boo and sings about Jesus as passionately and loudly as she possibly can!

Because of all the hardships in my life, I wanted to spare my daughter and her siblings of the same. Brittany is the joy and rejoicing of my heart! I'm so thankful for her wisdom that is well beyond her years. She has exhibited maturity and compassion since a very young age. I love that she is not materialistic, but cares about the deeper things of life.

She's always been a lady. When she was an adolescent, I said to her, "You're a lady; guard your reputation. Anybody can follow the crowd. Don't allow peer pressure to sway you from your values. While your peers clamor for attention by trying to stand out in negative ways, you can simply be as God designed you. Honor yourself and your Lord. It's a grace and an art." She did not let me down!

Her interest was in education. She didn't start dating until after she *graduated* high school. She chose an excellent husband of whom she waited seven years to marry. I'm not proud to admit that I had some early *unfounded* fears. I was wrong. He has grown on me and I am very thankful for him! She obtained a teaching degree and is now an exceptional educator of high school Biology. She goes above and beyond to *inspire* her students.

KNOWLEDGE WITHOUT INSPIRATION IS LIMITED.

Additionally, she implemented a recycling program at school and at home. She inspired me. She stewards her part of God's creation. She loves the simple life in the mountains. I appreciate how she keeps the extended family together and treats us with heartfelt and freshly made feasts at her home.

She and I are close friends now. Best of all, she is stepping into her own calling in Christ. My heart overflows knowing she will keep the ministry torch burning. There is much to say about her, but she is private and wouldn't want me to make a fuss over her.

Discussing my daughter reminds me of how honored I was to be her labor coach with her firstborn daughter. It was refreshing to watch her move gracefully through pregnancy, labor, delivery and breastfeeding. She embraced it and saw each phase as a privilege.

There has been a range of attitudes over a span of generations regarding pregnancy and childbirth. Personally, I absolutely loved being pregnant. Being an expectant mother gave me a sense of beauty, awe and purpose. My first pregnancy was under duress, but once I got over the shock of being pregnant while under the control of the abuser, I enjoyed the little life growing inside me. It's truly a miracle to be thankful for, especially knowing that some women yearn for the same.

In the days of antiquity, women squatted in the fields, delivered a child and soon were back to their harvesting. There was no epidural anesthesia. Generally speaking, women embraced pregnancy, labor and delivery as a natural part of life. Then the pendulum swung to medical births where women were completely sedated and then awakened *after* the baby was born.

Childbirth methods have since varied between medical, natural and semi-natural births with minimal medical assistance. I'm not suggesting which one of those methods is best for you. Each woman should choose her own experience that fits her personal needs. No judgment is being made here.

Woman-to-woman, I'm simply expressing issues of life.

OUR *ATTITUDES* ABOUT OURSELVES AND OUR CONDITION CAN EMPOWER OR DEFEAT US.

We can have an overall joyful experience or succumb to cultural misconceptions and be robbed of the true beauty of our womanhood. I pray for everyone to embrace the journey.

In modern society, I hear expectant mothers complain about how they are feeling. I get it. We all do that sometimes with valid reasons. It is sad, though, to hear *too much* complaining about being uncomfortable from those who seem to have forgotten how much they *wanted* to be pregnant and just couldn't *wait*. Be sensitive to other ladies who may be watching and listening. Many would give their right arm to be pregnant— no matter how uncomfortable they might become! Hold on to your joy. Don't let it be stolen. Start practicing going to the Lord for and looking to God's Word to maintain a healthy mindset. You're already giving *of* yourself for another life. Embrace that. When the baby comes with all of its demands, you will be ready to set aside your own needs and joyfully mother the child. Find time in all of that for yourself as well. This will ultimately teach your child that you respect yourself and so should they.

Often, this precious time of pregnancy is rushed. The timing of delivery is sometimes scheduled to an earlier date for non-medical reasons and sometimes for no reason at all. Some Moms chant, "I can't wait,

I can't wait!" Then after the baby is born, they miss being pregnant!

We can choose our attitudes. Our way of thinking affects our actual physical state. For the times when I *apply* the principles of God's word, abide in Him and His son, great results manifest. When I don't, I struggle. It's as simple as that!

It was never God's original intention for women to have pain during childbirth. Deeper insight regarding this topic is addressed on pages 39-43 of Katharine Bushnell's book *God's Word to Women*.

The original benefits from our loving Creator were lost due to sin. *However, Jesus Christ restored all that was lost. In Him,* we are no longer under sin's bondage. **The women, whose Lord is Christ, can have joy in childbirth**. Think about it. *God is not really into pain.* If He had wanted to leave us in a painful state of continuously paying for sin, He would not have sent his Son! Jesus freely sacrificed himself in our place. The least we can do is claim His victory!

Labor means *work* and effort, but it doesn't *have* to be literally unbearable. That may sound ridiculous to us ladies who have experienced hard labor, but it's possible and available to have a manageable labor and delivery. Fear of labor can be crippling. It's sad when women tell other women horror stories. Please think before you speak. Think about the state you are putting your fellow woman in before their due date arrives. Let's empower each other and coach each other.

There are practical techniques, preparations and confessions of truth that can empower women during that time. I'm not saying it won't get uncomfortable, but you are stronger than you think, especially with God's help and a good coach.

If you want epidural anesthesia, have it. No judgment. However, my suggestion is to be prepared for any scenario. Preparation and attitude can make a difference. For example, you could get stuck in traffic and have the baby in the car or any other variation of circumstances. Telling you to *relax* doesn't work, but showing you *how* does work! Therefore, whether you plan a natural birth or not, I recommend natural childbirth classes, books or videos and practice those techniques. Two of the many things they teach is breathing and having a focal point. Look *beyond* the discomfort. For me, I found a spot somewhere in the room and fixed my eyes on Jesus. I continue to use those techniques if other pain comes upon me. I had a bad tummy bug once and during the severe abdominal cramps, I found myself doing the breathing and relaxation techniques through the cramps! It kept me from pulling the toilet paper holder off the wall!

My prayer is for all expectant moms to have joy. Recognize the privileged gift of parenthood whether by birth or adoption. Holding on to that thought will carry us through the challenges. I have been crushed at times under the responsibility of it. My only strength is asking the Lord to help me and boy did I need help.

(I'm sure you're laughing right about now.) Raising children is challenging to say the least, but contrary to popular belief, we actually *do* have an instruction manual: It's called The Word of God! Jesus wants us to have joy. Jesus said, "These things I have spoken to you, that my joy may remain in you and that your joy may be full" (John 15:11).

God granted my prayers regarding my children. The reason I am telling you about them is not to bore you with a mother's bragging, but to testify that generational chains are broken and their lives are blessed. I continue to claim for them the blessings of Abraham plus the greater covenant blessings that Jesus Christ provided. Previously described were some testimonies that happened during their early childhood. The following describes more about them and my continued journey as a mother.

I'm reminded of my oldest son's nature. He has a reputation for jumping to the rescue. He tends to appear out of nowhere, take charge and reveal the depths of his heart. As mentioned earlier, he assumed the rescue role when his baby sister fell eight feet onto the basement floor.

When he was about nineteen, and I was not much older, we went to the lake with some friends to learn to water ski. This was a huge undertaking for me. My parents were afraid of water and so was I. Also, due to my previously described traumatic water experience, I never learned to swim. Years later, here I was playing in the lake! For a few moments, I was quite proud of myself. My son and I were having fun bobbing in the water waiting for the boat to circle. Suddenly, fear struck me! Even though I was wearing a life jacket, I started to panic. At first, I started laughing nervously. Intuitively, he recognized what was happening and took charge! He calmed me in his unique style.

About a year later, I was hospitalized with life threatening blood clots. Suddenly, he showed up and spent the night with me! How did he know I needed that? I never asked him to come! He chased away my fears by keeping me company and making jokes throughout the night.

My next son, Kelby, was a calm and quiet child. At age two, he was self-entertaining. I can still see him, playing quietly on the couch for hours. He was a delight. Most parents complain about the *terrible twos*, but no matter the age, bad behavior should not be tolerated. Some parents boast about the many *advanced* things their babies and toddlers achieve, but when a tantrum or delayed potty training happens, they blame it on their age or stage. These stages are tough for us parents to navigate, but we all need to know that it's wise to guide them toward self-control. Kids actually want boundaries because it centers them and makes them feel safe.

Safe. That word reminds me of the day I was cooking dinner while a very young Kelby was mowing the grass. Suddenly, his dad appeared in the kitchen and presented me with his severely mangled shoe. My heart flew out of my chest and I nearly fainted! Are you kidding me? His dad showed me the shoe instead of my son! Why? Was his *foot* mangled or cut off completely? I could barely breathe! I thought I would die! About that time, Kelby weakly walked into the kitchen appearing white as a sheet. At least he was *walking*. I was thrilled to see him, yet afraid to *look*. My eyes stopped at the front of his wet pants, then dropped toward his feet. His foot was completely fine! Not a scratch! Not even a scratch! My heart rate recovered. I praised and thanked God for protecting my son! How precious to us is our own son? It's moments like those that I worship God who gave His very own Son for our sakes! The magnitude of God's love is beyond my full comprehension! Because of God's Son, our sons and daughters have help, hope and freedom.

Adult Kelby is often asked to pray at family dinners. We think his prayers rock heaven and our hearts! I'm also proud of his work ethic, but would like to see him relax and be able to enjoy family as much. After diesel college, he quickly became a foreman. Now, he is establishing his own business. I pray for a deeper revelation of grace, joy and rest for him.

His wife is becoming my friend as she shares with me her developing journey with the Lord. Another prayer answered! What a treasure! As a matter of fact, while writing this chapter, she was in a significant automobile accident and called me to say that she was rescued from the vehicle without a scratch anywhere! No injuries! No pain! Nothing! If I told you the details and you saw the photo of the totaled vehicle, you would agree this was a miracle.

After the car was towed, she returned to it and gathered her belongings. She noted the Bible verse I had given her years ago did not move from its place in the car! She later recalled, although the car went out of control, she felt as though she had not been there. She was protected and the paper didn't move! Thank you Lord! No greater pleasure than to know your family speaks the praises of thanksgiving. I enjoyed her calling me with both of them on the phone sharing her testimony.

Telling you about Kelby reminded me of the developmental stages of childhood in general. I'm thankful that he was an easy child. Well, he was easy until adolescence. (Yes, go ahead and laugh. I know that you are laughing!) Those years were challenging for all my kids! It's not easy to discipline children and certainly not easy to discipline adolescents, but making *excuses* helps no one. It's so tempting to give in when they protest, but consistency will overcome and all will be greatly rewarded. The time you invest upfront will help you when they progress to the next thing you will need to teach them. There is always the next thing.

Love esteems another higher than self. That's a difficult lesson for tiny children to grasp, even into young adulthood and for the newly married. Therefore, the sooner we all learn this, the better it is for everyone. When we are young, we want so many things for ourselves. Our thoughts revolve around the idea that there is so much life to live and we are eager to grab it for ourselves.

SELF-CENTEREDNESS MUST BE SET ASIDE
FOR THE COMMON GOOD.

We are doing our children (and society) a disservice by allowing them to think *that the world revolves around them all the time*. The kids eventually get out in the world and suddenly discover they can't have their way all the time with everything and everyone. The shock comes that other people also have needs.

A common cliche` says, "You only live once." I cringe when I hear that! It's often said to justify doing things that might not otherwise be done and it communicates that this is the only life. However, there *is* another life to live and that life is eternal. Jesus decided in the garden of Gethsemane to deny his own needs for the greater good. He was greatly rewarded! Eternity is a very long time!

Speaking of time, one of my concerns regarding today's generation is that some children are *too* busy. There is an enemy competing for worship who tries to steal everyone's time. I noticed that when street drugs and promiscuity became prevalent, society developed a new parenting pattern. Parents lovingly believed they were doing a good thing by keeping their kids *so busy* in sports and other activities that they wouldn't have time to get into trouble. Sounds good. Sure, there is also team building and problem solving and fun. Sounds good, right?

Yes, there is plenty good about all that, but what about leaving some wiggle room for children to also explore ways to enjoy God. I'm not talking about simply attending Church one hour a week. I believe God likes sports and fun, but He also likes for us to know Him and the real power we need to know about when trouble comes. The activities of this world can't fully help us when the rubber meets the road.

Children can learn through conversations about godly matters. Allow children to see examples set by the parents' lifestyle. If they see your joy and reverence for the Lord along with the magnitude of the power manifested from studying God's perfect Word, they will see there is something really real therein. They need to know that the Bible is not some dusty book that nobody understands. They need to see that it is living and breathing and not some made-up collection of stories from which each *different* person draws a different opinion. Children need (we all need) THE Truth. We need something we can hang our hats on and trust. Lifestyles and activities display our priorities. Who is our priority in the line up? Who gets our worship?

It's a matter of the heart. The Lord deserves our continuous and intimate abiding with Him where He has preeminence. This can be enjoyed simultaneously while busy working and playing. Of course we can! Why not? It's fun! It's not a burden or drudgery! The greatest gift we can pass on to our progeny is to pray for them to be drawn to the Lord and hunger for God and all of His Word. Love will be the result when we hang out with Him in a real relationship and reverence. He is love. Once we meet Him, we can't settle for less! Otherwise, success without love is lonely and without sustenance.

Some may mock these words, but if they're honest they will admit that relying on other things, no matter what they are, will at times fail. The enemy's pride became so big that he declared himself bigger than God. Misplaced pride causes a fall. Jealousy is also an extremely destructive spirit. My daughter mentioned that she recently realized the seriousness of how evil jealousy really is and the destructive effects of it. We must take authority over it in the name of Jesus. As parents we can monitor behaviors of jealousy and pride and ask for the Lord's help for us and our children.

We can fall behind enemy lines if we become *too* busy for God. We can get out there too far and flounder around in never-never land. Some become depressed, not knowing how to cope.

WHEN WE FEED ONLY FROM OTHER SOURCES, WE BECOME SPIRITUALLY ANEMIC.

It's much better to spend time feeding from the Lord's table.

We must truly know that <u>God</u> is <u>good</u>, trustworthy and bigger than all of our troubles. He is not mad at us. We don't have to be perfect to talk to him. We must teach kids this often and early while they are listening. Those who have no place to go, turn to drugs, suicide, addictions, gangs and some retaliate by performing unthinkable havoc in schools. Any range of discontentment, confusion, loneliness, hopelessness, destruction or anything else that lies between those extremes cannot be swept under the rug. It must be nipped in the bud with the power of Christ Jesus. Kids need our real God who is powerful and has real answers. Kids don't want a wishy-washy religion. That will not help them. They are smarter than that. They want more. God wants them to want more. He wants them to choose Him. He wants a relationship with us. He does not want us to choose evil. He wants to protect us from the evil one.

Children can learn early that prayer is not some boring ritual, but they can actually talk to God and ask Him questions. They can look into the timeless scriptures for answers that address every issue known to man. There is nothing new under the sun. Oh sure, there is modern technology and such, but the concepts of life remain the same. It just has a different appearance. The enemy alters appearances in an effort to better trick us.

The true God bases everything on love and light. (Society as a whole, always darkens when it moves farther from the true living God and turns only to human intelligence and idolatry. There are many counterfeits.) The effects of this pattern is repeated in the Bible and in history books, yet we fail to learn and history repeats itself. Each child has the opportunity to make a difference. Each parent has the opportunity to influence a child.

The Internet is a good and powerful tool. Google is amazing. I go there often and I love it. We can ask it most anything and get an instant response, but don't forget to seek God. Believe it or not, there was a time when people went to God first. He has not been replaced!

Sports, activities, work, family and social media are healthy and important. They build social skills, community and self-confidence. The balance gets tipped when they become more important than the God who created everything and our Lord who redeemed us. Self-confidence is fine unless it becomes bigger than "Godfidence", as Minister Todd White would say. I like that term! *Godfidence.* Yes, our ultimate confidence is in the Lord.

We can make parenting mistakes whether we have a Bible open every second or whether we spend every second on a ball field or in front of an influential television show. A big part of my mothering goals was to show by example the importance of education and the responsibilities of taking care of a family. I also worried that I had neglected them by being too busy with work and school. While I focused on improving their *future*, I missed some of their *present*.

My own children could have had more time for play, sports and other activities than they actually received. I made many mistakes. As you can see, my story has ups and downs and events go back and forth. Life is a battle. We get knocked down, but we get back up again! Let's help each other grow and find joy in the rough times. Things usually work out fine. More victories come by laying a strong godly foundation early and receiving grace. We know there is power in the name of Jesus! Yes, we have *heard* that said, but when we really get it, when we actually *really get it*— the manifestation of that power breaks forth mightily.

With God's provision, my children had their physical needs met. They had decent and warm clothes to wear like fleece hooded sweaters. When I was growing up, I yearned for gloves and something to keep my head warm. My snow gloves were old thin socks which became instantly cold and wet. A thin linen headscarf failed to keep out the cold.

I learned a funny fact after my kids were grown. They said that as soon as the school bus pulled away from my sight, they stripped off the sweaters! I guess they didn't understand how much I wanted them to have warm clothes! I had no idea they were too warm or too embarrassed to be bundled up like that! Sometimes, no matter what we do, the kids have a mind of their own.

When my siblings and I were growing up, we didn't own a toothbrush and there was no money to go to a dentist. This would not be the case for *my* own children! Their baby teeth were brushed by me so they would learn to faithfully brush their own teeth. My first trip to the dentist was after my eighteenth birthday while working my first steady job. I called it my refugee year.

My teeth were in such neglect that it required three dental visits to achieve sufficient cleaning. I'm sure this sounds completely foreign to the modern mind in America. Although my teeth were in ridiculous disrepair, the dental staff never looked down on me. Also, the precious nonjudgmental dentist allowed me to pay installments for his charges. Too bad all people are not kind like that. To this day, I get angry when I hear some people make fun of those who have teeth in disarray. They mock them never knowing *why* they might be in that shape.

The remaining dental work was to be done after moving to the mountains, but the dental office there required all the money upfront. I went to the bank and asked for a loan. I didn't know anything about applying for loans. Up to that point, I didn't even have a checking account.

God placed another person in my path— a loan officer. He looked at me strangely, listened to my request and asked, "What do you have for collateral?" I questioned, "What is that? What does that mean?" He gently replied, "Nevermind. I know you have a steady job. There's just something about you that I trust. I will arrange small and affordable monthly installments." I thanked him profusely and floated out the door praising the Lord!

Toothbrush. That reminds me of Thomas who walks around the house with a toothbrush in his mouth. I previously mentioned him. He was the little boy who reminded me of when the lamps didn't run out of oil. One day, around age four, he answered a knock at the door. I heard the jovial visitor ask, "Who are you?" I arrived on the scene as Thomas put his little hands on his hips, straightened his shoulders and replied, "I'm a son of God! Who are you?" Needless to say, the man and I stood there stunned! That let me know that my children received a good foundation regardless of my own shortcomings. We all should know who we truly are! (See Ephesians 1:6 and 2:6.)

Thomas has a nature like mine: not afraid to show affection. Like all of his siblings, he worked while attending school. During high school he worked at a local nursing home. He understood delayed gratification, invested his time and set his sights on a career goal. He fulfilled the requirements and eventually applied to medical school. Rarely taking recreation time, he worked and studied diligently preparing for his and his anticipated family's future.

One of my biggest embarrassments is that I didn't have the finances to pay for my children's college tuition. On the other hand, some parents pay for everything and their kids drop out or get kicked out of college because their grades are poor. Sometimes we don't fully appreciate or steward what we have when we don't earn them for ourselves. Some feel less invested if they don't have any skin in the game. When we are spending our own money, we are less likely to waste it. It's a good thing for children to be independent and responsible. It counteracts the *entitlement* syndrome and they learn to work without laziness. Being a loving parent does not mean doing everything for the kids no matter what their ages.

Like me, my children obtained student loans. My only consolation is that they understood the bigger picture. I'm sure my children would have much appreciated more financial help from me, but they didn't *expect* it or think that it should be simply handed to them. They embraced ownership and responsibilities of their own. Having said all of that, there is a deeper truth. Don't go to the extreme. We cannot earn everything. We could not *earn* salvation by our works. God is a giver and His grace is unmerited favor. Our response is praise, thanksgiving, loyalty, stewardship and worship!

Nowadays, I want them to understand that Jesus is our perfection, our sufficiency and our rest. Our jobs are not our sufficiency. For their sake and mine, I wish I had learned sooner what it *fully* means to enter into *the Lord's rest*. I'm still seeking the fullness of it. (See Hebrews 4:3.) Christ brought us through to the place where we can rest in His finished work. Odd as it may sound, we can rest while we work. We can rest in His presence.

I'm making payments on my school loan. They have fully paid theirs. It would've been so nice if I had helped the children more. At the time, I did the best I knew how. I did give them a leg up in other ways, although maybe not quite as high as other children. At least they had enough of a generational leap that they and their children will benefit at an earlier age than I did. I was born with a wooden spoon in my mouth instead of silver. However, with every step of a deeper revelation of the Lord and how to receive His abundance, we have all made progress! No matter what the playing field. Every individual can work it out with our mighty Lord.

During the college years, I was able to help Thomas get a position in the same surgical department where I worked. He was a quick learner, paid attention to detail and the surgeons were impressed. His path was redirected to the arena of surgical implants and instrumentation. His skill set and medical background equipped him to teach the insertion techniques, associated pathophysiology and the advancing technology for best patient outcomes. Navigating this arena is demanding in ways most people don't realize. However, Thomas is a tenacious worker and relies on the Lord to overcome the challenges.

I'm thankful that he always made an effort to keep a close relationship with me. As a father, he excels and leads his family with patience and godly council. His bedtime routine of praying with his children is never rushed and surpasses all I've ever witnessed. His children display the fruit of his legacy in Christ. They carry a presence of the Lord that is quite noticeable. When they enter the room they bring joy and love in such a way that you just can't get close enough to them—hoping to get some of it on you! They are well-behaved. Some of the words that come out of their mouths drop straight out of heaven. The way they make an effort to reach deep into the hearts of the people around them is unique beyond their years. They do it in the most unselfish way and is a display of honor. I know, I know what you may be thinking. Every grandmother feels that way. However, ask *anyone else* and they will tell you the same thing. I must stop here or I will go on and on about them forever and about their mom. Their entire family has overcome assaults from the evil one. Another well of prayers answered!

Any of us can fall into the enemy's trap, but let's not stay there. Let's not intentionally destroy others. My second husband and I set out to be good parents. We vowed our children would not witness disagreements or feel insecure because of us. We were not going to have chaos in our home or destroy each other. Instead I soon discovered the opposite: extreme silence. Lonely silence. The children never witnessed real life problem-solving. We simply hid things under the rug. We were remnants of the effects of life's prior deceptions that had damaged us.

We stuck to not allowing chaos in the home. However, when the divorce happened, the kids were stunned because they didn't know anything had been wrong. They could not understand the cause of the separation.

Through the years, I taught my own children everything I knew at the time. Now what? The divorce seemed to mock me, saying I had failed them miserably. During that dark time, under extreme guilt, I couldn't bring myself to pray. I felt I didn't deserve to speak to God. This is a dangerous mindset that tricks us out of *receiving* God's help.

Sure, I had repented, but I had to *receive* His grace and shed the spirit of unworthiness. After I recovered my prayer life again, I prayed that my children had received enough nurturing to make good choices and that God would protect them from any effect of my mistakes.

Although there were some rough times in my childhood, I knew my parents did the best they knew how at the time. However, with humility, we can learn from our own mistakes and from the mistakes of others. I prayed my children would overcome a broken family, as I eventually did. It seems that every generation thinks they can do things better than the last, but we ultimately discover that we all desperately need constant divine help. If we feel we are drifting, we must call upon the Lord all the more!

I prayed that my children would marry peaceful and loving spouses who would *share* in their dreams and work alongside them. I prayed they would have companions to help propel them forward in their childhood dreams of which they had already worked so hard to initiate. I prayed for their lives to be free of fear and destruction. A parent never loses the desire to protect their children, no matter their ages. It has been heart-rending watching my children go through some hardships. Those can be the darkest hours for a mother. When things seemed unbearable, I had to lay them at Jesus' feet and realize that no matter what, I have the Father and the Son. It was not easy, but one thing is for sure I cannot survive without the Lord's promises and His strength.

Perhaps we can show grace from generation to generation as our heavenly Father guides each of us. God covered me and them through it all and we overcame by the blood of the Lamb. We call on you Lord, to continue under your light and not be blinded or seduced.

There are many different disadvantages in this world. Everyone has to make individual choices. Blaming others only leaves us stuck in the mud.

OUR FATHER IS AN EQUAL OPPORTUNITY GOD.

I personally know some alcoholics who got stuck in bitterness because they blamed other people and circumstances for their own predicaments. Alcohol falsely claims to make one happy and momentarily it appears to do so. However, it is actually a downer, a depressant.

It's a trap that falsely promises to make us forget our problems. This brief so-called escape demands more until one day, unsuspectedly, the drinker is under the tight grip of addiction. We cannot change the past, but we can take authority over our present. We can stop the cycle from passing to the next generation. **We don't have to allow brokenness to control us.** We decide what we allow. We decide to overcome. We do it through Christ.

Throughout this chapter and elsewhere in the book, I have broadly shared my heart as a mother. As you know, there is a wide range of situations in this world. Some parents stay in a destructive marriage as they say, "for the sake of the children." That statement needs serious evaluation. If the children and a spouse are in danger of their lives and the children only live with an example of violence, how is that environment good for the sake of the children?

In the marriage relationship, one person can't do it alone. If we are unequally yoked, there will be difficulties. I pray that you go to the Lord and ask for His plan for you and the children. Ask Him if the dangerous family member is ever going to change and choose the Lord. The Lord knows the future. Pray for the person and forgive the person. However, it is not the Lord's will for lives to be tortured or killed. Therefore, ask the Lord to give you specific instructions regarding your situation. Ask Him what He wants to do about it. He will show you what steps to take and when to take them.

Prevention of bad situations is, of course, ideal. As parents, with the Lord's help, we can raise our children to be the kind of spouses and parents that He desires. I know we all *think* we are doing all that. However, are we?

We must choose our mates wisely. Better yet ask the Lord to choose them. Know this, there is not a perfect person out there. Choose a mate who has humility to the Lord. Children will see this and we pray they do the same. If *true* humility and surrender to the Lord is present, then the Lordship of Christ will sustain the relationship.

Pray before you marry and preferably, don't pick an ax murderer. Seriously, some of us spend more time and effort picking out a television, a wardrobe or a computer than we spend choosing a lifelong mate. How many of us have spent tons of time combing over the specifications of a piece of technology? We carefully check consumer reviews. We compare our potential purchase with all the other models and ask all our friends about their experiences. Yet when it comes to seriously evaluating who we will marry, we don't take the time to check for compatibility. One wink and we're at the Church with wedding bells ringing! For a quick and really funny clip with a serious message, watch the YouTube video: *What's Your Motive* by Creflo Dollar.

I'm not saying you should be afraid of marriage or having children. Even with the best preparations we must put the Lord in preeminence and trust His leading. **We cannot rely on other humans to fill a**

void that only the Lord can fill. Asking our spouse or our children to make us happy is not fair nor is it possible. It sets them up to fail, then the relationship fails. If we realize that, we won't be destructively disappointed and seek other sources for our joy. The joy of the Lord is our strength.

We know that some children have been raised in unbroken homes with all the advantages, but some of them also go astray. Others have been raised in impossible situations and end up becoming the most successful of overcomers. This is not to say we all shouldn't strive for the best right out of the gate, but if we find ourselves on the other side of regret, we cannot let guilt steal the remainder of our lives, our victories, or our peace. What good would that do anyone? Instead, God will receive all the more glory if we bounce back and glorify Him!

I received a great amount of healing when three of my children told me that they understood *why* I got divorced. None of us condone it, nor should we. What they were really saying, was that they forgave me. I cannot sufficiently express how humbled I was by their grace and forgiveness!

To summarize this chapter, let me say that from the moment a mother-to-be realizes that a child is in her womb, to the moment the newborn wraps its tiny hand around her finger and for as long as Mom lives, most mothers' hearts are overwhelmed for their children. We help them become independent, then we miss them when they don't need us anymore. I wonder if God misses us when we run off after He pulls us out of the ditches. I'm sure he misses us when we are out there trying to figure things out on our own.

Grown children sometimes think that parents should not be concerned about them if things are not going well. I regret all the pain and fear my parents went through while I was with the abuser. I wish my parents were still alive so that I could honor them more for what they endured raising me and when I was older trying to find my own way. Of course I loved and honored them, but I could have displayed it better.

After we leave our parents' home, we should continue to include them in our lives and protect their hearts. This scripture should not be taken out of context: "Leave your father and mother and cleave unto your wife." In ancient days the engaged couple lived with the bride's parents a year to learn how to get along with each other and the entire family. This custom was also part of God's plan to protect them, especially the woman according to Katharine Bushnell's biblical study noted in her book *God's Word to Women.*

Meanwhile the groom's father helped build the house to be ready on the wedding day. The father was the only one who knew when things were *ready* and *he* announced the *day and the hour* for the couple. No man knew but him. This is a physical example for our learning, sort of like our heavenly Father knows the day and hour when His Son will return and when that marriage supper will be. By the way, the phrase of scripture, "No man knows the day or hour" also has to do with determining the very first moment the faint sliver of the new moon came into view because the High Priest of the Old Testament required two witnesses (the watchmen) to mark it and come report to Him, then the trumpets would be blown for the feast.

> Honor your father and your mother, as the Lord your God has commanded you, that your days may be long, and that it may be well with you in the land which the Lord your God is giving you. (Deuteronomy 5:16, NKJV)

Today, my children are independent, successful and blessed. Of course they are independent, no surprise! Mission accomplished! I taught them to do things on their own and survive should something happen to me. I wanted to ensure their survival. I felt kind of like a lioness that teaches her cubs to hunt and hide. Later, I realized that was not an entirely healthy mindset. Because my own life had been under threat, I carried that mentality too far and for too long. A better balance is to prepare our children to function without us if we were to step out to the grocery store or be in the hospital for an appendectomy. In other words, teach them to be their own person and not your appendage so they are not devastated if you walk out of their sight for one moment.

I displayed all the love in my heart to them, I loved them up and squeezed them tightly, but I didn't do everything for them. They made their own beds and had household chores. They grew up and began to find their own way. Although they have their own lives, I desire to spend time with them and exchange impartations of wisdom, fun and mutual respect.

How amazing would it be if we could all go back and be better parents to our children and better children to our parents regardless of our ages? Oh my, as I write this, I'm catching myself in a bad habit! Recently, I decided to stop saying *should've, would've, could've* and *if only.* Obviously, I still need the Lord's help in doing so. At least I'm getting quicker about catching thoughts of regret. My goal is to lay down my burdens.

For a long time after the divorce, I cried myself to sleep night after night worried that my children would not realize all the dedicated mothering that took place beforehand (and afterword). I worried that they would remember only that I left. In reality, I didn't actually *leave* them. During the adjustment I saw them several times every week, was readily available and soon we developed life together again. Also, there were other circumstances out of my control, but was reality in their memories?

There is no benefit in becoming paralyzed by guilt for mistakes already made. Every time a relationship deficiency popped up between me and my children, I instantly blamed myself. In reality all families have problems, even families who never divorce.

Chapter 34

SANITY IN THE RAGING STORM

STORMS POP UP WHEN LEAST EXPECTED. I'M going to tell you about a big bump that came in the middle of the road! Actually, the following was more like a crater that swallowed me. Nine years after my escape from the abuser, there was a reintroduction of the past. I randomly decided to visit the grandmother of his children. You remember my telling you about her earlier and that she treated me well. His children never left my heart and mind. I missed them terribly. I never dreamed that two of them would *happen* to be visiting their grandma at the exact same time that my son and I came to visit her! What an emotional surprise! Although I cannot describe the joy in my heart to see those girls, the news I discovered during this visit induced the darkest of all my dark days.

Once inside their grandmother's home, the girls immediately fell into my arms and clung for what seemed like forever groaning with torrential tears that soaked my shirt. We finally broke away from our huddle and could barely see each other through tearful eyes. Without sitting down, they began pouring their hearts out about what happened to them after I left. Suffice it to say, the abuser was sentenced to forty years in prison. (We learned that he was released after serving less than twenty.)

I will protect the privacy of the children. To express it all would take another book, which should be written through their eyes. They are beautiful individuals. If you see them at a social function, please don't say, "Hey, aren't you that..." "Isn't he your...?" No! Instead, simply say, "It's so good to see you! You look amazing! What's new with you?"

As thrilled as I was to finally see the girls again, the pain was equally too much to bear! I cannot adequately describe the scene that day as we reunited and all the raw emotions that flowed like a volcano. We were the ones who truly understood what we all had been through together. Our love and bond was strong. My guilt seemed stronger. I blamed myself for all that happened to them after I escaped. I thought they had been taken out of the home when I called for help.

I looked around for my son and found him in their grandmother's bathroom vomiting. I thought that he had been in the kitchen with the grandmother while the girls were telling me about their horrors. The shock of it all was too much for him as well. I had never told him details of our past. He was only two and a half when we escaped. I assumed he didn't remember the violence. I had focused on a new and positive life-style for him.

The visit at grandmother's house was coming to an end. As upsetting as it was, we were also thankful to be reconnected. We didn't want to part ways. Therefore, my son and I followed one of the girls to her house to continue our visit.

Afterward, on our long drive home, I discussed everything with my son and tried to comfort him. I prayed that his heart and mind would heal from that traumatic encounter. I pray he clings to the fact he has a perfect heavenly Father who is faithful, good and trustworthy. God is the best Father any of us can ever have. He loves us and will never disappoint us.

My son and I arrived home. Exhaustion and devastation was evident on our faces as we walked inside, but we were not greeted with any display of concern. No attempts were made to comfort us. The only comment made was, "All that happened a long time ago; you should be over it by now."

I wasn't. All the horrors of my past, plus more, had just been laid out in plain view. Dumped like a bag of bones all around my feet! The reality about what happened to the children hurt me much worse than anything that had happened to me. Also, memories that I had suppressed, returned like a flood. This time, I couldn't crawl my way out, as this hole was deeper and darker than any place I had been. I went to work, but could not function. How I drove there, I don't know. My mind was stuck on the children. I couldn't bear it and was becoming unglued!

At work, I literally could not stop sobbing. Uncontrollable sorrow had overtaken me. My co-worker had no idea what was wrong, but she put her arms around me, pulled me out of the chair and walked me down to the Emergency Room. Once there, they put me on a stretcher and injected a sedative. I had barely slept at all since seeing the girls again. The sedative wore off and I was still lying on the stretcher, not quite sure where I was at that moment. A gentle and concerned doctor asked me what was wrong. I very briefly explained. He asked if I had talked to anybody about that and I replied, "Nobody wants to hear bad stuff." Nobody seemed to care except my friend Wendy. The doctor referred me to a psychiatrist. I eventually went for only a couple of visits and the practical help was useful.

Meanwhile, I couldn't cope. One night, I found myself lying on the cold kitchen floor staring at the dust underneath the refrigerator. I felt my mind slipping away. I cried out for God to help me. I relied on my heavenly language, because my own mind seemed to be dying. After the pleading prayer, light came in and I felt better. Actually, the Lord saved my sanity. (See 2 Timothy 1:7)

The next day, I called Wendy, who continued to comfort and teach me from the Word of God about how to cope, hope and heal. Although this process of healing continued another twenty years, it was a strong foundation. The speed of healing depends on our ability to receive it.

The girls and I still have a relationship. In fact, they continue to call me Mom. The oldest daughter and I have a special bond. Not only did we survive together, but we also tried to protect the younger children. Even though I had no legal authority or means to take them with me, I thought the help I requested was going in to get them out of the home as soon as I escaped. Thankfully, I have been redeemed from the guilt.

The fact that guilt had tortured me, should be of no surprise. We have an accuser. In the book of Revelation we read, "...for the accuser of our brethren...which accused them before our God day and night" (Revelation 12:10). However, I'm so thankful that Jesus "...ever liveth to make intercession for them" (Hebrews 7:25).

God's living word is real in our everyday lives. My testimony declares that I claimed Psalm 147:3 and carried it in my heart. The atomic power of that living and breathing word saved me. I highly recommend it. "He heals the broken in heart and binds up their wounds." (Psalms 147:3)

Grace was extended to me again. As I was writing this book. The lovely woman, whom I still call my daughter, said to me, "Momma, you were barely older than us. You were just a child. You tried to help us. You raised us as your own. I was glad to see you get out. You took your little son with you and I knew you would try to help us." All I could do in response was cry tears of thanksgiving mixed with regret, but awed by the grace of God and the wise, forgiving and graceful heart of my amazing step-daughter. Correction— daughter. She couldn't be anymore my daughter than if I had given birth to her. She is stronger than all of us. I admire her more than she will ever know!

Chapter 35

GUILT VERSUS GRACE

GUILTY FEELINGS ALSO CAME WITH BEING divorced and remarried. I will not make excuses. Although there were plenty of reasons it happened. Only recently was I able to again crawl out from under guilt's bondage and receive grace. God's design does not allow abuse.

God's heart for marriage was to protect women, not enslave them. Initially, the couple's living arrangements were in regard to the bride's family. Part of this was for women's protection. For example, *some* of the husbands would sell the services their wives as sex slaves if finances were low. For further insight on this topic and much more, see the Biblical research book: *God's Word to Women* by Katharine C. Bushnell. In her research, she honors 2 Timothy 2:15. There are more scriptures and truth behind the scriptures than the few commonly known verses. We can casually read across a scripture over a muffin or we can search the matter out with a pure heart of humility.

As people, we are sometimes too quick to make a judgment call without knowing the whole truth or the deeper truth behind God's amazing principles. Are we worshipping only a law in and of itself or do we look at God's intentions behind the law for our own wellbeing? With God, there is always more. His love is behind everything. If we cannot see His love and mercy behind it, we must pray and look deeper. Let's not forget that those who *only* looked at the rules, missed the Lord of grace standing in front of them and ordered the crucifixion.

Not everyone has had the same level of nurturing and training about *how* to live victoriously in the marriage arena, or in many other areas for that matter. I understand the sanctity of marriage. I do not advocate for divorce and I was already punishing myself more than anyone else ever could. Do people who point fingers have any clue what it's like to live in fear, danger, loneliness and bondage. Those descriptions are not God's definition of a marriage. God does not put that together!

Some people continue casting stones. The first Sunday after my divorce was finalized, the entire message was the labeling and personal judgment of "sinful divorced people." We are to judge evil and we are to judge sin, but we are not to attack people. Our job is to speak the truth in love and turn them from darkness to light. Not kick them when they're down.

WE CANNOT PERFECT THE FLESH. WE NEED TO SEE JESUS BIGGER.

Crippling feelings of guilt and unworthiness temporarily kept me from praying and from reading God's word. Deep in the trap, sin-consciousness had seized me and I was blinded from accessing those two lifelines. That was a lonely time. *I felt I had let God down and that I had lost all credibility.* I wonder if Eve felt the same?

IT SEEMED AS THOUGH I HAD PUNCHED THE LAST TICKET AND WOULD HAVE NO MORE PASSES.

Wake up! Snap out of it! That's exactly where satan wants us to be. He wants us to think that we are totally lost and that we should give up completely. Don't do it! Instead, shout GRACE! GRACE to that mountain!

What happens, if you confess a sin and you are *all good* for that moment. Then, while crossing the street, you unexpectedly you see a gorgeous person, suddenly lust in your heart and accidentally get hit by a truck and killed? What then? There was no time to repent! We cannot confess sinful *acts* fast enough to keep up with them. When are we ever going to get it? **Jesus is our righteousness!** His sacrifice was a complete work! He went into the Holy of Holies once and for all. That is why we serve and praise him as Lord. Otherwise, we would praise ourselves for being all goody-goody. If people could be perfect all the time, we would not have needed a savior. No one has done a perfect work except our Lord. Thank you Jesus! Of course we do our very best to live and behave as he wants us to, but we cannot perfect our flesh. Ask Paul.

After the divorce, I underwent a minor surgery and afterwards sustained an extensive blood clot in my leg that moved to my lung. This condition carries a high fatality risk. I was immediately hospitalized and started on a blood thinner. First thing the next morning I was to have a filter placed in a major blood vessel to prevent any more clots from traveling to my lungs or heart. During the night, I was alone and afraid. Every move I made in bed was slow and easy. I didn't want to sneeze. I felt as though I could hear the blood flowing (or not flowing) in my veins. I tried to pray, but I couldn't. I remember thinking that I didn't deserve to pray.

> Suddenly I heard, "That's right, you don't deserve it; that's why it's called grace. It's a gift."

Thank you Lord! Forgiveness was there all along! I *received* it (again) and was able to reclaim my relationship with my redeemer! He had never left me! I had temporarily been too blind to come to Him because I had been deceived by a spirit of unworthiness. Thank you Lord for reminding me that *you* made me worthy. I can never be worthy on my own. Full sharing returned with the love of my life, my God and His Son and I no longer quenched the Holy Spirit! In stepped truth! "My righteousness I hold fast, and will not let it go: my heart shall not reproach me so long as I live." (Job 27:6)

Why carry around dead weight? Had I remained under the weight of sin, I would've been no good to anyone. My testimony would've died. Where is the profit in that? Be free and God gets the glory!

As we are forgiven, we are commanded to forgive others again and again and again. God forgives us again and again and again.

JESUS IS A *CONTINUOUS* SAVIOR.

God's mercies are new every morning. Grace is enough. It is sufficient! Ask Paul.

In contrast, the evil one reminds us of our continuous failures and tells us that repeat offenders are without hope. He roars the loudest in those moments. He wants to make sin bigger than grace. He wants to steal us away from our rightful standing wherein Christ has made us righteous. He cannot legally do that! Don't listen to his lies. Feelings of unworthiness cause us to shy away from Him and feel naked. We are not naked and ashamed. We are *covered* by the blood of the lamb!

We reply to the accuser, "It is written! Romans 8:37-39." Forget about ourselves and everything else and sing praises to the Lord so loudly that it blocks out the enemy's voice. The enemy will flee because he hates Jesus and he hates praise. Praise hurts the enemy's ears! Therefore sing, "**Nothing can separate us now!**"

> For I am convinced that neither death nor
> life, neither angels nor demons, neither
> the present nor the future, nor any powers,
> neither height nor depth, nor anything else
> in all creation, will be able to separate us
> from the love of God that is in Christ Jesus
> our Lord. (Romans 8:38-39 NIV)

You see, it comes down to this: Did Jesus take away sin or not? Of course He did! The sacrificial flesh and blood covenant of Jesus Christ met all the legal and binding requirements once and for all for the full payment of sin.

If the judge said, "Not guilty. You no longer have a death sentence." Would you sit in jail or leave? Receive the gift! What else would we have Jesus do? What more could we possibly add to what he already accomplished? If we don't continuously receive what *He* did, it's like saying we can do it better. It would be like saying, "Hey, Jesus, you could've skipped the beating and crucifixion. We think we can be good enough." No! How crazy would that would be! We needed a savior and God gave us His best! As a parent, can you imagine doing that? Can you imagine a greater love?

The ball is now in our court. Jesus already made His play. It's up to us to receive it. We run that ball down the court, dodging all the devils trying to block it. We *keep control* of that ball all the way, yelling with each maneuver, "Jesus made us righteous!" Slam dunk it in the basket and praise His holy name! Jesus is our game-changer!

I want everyone to know the extravagant love that the Lord has for us and the joy of knowing Him. It surpasses everything our hearts can imagine! We thankfully honor Him. He was not a temporary fix until our next wrong move. *The cross cannot be reversed. The covenant does not have an expiration date.*

If we find ourselves on the other side of regret, we need to know how to receive forgiveness and not disappear from God's ultimate plan. Don't allow self-righteousness or sin consciousness to linger. If we think we can only receive from God when we are being *good*, we have *fallen from* grace. Let's not fall to a lesser place. Jesus paid the debt. If your mortgage were paid in full, would you keep on making payments?

> Now if we died with Christ, we believe that we shall also live with Him, knowing that Christ, having been raised from the dead, dies no more. Death no longer has dominion over Him. For the death that He died, He died to sin once for all; but the life that He lives, He lives to God. Likewise you also, reckon yourselves to be dead indeed to sin, but alive to God in Christ Jesus our Lord. (Romans 6:8-11, NKJV). For sin shall not have dominion over you, for you are not under law but under grace

(Romans 6:14, NKJV). But he giveth more grace. Wherefore he saith, God resisteth the proud, but giveth grace unto the humble. (James 4:6)

In humility, we are thankful. **No one ever sinned less by focusing on sin.** Rather we take authority over it by focusing on the Lord. (See 1 John 1:6-9 and 1 Corinthians 5:21.) When the Father looks at us, He sees Jesus. He does not see sin. We come boldly to the throne of grace. *We are free to pray.*

Simply having *good morals* does not make us *okay* with God. The only way we get to the Father is through Jesus the Son. It's His righteousness and not our own. When we turn to the living God, believe that Jesus is His Son, recognize that we are covered by His Son's blood and submit to the lordship of Christ, **God remembers our sin no more.** "For as the heaven is high above the earth, so great is his mercy toward them that fear him. As far as the east is from the west, so far hath he removed our transgressions from us." (Psalm 103:11,12, KJV)

Why am I telling you all of this? I speak it because I need to hear it over and over again until it's engraved on my heart. We cannot hear it too much. Faith comes by hearing and hearing and hearing the word of God. Hold fast to these truths.

The law was a mirror that made us aware of sin. Where there is a law, there is a demand. Sin was imputed to Jesus and he made full payment for it. We can't pay a debt that is already paid. God is a just God. He abides by His covenant.

> For if by **one** man's offense death reigned by one; **much more** they which receive abundance of grace and of the gift of righteousness shall reign in life **by one,** Jesus Christ. Therefore as by the offense of one judgment came upon all men to condemnation; even so by the righteousness of one the free gift came upon all men unto justification of life. For as by one man's disobedience many were made sinners, so by the obedience of one shall many be made righteous. Moreover the law entered, that the offense might abound. **But where sin abounded, grace did much more abound:** That as sin hath reigned unto death, even so might **grace reign through righteousness unto eternal life by Jesus Christ our Lord**. (Romans 5:17-20, bold emphasis mine)

Be aware of religious spirits who try to talk us out of what those scriptures say. They mock the grace message and accuse us of using it for a license to sin. My loves, how can we sin if we are dead? We are dead, but

Christ lives in us. We are Christians. Christ-in. We *have* been translated into His kingdom the scripture tells us.

Overwhelming thankfulness makes us *want* to honor Him with our behaviors and our hearts. We can put on the *breastplate of righteousness* along with the whole armor of God (Ephesians chapter six). Don't remain under self reproach! Receive the blessings from the Lord. "Beloved, if our heart condemn us not, then have we confidence toward God" (1 John 3:21).

We then have confidence our prayers will be answered. We stand before Him in full relationship, which is an awesome place to be. "Thou wilt show me the path of life: in thy presence is fullness of joy; at thy right hand there are pleasures for evermore" (Psalms 16:11). Let us hold fast to the righteousness of Christ. "Heaviness in the heart of man makes it stoop: but a good word makes it glad. Let's honor what He accomplished for all the world to see!

Don't remain balled up in a trap, bearing no fruit? Get up! We are raised with Christ in newness of life. Sin does not have dominion over us. Let Christ reign. We reign with Him. He knows those of a contrite spirit. He understands we don't want to disappoint Him. We repent and keep moving. It's important that we keep moving!

To the praise of the glory of his grace, wherein he hath made us accepted in the beloved. (Ephesians 1:6, KJV) How ridiculous would it have been had I continued to listen to the religious spirits telling me that I was not qualified to be a minister? How ridiculous?

Some of the self-righteous Pharisees thought Jesus wasn't qualified. They said the fishermen were not qualified, but Jesus called them. He qualified them.

How dare we feel the sting of rejection without remembering Jesus who was rejected and killed for our sakes? Let's not reject His Lordship over the weight of sin that so easily besets us. Let's not reject the power that He gave to us.

There are two main reasons why the grace message is criticized by some: first, the devil does not want you to receive grace. Second, many people and some ministers get nervous and think that if sin is not preached people will think it's okay to continue sinful acts. On the contrary, we are so overwhelmed with thankfulness and love for our redeemer that we WANT to please Him. We can't help it. He deserves it. When someone wants to do something, it is a genuine and lasting thing. A true heart's desire is opposite of being shamed into it or forced into it. Fear is not a good motivator. That kind of motivation is usually short lived. When sin is the only message preached, some people give up or live in misery and self-reproach. The Lord didn't suffer for that to continue. He loves us much more than that!

Do you see the scheme the enemy plotted to prevent me from walking in the fullness of God's plan for my life? Are there similar lies and schemes happening in your life or in the life of someone you know? The evil one says, "You're too poor, too rich, too black, too white, too skinny, too fat, too ugly, too old, too young, too sinful, divorced, too stupid or too smart. You don't have the right clothes. You don't have enough education. You are overeducated. You can't do anything right. You did a sinful act after you were saved. You will never make it and you are not good enough." However, God says, "For I know the plans I have for you, declares the Lord, plans to prosper you and not to harm you, plans to give you hope and a future." (Jeremiah 29:11, NIV)

Therefore, let's partner with the words of the Lord. Speak them over and over until they are engraved on our hearts and manifested. Continually declare and decree that the blood of Jesus *is* good enough.

I also beg you to read the entire word of God and establish a firm foundation of His truths. However, please do this with the firm intent of seeking His face and to get to *know Him*. Knowledge, for the sake of knowledge *only*, is not transformational. Believe it, be inspired and do something with it.

We must have a relationship with the author of the treasure book, that love letter, that Holy Bible, that perfect Word of God. We must personally know and experience our redeemer Christ Jesus and the Holy Spirit will guide us into all truth.

Please don't be intimidated by the Bible. Anyone who seeks to understand can understand. God would not give us His word without giving us the ability to understand it. The simplicity of Christ is more wisdom than all the knowledge in the world. Without Jesus giving us the understanding, even the most schooled scholars won't understand it. Ask for understanding. He will not withhold. *"Then opened he their understanding,* that they might understand the scriptures" (Luke 24:25). For more insight, I refer you to the thirty minute audio teaching *Jesus Gives Us Understanding* (See references.)

Receive Jesus Christ as your Lord and receive the baptism of Holy Spirit. We need that power to walk it out and the manifestation of Jesus' faith. Faith is one of the manifestations of the spirit! Christ's faith adds to our mustard seed faith. Christ will multiply our faith just as He multiplied the bread and fishes. Come to Jesus! Come and dine, as Jesus invited His followers to dine in the Gospel of John, chapter twenty-one.

We partner with the *living* word, Jesus Christ. We partner with the covenant of Jesus' flesh and blood, the ultimate atonement. Jesus is our High Priest.

> Having therefore, brethren, boldness to enter into the holiest by the blood of Jesus, By a new and living way, which he hath consecrated for us, **through the veil, that is to say, his flesh;** And having an high priest over the house of God; Let us draw near with a true heart in full assurance of faith, having our hearts sprinkled from an evil conscience, and our bodies washed with pure water. (Hebrews 10:19-22 bold emphasis, mine)

For we which have believed do **enter into rest**, as he said, As I have sworn in my wrath, if they shall enter into my rest: although the works were finished from the foundation of the world. (Hebrews 4:3, bold emphasis, mine)

We cannot *rest* under the weight of sin. We cannot rest in unbelief. Therefore, if you are so compelled to do a work, then the work is to believe! The commandment is to believe and have rest. To please God: *believe* His words. We do not keep making sin offerings. ***We do not insult the holy, perfect sacrifice of our Lord Jesus.***

Not that we are sufficient of ourselves to think anything as of ourselves; but our sufficiency is of God; Who also hath made us able ministers of the new testament; not of the letter, but of the spirit: for the letter killeth, but the spirit giveth life. (2nd Corinthians 3:5,6)

But their minds were blinded. For until this day the same **veil remains unlifted** in the reading of the Old Testament, because the veil is taken away in Christ. But even to this day, when Moses is read, a veil lies on their heart.

Nevertheless when one turns to the Lord, the veil is taken away. (2 Corinthians 3:14-16 NKJV)

We were blind, but now let's see! We were lost, but now we're free! Let Jesus remove the veil of deception. Let the veil come off and see grace!

God knows the people who truly love Him and want to serve Him and He knows the people who reject Him. He has mercy on those who truly seek Him. "...the mercy of the Lord is from everlasting to everlasting upon them that fear (have reverence for) him and his righteousness unto children's children." (Psalms 103:17, parenthetical added for explanation.)

We do not frustrate the grace of God. Our lights must shine! Sometimes it's difficult to shine if we are struggling, but we can ask the Lord for strength and a bigger revelation of his Grace. With Jesus, all things *become* new. We are new again and again, in every continuous moment, as we receive His full redemption.

Chapter 36

BACK IN THE SADDLE

STARTING OVER AGAIN. WITH THE LIGHT shining brighter, life started falling into place. I was able to function socially, economically and spiritually. I continued my education. The pressures of secular work were more manageable. I began to walk in victory. I was not doing it perfectly, but when I applied the scriptures, received grace and kept my eyes on Jesus, victory manifested! All of God's promises are "yes and amen" in Christ according to 2 Corinthians 1:20. In other words, God keeps all of His promises to us. The word *amen* means *so be it*. As Rev. Tom says, "We can't allow our doubts to be bigger than God's promises."

Once I received grace *again*, I allowed myself to resume and *enjoy* intimacy with the Lord. I quit hiding from Him. Oh, how I had missed that closeness! My isolation was of no one's fault but my own. I love what the scripture says here, "Because he hath **set his love** upon me, therefore will **I deliver him:** I will set him on high, because **he hath known my name."** (Psalms 91:14, ASV, bold emphasis.)

How glorious to live again in that childlike faith! Have you ever stopped to think about why it's called childlike faith? Children know that they can't do everything on their own and they will ask for help. Children are not self-righteous. Most children, by nature, trust in all the possibilities. Unfortunately, sometimes as we grow older and life goes sideways, some of those beliefs get stolen.

May we never become so cynical that we forget our childlike faith. I was able to crawl out from under a rock and stand on The Rock, Jesus. Of course, there were many hurdles along the way. The good news is, the closer we snuggle up to Jesus, the harder it is for the enemy to get to us.

With wide-eyed wonder, let's remain in awe of the Creator of the universe. Like children, receive the reward of your expectations! "...without faith it is impossible to please Him, for he who comes to God must believe that He is, and that He is a rewarder of those who diligently seek Him" (Hebrews 11:6, NKJV). If I lighten up, like a kid, joy comes and results follow! I'm normally much too serious. I want to become more childlike!

I have enjoyed my professional life. I studied human anatomy and physiology. It's fascinating how wonderfully and beautifully we truly are made. The intricacy of the human eye is only one example of a miraculously functional and beautiful organ. Looking with that organ at our other organs further takes my breath away! Breathing. Yes, what about that divine design of breathing? We go to sleep and our bodies keep on breathing throughout the night! Automatically, the heart keeps on beating. Looking through a microscope is a journey into the otherwise unseen world of a truly incredible creation. Do I even mention the subatomic? I remain in total awe of my Creator! How much more is the wonder and awe of the spiritual connection with our God!

Each organ is individually amazing! Working together, as a whole, is above extravagance! It is such a phenomenal picture of how the Lord's Church, The Body of Christ should function with each part making up the complete whole with Jesus as the head. How can anyone possibly fail to admit the creative genius and greater purpose? How much more uncharted and limitless is the holy spirit living inside us? Why seek temporary thrills and neglect the endless possibilities of living as spirit filled sons and daughters of the most high God?

I never get tired of looking at God's handiwork and specializing in surgical assisting has given me great joy. It's a pleasure to pray for the patients and for our team during the procedures. I have no doubt that God gave me the desires of my heart.

The more I fall in love with Him, the more He becomes my everything. Former dreams seem less important. However, He wants us to have the desires of our heart and work heartily unto Him. He delights in our enjoyment of the things our hands find to do.

But seek ye first the kingdom of God, and his righteousness; and all these things shall be added unto you. (Matthew 6:33, KJV)

Let them shout for joy, and be glad, that favor my righteous cause: yea, let them say continually, Let the Lord be magnified, which hath pleasure in the **prosperity** of his servant. (Psalms 35:27, KJV, bold emphasis mine)

Chapter 37

SCHOOL, PART II

IWORKED WHILE CONTINUING TO CHIP AWAY
at more college classes. At age forty-four, I graduated with my second degree, a Bachelor of Science in
Nursing from the University of Phoenix. I wondered.
Could I possibly be accepted into the Master's program
at Duke? I will never forget the application process or
their grueling entrance exam, but my *acceptance* letter
came! I ran up and down the hallway, jumping and
laughing and praising God!

Looking back, I could see the orchestrated stepping
stones that had prepared me in many ways. Along my
journey, I misinterpreted some things as roadblocks,
but they ultimately proved to be blessings. For example,
I included my nursing-related legislative endeavors,
community service and other life accomplishments on
the essay portion of the graduate school application.
The acceptance officers viewed it as being well-rounded.
Thank you! I viewed it as a long and grinding road.

I wasn't out of the woods yet, because I knew acceptance into Duke also depended on a high score on the college entrance exam. My determination level outweighed my confidence level. I furiously studied night and day. I carried extensive notes, flashcards and the prep book with me everywhere I went, vacation included.

I scored high enough to be accepted, but the application officer suggested that I retake the exam to see if I could bring my score up just a little. Back to the grind with more vigor, if possible, I studied and retook the exam. After taking the entrance exam *twice*, I made the exact same score! My husband John and I laugh about this now, but it wasn't funny at the time. Everything considered, Duke accepted me anyway! Thank you, Lord!

The Duke Chapel was a point of encouragement. It came into view at the end of my long drive. I could see the top of it from the interstate exit. Stately, it towered over the trees. I was in awe of its beauty.

On the first day of school, I found my way across the massive campus to the orientation auditorium. I felt accomplished simply having located it. Suddenly, someone grabbed my name tag, hugged me and shouted, "You're number five!" I wondered what that could possibly mean. Soon, I realized that I had met yet another person that God had placed in my life. She was tracking down all the students in our specialized Acute Care Adult Nurse Practitioner program. There were not many students in our specialty and I was number five. I smiled, knowing that five is the number for grace!

The massive auditorium was buzzing with student body chatter. The microphone screeched as the speaker sternly commanded everyone to take a seat. On command, my bottom instantly clunked into the seat. Looking around inside this grand auditorium, I was surrounded by obviously intelligent and well-bred students. I wondered, "What am **I** doing here? How can I do this?" In fear, I took a gulp. Then, I clung to the promise of Philippians 4:13: "I can do all things through Christ who strengthens me."

Although I remained anxious during my drive home, I was very thankful that I was a student of Duke University! Suddenly, I remembered my teenage years of not being permitted to go to high school. I recollected the television sitcoms from my teen years that showed the bedrooms of teen stars with *university pennants* on their walls. Back then, I was broken hearted, thinking I would never have those things on my own wall from a *real* university. Silly as it may sound, the first thing I bought after graduation was a Duke pennant, which hangs in my office today. Also hanging is a graduation present from John. He gave me an official university frame for my Master's degree, which includes a photo of the Duke Chapel—how appropriate!

The Lord answered every prayer. In the early 1980's, I declared a five-year-goal on a job application. Twenty-four years later, that goal came true. I indeed became a surgical Nurse Practitioner as declared, but also became a self-employed Nurse Practitioner! Sure, it took a lot longer than five yearsl, but it happened! "Take delight in the Lord and he will give you the desires of your heart." (Psalms 37:4, NIV)

A funny thing happened on the second day of class. The teacher announced, "Turn in your case study." I panicked! What? When did she assign that? All the color drained from my face, as I turned to my class-mate and asked, "Case study! What case study?"

Addie couldn't get over the look on my face as I ran out of the classroom. I quickly banged out a case study in the computer lab next door, raced back into class and planted it on the professor's desk! We've laughed over that scene so many times. John really thought it was funny because he knows me so well. He knows how upset I get when my ducks are not in a row.

Other experiences were not as funny. In order to catch up, I put in many hours of study and pushed harder than my classmates. I simply didn't have the caliber of educational background for this level. I lacked the solid elementary and high school funda-mentals and had to get them on my own.

Young people, please stay in school. Being a student is much easier without the added demands of adult life. It can be done, but why do it that way if you can avoid it? Out of this passion, I developed a program titled *Peer Partners, Not Peer Pressure* and presented it to the local high schools. One of the major topics advocated was against dropping out of school. I did those presentations during my college years and still have the slides. Recently I have been thinking of revising them with updates regarding today's concerns inside the school atmosphere and re-present the program. I need an avenue to speak freely in a public high school setting or find another venue where I can reach the young people outside their usual organizations.

While navigating graduate school, I tried to hide the victim mentality and lack of self-confidence. I caught myself looking at my clothes to see if I fit in with my classmates. I wouldn't talk very much. I kept my head down so I wouldn't see any potential looks of disapproval. I silently scolded myself, "You're clothes are good. No one thinks you're stupid. Get a grip! You're fine now, so act like it! To receive honor, I must display honor. "

Our body language and our countenance is on display. *Feeling* inferior makes us *look and act* inferiorly, which is repelling to other people.

BONDAGE ON THE INSIDE MAKES US APPEAR BOUND ON THE OUTSIDE.

We should *not carry* bondage for others to see. Those bad habits must be broken because they attract abuse. Kingdom thinking brings the kingdom. Let's speak and act in such a way that we declare and attract God's kingdom.

Addie became a good friend. After we got to know each other, she invited me to stay at her nearby apartment anytime I wanted. This eased the burden of the long commute to school. Her hospitality was yet another example of God's provision! She was well-educated, having three degrees before she got to Duke. She came from a lawyer father and a well-educated mother. Surrounding myself with successful people has been another habit that has helped me grow. I learn a lot by listening and observing.

At the age of forty seven, I graduated from Duke University with Honors. John was so excited that he rented a limousine to take me and a few proud family members to graduation. Who does that? He should be rewarded for all he has done for me!

Addie said to me, "You've earned a place at the table." I will never forget her saying that. Her comment was a great graduation present and I felt valued! God gives us wisdom and skills. Examples of this are beautifully described in places like Exodus chapter twenty-eight to thirty-five. Since then I have had an even greater revelation of Ephesians 1:6. Thank you Lord for giving me a place at the table. King David put it this way, "You prepare a table before me in the presence of my enemies; you anoint my head with oil; my cup overflows." (Psalms 23:5).

My posture didn't stoop while I was striding across the University field to receive my diploma. My countenance was bright. I spotted Mom! She stood out in the massive crowd wearing huge sunglasses prescribed after her cataract surgery! They blocked the sun, but I imagine also hid her own disappointments regarding her lack of opportunity. Knowing her, tears of pride and joy for me overrode her own pain. She knew how to rise above pain. She was experienced at that for sure.

Mom used to tell me, "Be patient. God will move you to the next place He wants you to be." This declaration was prophetic and comforting. I knew it was time to move on from my first post graduate job. Mom was correct. A door opened for me to start my own practice! My business launched doing what I had always wanted to do: specialize in surgical assisting.

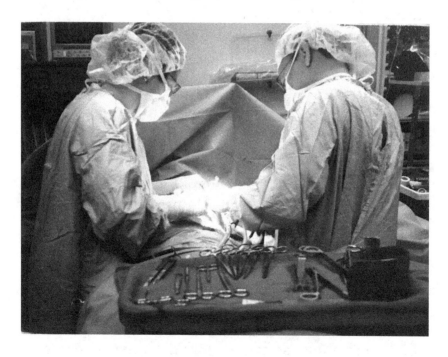

I opened my business account with only one hundred dollars. I knew I had to put feet to my faith! It took four months to receive the first reimbursement. The pipe had to be filled before it could come out the other end. No matter! God is a blesser. That's who He is and that's what He does!

Self-employment was exciting and worth fighting for. I asked the Lord for wisdom to navigate the business world and its many professional standards. I hired a billing company. Also, I personally bird-dogged unpaid claims. My efforts paid off! My income far exceeded my first fast food job that paid only $1.50 per hour. Many surgeons called me and requested my assistance. God heard every prayer!

He brought Goliath down to my size! One of the largest health insurance companies had a policy in which they sent physician extender reimbursements directly to the patients instead of to the provider. The patients were instructed by the insurance company to forward the payment to the surgical assistant provider. In this case, that would be me. I don't have to tell you what often happened. More than a few checks never made it into my hands.

To remedy this problem, I applied to become an in-network provider with that insurance company. That was not so simple. That particular company's policy didn't contract with non-physician providers. This made no sense to me. All other insurances paid me directly as a qualified and certified mid-level provider. This particular company, also, was already paying me for my services anyway, so why not send the payment *directly* to me? The battle to correct this problem was fierce and lengthy, but the stone of grace was slung and favor took down the giant! I became the *only* non-physician provider to ever be contracted with them! Victory!

The Lord becomes sweeter to me every day. The Master's Degree and the doors it opened gave me great satisfaction, but nothing satisfies me as much as The Master, Jesus. I would give it all up to work full-time for Him. I know He has the very best benefit package! Ahh, what am I saying? I already work for Him! "And whatsoever ye do, do it heartily, as to the Lord, and not unto men." (Colossians 3:23)

Not *everyone* must go to college. Nobody should feel guilty for not having done so. There are many ways to fulfill the life the Lord gives us and all are important. My story is not to say, "Hey, look what I've done." Instead, I write to say, look at what the Lord has done! "...for the testimony of Jesus is the spirit of prophecy" (Revelation 19:10). Testimonies call it forth, "Jesus do it again!" May my testimony be an encouragement. Where there's a will, there's a way. Jesus is *The Way*.

My parents couldn't afford to send any of us to college. That's okay. I went anyway. I'm still paying school loans at almost fifty-nine years old. For me, personally, I view it better than never having gone to school. It makes no sense to blame others for failed dreams.

It makes no sense to make excuses and later have regrets. Excuses are another form of lies. The enemy tells us a million reasons why we can't do something. Whenever you catch yourself saying *I can't*, switch that statement to **I can** *do all things through Christ* who strengthens me (Philippians 4:13, KJV). How many things can you do? All.

ACCUSERS AND ENCOURAGERS PEPPER OUR LIVES.
HANG OUT WITH THE ENCOURAGERS.

Whatever you need to do, whatever it is, never give up! In fact, just before I opened my business, I read Joyce Meyer's book, *Never Give Up*. She speaks of well-known and highly successful people who were told to give up, but they didn't. They went from rags to riches and contributed significantly to society.

One of the most amazing things that happened to me was being able to take that *one* college class so long ago while under the control of the abuser. At one time, my only goal was to sleep at lease a couple of hours and live to see the next day. Look at me now: I'm spiritually fulfilled, prosperous and safe!

Start with one thing, and then keep going no matter what. How do you eat an elephant? One bite at a time. Education is a key that I value and there are other keys, but Jesus is *the* key. It is He that holds all the keys that pertain to this life and life eternal.

Jesus said, "And I will give unto thee the keys of the kingdom of heaven: and whatsoever thou shalt bind on earth shall be bound in heaven: and whatsoever thou shalt loose on earth shall be loosed in heaven." (Matthew 16:19)

Execute that authority, especially when those influenced by darkness are coming against you. Also, don't be afraid of wanting better things. God gave us capabilities to do the amazing. He designed us to give Him glory—to reflect the glory of the Creator. We have been to the moon. We have made extraordinary discoveries. God's people should be bright and shining stars. What if we ask God for the wisdom to change the things we can and for *His power to change* the things we cannot? Don't accept the status quo.

Our blessings are as close as a whispered prayer. Many things we pray for have already been given to us by the finished work of Jesus. Our job is to *reclaim* them from the thief who came to steal, kill and destroy.

Claim life. The view from the window of my currently fabulous home showed the glorious glow of a brilliant sunrise. It illuminated the entire tree line and my entire soul. I'm free! I survived, and I'm alive!

I missed many sunrises while working inside windowless operating room walls for long hours before and after daylight. *The light is always there whether we see it or not.* I'm overcome with thankfulness as

253

I witness the breathtaking sunrise this morning. I've been granted four months off work— time that was carved out by the Lord to write. Joy flooded in and praises sprang forth to the Creator of the golden sunrise. I'm blessed exceedingly abundantly above all I could ask or think (see Ephesians 3:20).

The word of the Lord comes to me usually when I'm in the space between sleep and wakefulness. One night I heard, "exceeding power". Instantly, I knew the scripture to which He was referring, *"And what is the exceeding greatness of his power to usward who believe, according to the working of his mighty power."* *(Ephesians 1:19).*

A few nights later I heard this address, "Matthew 21:22." That scripture promise has been and continues to manifest in my life! He is faithful. A different night, I was attacked by darkness. Once awake, while trying to settle down and wondering if I dare return to sleep, I heard, "Hebrews four." As I read it, an instant and palpable peace flooded me. All fear left! I mean *all* the fear left. He has been teaching me about *entering into his rest.* He whispered to me the scripture and then *demonstrated* it. It was as if to say, "See, that's how it works! That's what it means! You believe in me, now *experience my* rest!" Oh, the sweet reality is truly overwhelming! Abiding with Jesus is key.

The more time you spend with someone, the more you get to know that person and experience the benefits of the relationship. Trust builds. Love builds.

THANKFULNESS AND PRAISE IS LIKE WATER AND FERTILIZER THAT PROMOTES THE GROWTH OF THE LIFE INSIDE THE SEED.

Without Jesus, I can do nothing. He said, "I am the vine, ye are the branches: He that abides in me, and I in him, the same brings forth much fruit: for without me ye can do nothing." (John 15:5).

Chapter 38

HEAVEN SENT

THERE ARE MANY DOORS, BUT JESUS IS THE door. Through Him all other doors open, which reminds me to tell you about my present wonderful husband. At the time of this writing, we have been married twenty three years. He supported me emotionally throughout graduate school. He is such an effective encourager who leads patiently and gently. Companionship is his forte`. The Lord knew I needed someone exactly like that! The painful and lonely years were gone! I'm so glad I didn't stay in the wilderness!

John honors Christ as his head and therefore loves me as Christ loves the Church. That is a marriage designed and put together by God. It took me a long time to learn how to receive such a blessing instead of staying in the self-preservation defensive mode. I always wanted a relationship like this, but had grown to think that it didn't exist. Was it too good to be true?

You know what they say, "If it's too good to be true, it's probably not true." Sometimes I think that's why some people have trouble believing the gospel. It is so incredibly good that they just can't believe it! It's too good to be true! Oh, but it *is* true!

God is good beyond our wildest imaginations! He wills all goodness toward you with nothing lacking! The enemy lied to Eve, perhaps insinuating that God *wasn't all that and a bag of chips*. Was God too good to be true? That question, that doubt is still placed in the minds of people today. Distractions and seductions are everywhere. "Surely there is *more* for you in other places, look over here," said the spider to the fly!

Lord, open our eyes and have us receive all your goodness. Sometimes, I don't think I deserve my present husband, John. He had to unpack a lot of my baggage. How many of us have trouble receiving from people and trouble receiving the grace of God?

Although some people accused me of leaving my second husband for another man, that could not be further from the truth. My second marriage was over five years before I met John. I won't breach the privacy or honor of the other person or his family, whom I love. He didn't know *how* to display simple everyday affection. He was a product of being raised in a time and culture where some men did not show those emotions. Growing up, he was expected to do hard physical labor, be tough and keep quiet. I was also a product of a damaged past and saw my second husband as a safe place to be. He was one hundred and eighty degrees opposite of the abuser, yet we lived in silence. I don't blame him that he didn't know how to display what I needed and I wish I could have lived without it. There were other chains to be broken and free will is a part of that. I pray the veil comes off of everyone who struggles to overcome. Everyone must be invested for relationships to work. I pray he forgives me. I forgive him.

As mentioned in a previous chapter, I died a thousand deaths from a guilty conscience after the divorce. However, I cannot thank God big enough for forgiving me and not leaving me under my self-inflicted guilt. I don't expect people to understand this. As crazy as it sounds, the turn in my life's path opened doors to serve God. Some people won't understand that. I don't even think I understand it, but some things cannot be explained with words, but rather by the fruit.

It turns out that I wasted too much precious time feeling guilty about being divorced and remarried. John is considerate, gentle, kind and compassionate. He displays love. I highly resisted him at first, but I'm so glad we are together!

John and I have so much in common. He taught me that it is actually okay to have fun. He got a thrill out of taking me to Walt Disney World and I was like a kid at age thirty-six. I loved his spontaneity. He loves to give surprises. Late one night, on the spur of the moment, he put a mattress and blankets in the pickup bed that had a camper top. The children were sleeping at our house. He came back inside and told me not to wake them, but to pack them a change of clothes. Without waking them, he carried them and laid them in the truck. We drove off into the night as I lay with them on the mattress. This was a mystery trip for me as well. The children awoke with the sunlight and curious glee. Finally, they saw road signs to Busch Gardens Amusement Park. Oh, you should have heard them squeal with excitement! This was only one of many adventures. However, our best adventure is currently enjoying God's Kingdom and The Promised Land together. We're on a mission for God and for each other.

We enjoyed road trips across the western United States and saw the vast beauty of God's creation. "God's majestic mountains are breathtaking," says the grown up girl from humble beginnings where her childhood neighbors never left the county!

John gives me joy, and the Lord gave me John. The desires of my heart were granted. In the winter wonderland of Breckenridge Colorado, another dream came true. I rode in a one-horse-open-sleigh! It was just like the Christmas cards! Perfect! As a bonus, John also took me for a ride in a horse-drawn sled through the woods in the beautiful mountains of Glenwood Springs, Colorado! As usual, there is always more with God.

One summer, John, my daughter and I flew to Las Vegas, rented a car and drove a large loop across the West. We were gone seventeen days and spent only one night at each new place. This adventure was unplanned and unforgettable! Hardly a week goes by that we don't think of that special time together and the beauty we saw!

John carries a peace. He encourages me to rest and play. No matter how long it takes, he waits patiently for my attention when I'm working on professional projects and long projects like this book. He improves my life, but too many times I have made his more complicated. He loves me as a person, not because of my duties. He doesn't care whether I do or do not have a five-course, home-cooked meal on the table and all the chores completed. I can walk in a room and he instantly knows if I am sad, worried, confused, afraid or excited. I feel his love. We make each other happy, but we do not *depend* on each other for happiness. True joy comes from Jesus Christ.

God sent me this amazing man, but I didn't *fully* trust him until about nineteen years into our marriage. Prior to then, I had unfairly measured his every move against past exposures to men. I was burned out before I met him. Quite frankly, I had given up and had come to the realization that the fairy tale didn't exist. No, the fairy tale does not exist, but I finally learned that a marriage truly put together by God is far better!

The enemy attacks marriages because he knows the power behind husbands and wives equally yoked for God's purpose. A marriage *truly* put together by God is an example of Christ with His Church. Often we think that God put a marriage together, but sometimes it's only two people who jumped the gun walking only by the flesh or simply not seeing the big picture. I praise God for His mercy and forgiveness when we humans make mistakes. I'm so thankful for his mercy that restores the missing pieces.

Love conquers all. I intermittently began to soften and let go of the shell I had put up due to the past failures. I'm still overcoming bad habits and asking for the Lord's help to be a better wife to John. Also, watching him grow deeper in Christ makes me appreciate him even more. I love watching his love for the Lord on display. Often he sits alone for hours playing the guitar and singing praises to the Lord. Just him and the Lord. I get the benefit of hearing that from another room and am overcome with thankfulness. I'm truly seeing him the way that God sees him.

I must continually remind myself to consciously watch my attitude and my tongue. You see, damaged people must receive true healing so that we don't continue damaging the ones we love. Weakness must be identified and addressed so that a healthy spirit-filled life can blossom. Sin has no more dominion over those who are washed in the blood of Jesus Christ. We can choose how to speak and act. Our Lord will strengthen us.

Nowadays, I tell John that I think God has a special mansion waiting for him that includes many rewards for his patience and kindness toward me. He shyly smiles, but I'm very serious when I say that. During my dedicated time writing this book, he was my biggest fan. He entertained himself and picked up my other duties. Many times, he brought food to my secluded space so I could continue typing without interruptions. We got a chuckle when he had too many things in his hands and spilled food all over my lap and my laptop!

He has been a constant comfort. Many years ago, I freaked out while we were on vacation. It was a rainy day, so we went to a shopping mall to see a movie. Walking back to our car, we discovered it had been vandalized. They wrote with a big black marker, saying things like "Bitch we see you." I don't remember what else was violently marked all over it. The headlight was broken. I had an immediate mental meltdown right there in the parking lot. This continued and I allowed it to ruin the remainder of our vacation. I was convinced that the abusive ex-husband had found me; as he always claimed he would. I imagined all kinds of things. I thought he had watched us go to the movie, watched us come out to the vandalized car and would probably try to follow us back to the hotel. I had no sense of reality. I barely slept for the remainder of the vacation and looked over my shoulder everywhere we went.

John gently tried to calm me. He said that random vandalism happens all the time and that it was probably some punk kids who were bored and up to no good. You see how grateful I am for John? He could have been annoyed with my instability and irrational fears. He could have been more concerned about having his own good day, but he was more concerned about me. He didn't scold, make fun or ignore me. **Love is patient. Love is kind.** God knew I needed a husband like this. He is a gift from God. It's easy to distinguish the marriages that *God* puts together in contrast to the ones that He didn't. That is an important concept to grasp.

Years later, John was out of town and some guys tried to break in through the window while I was home sleeping. Thankfully, our dogs startled them and they ran. I was completely undone. I couldn't sleep for months. I had an alarm system installed. My son, Kelby, spent several nights with me so I could sleep while John was away working. John and my entire family tried to convince me that it was not the abusive ex-husband who tried to break in our home. I could not be convinced, even though several other homes in our neighborhood had also been invaded.

A week before the attempted break-in, a car lingered in front of our home. I was standing in our driveway at the time. The car eased up, eased back and eased up again. Then the driver raised a camera and snapped a picture. I immediately panicked thinking that my ex-abuser had sent someone to scope out my premises. The attempted home invasion the week later, added fuel to my fear.

John came home and tried to calm me by saying that it was probably someone from the bank doing appraisals in the neighborhood. Of course, I didn't believe that. I was convinced I had been *found*.

Most men would be weary of dealing with my fears, but not John. If he was, he didn't let me see it and he didn't give up on me. He always understood that I had been traumatized, but until he read this book, he didn't know to what extent.

For anyone out there who is under any level of abuse or bondage from a so-called friend, boyfriend or spouse, coworker, parent or child, please understand that you *do* have options of freedom through Christ. He came to give us life more abundantly. Jesus is our true means of escape. I have seen others turn to alcohol or drugs as a form of escape, but those addictions have created more destruction than the original troubles they tried to medicate. Please be careful. Alcohol can sneak up on you, pretty soon it has grabbed you before you realize that you have depended too much on it.

Although I had escaped physically, I was still in bondage mentally. This spilled over to all aspects of my personality. It was exhausting. I praise the Lord that not long after that period of time, I received deliverance from the spirit of fear!

Life is totally different now. I am free. I began to understand the fullness of the godly union that John and I have when we were ordained as ministers on March 20, 2016. Since then, I've had a deeper revelation of God's larger purpose that goes beyond just the two of us.

We can decide to be an agent of change or remain stuck in the mud. My story bounces back and forth from one topic to the next, but that is the story of my life. Life is not always nice and in order, but we can know the author of life itself. The remainder of this book turning in a new direction. May changes take place in your heart also.

Chapter 39

COVENANT

A MAN HAD BEEN GIVEN AUTHORITY TO RUN a kingdom. The one who gave him the authority was good. So good in fact, that he provided him and his queen everything. They had a relationship with the provider. There was fellowship and peace in the land. The man was asked not to choose one of two options.

Unfortunately, there was a threat to this kingdom. The enemy wanted the man to breach the original contract and contract with him instead. The aggressor knew that if this effort succeeded, he would gain rulership and power over the people. He wanted to steal the worship relationship and have it for himself. His pride was big. He wanted to be served, so he lied. He wanted to discredit the true Master and giver of the kingdom. Even though the people had already been given everything that was good, the deceiver wanted them to think that there was more that was being withheld from them. Seductively, the enemy went in the back door (through the queen) to get to the man. The original covenant was broken. The deception was successful and the kingdom was legally transferred over to the deceiver.

One man had lost dominion and *all* the people in the kingdom were taken captive. Therefore, one man would have to pay the price in full in order to legally restore the broken covenant.

Mercy and compassion was extended and a hero was promised! He, alone, would win back the kingdom for everyone! As you might guess, the enemy of the hero continued to blind many people with lies to prevent them from trusting in the promise.

Thankfully, some of the people believed regardless of the circumstances and waited for the promise. He came! Many people listened to the voice of the hero who cared more for others than he did for himself. Those who chose the genuine hero as their Lord, became protected citizens under his new covenant! One for all and all for one. One person can make a difference!

Unfortunately, other people saw the hero with their very own eyes, yet didn't recognize him. They continued listening to the one who had stolen the ears of the people and remained in unbelief. Those unbelievers perished outside the city walls.

THE ENEMY WANTS TO DISMANTLE A CONTRACT AND STEAL THE DEAL FOR HIMSELF. *IF SOMEONE HAS TO STEAL YOUR ATTENTION TO GET IT, THEY DO NOT DESERVE IT!*

Genuine love is given, not stolen. In our haste to be loved and to give love, the genuine is worth the wait and to be inspected. 1 John 4:18, 19 tells us that perfect love casts out fear and we love him because he first loved us. There is a perfect love.

Near the beginning of this book, I mentioned that when I was very young, I didn't understand the meaning behind the story between Abraham and God as depicted in Genesis chapter twenty two. However, without a shadow of a doubt, I knew that God was a very good God and I trusted Him. Therefore, I figured there had to be a deeper meaning to that story. Many times we don't understand things, but if we trust God and keep seeking Him. He will help us come to the place that he wants to bring us.

Now, I see that Abraham was an example of the first covenant. He was a *man* who rose up at the pivotal moment and worshipped God big enough to cut the covenant with Him. God was moved by Abraham's loyalty, trust and love. God honored Abraham's worship so much that He provided no less than his own love sacrifice! That ram in the thicket! Such a powerful foreshadowing of God's ultimate provision. (See Genesis 22:13.) For God so loved the world that he gave! (John 3:16)

God is a giver, not a taker. He's a blesser! When you are looking for love, look for those qualities. God's Son, Jesus was a giver! He redeemed us! Through perfect obedience and perfect love, he sacrificed his very own flesh and blood. "Greater love hath no man than this, that a man lay down his life for his friends." (John 15:13). Jesus cut the *new* covenant with our Father God and trusted Him to resurrect Him with all power and glory! Trustworthy is He to resurrect us also, who believe.

Eve was deceived. Adam and Eve fell behind enemy lines. When there is a war, there is a sacrifice. The good news is, the war was won by Jesus! He is worthy of all of our love!

True love is sacrificial, but don't sacrifice *your* love to the enemy. Beware of lies in disguise. Beware of seduction. Beware of entering into any agreement or relationship with those who are self-serving, controlling, chaotic and opposite of sacrificial love. Avoid entering into a covenant with the enemy.

Chapter 40

GET REAL

THIS BOOK OPENED WITH THE GRIP OF DEATH around my throat, but a higher power loosened the grip of evil. I was not alone; unseen help arrived! Suddenly and strangely, the evil let go of my neck. The abuser fell over onto the floor into a strange deep sleep. I was saved again at the cry of help!

How did I get in the evil grip and why? Deception. A lie got me there, and for a long time. A lie made me believe there was no way out. Some people might say, "Well, if that higher power was so big, why were you not safe at all times?" I will reply with the words of my Lord, "These things I have spoken unto you, that in me ye might have peace. In the world ye shall have tribulation: but be of good cheer; I have overcome the world." (John 16:33, KJV, bold emphasis mine.) Overcome He did and He helped me overcome! We are in a battle and we must know the battle cry! We must belong to the captain of our salvation, otherwise we truly are without hope.

There is a way out, unless one chooses to stay in bondage. Had I stayed under the lie, I would most likely be dead and you would not be reading this book. This chapter was saved until now in order to allow the story to unfold and speak for itself. Hopefully, a wide range of people are reading. Those who are living rich and peaceful lives have this opportunity to find deeper com-passion and perhaps a new understanding for others.

Unfortunately, too many victims keep staying in the situation no matter how much help they receive. Some get out, and go back, they get out, they go back. I did that once, at the beginning, because I truly was deceived and under tremendous control and fear. However, I praise God I got a second chance to get out and stay out. I'm ever so thankful that my eyes were opened to realize that the cycle was not going to break. Recently, I heard a statistic that counselors sometimes see an average of fourteen relapses in each case of trauma and addiction.

OH, BUT I LOVE HIM...

I have heard that statement from so many abused women and it breaks my heart. Is it love or is it decep-tion? Is it a marriage or steal, kill and destroy? Love is a wonderful thing, but love does not require one to be neglected, beaten or worse! Unconditional love, does not mean unconditional approval. The Tomberlins spoke that to me and it set me free. I pray for everyone to receive the truth. Otherwise, when people see victims repeatedly returning to the den of hell, they stop trying to help them and turn a blind it to *all* victims. That problem often causes other victims who desperately need help getting free to become stereotyped and gravely misunderstood. Some are in grave danger. I pray they find escape.

I pray for those who feel hopeless in *any* area, no matter how big or small. Lies of hopelessness have taken some people to the point of suicide. Don't fall into that trap! Think about the ridiculousness of those deceptive thoughts! Where is the logic? **What sense does it make to try and fix something bad with something worse?** Be of good cheer. If you need an answer, there is always an answer! There is always a way out. Jesus said, "The thief comes only to steal and kill and destroy. I came that they may have **life** and have it abundantly." (John 10:10, ESV, bold emphasis, mine).

This book's purpose is to save lives, not merely to provide an interesting read. The goal is to capture the attention of everyone, unbelievers and believers alike. It's impossible to express in full color each event along the way without telling the source of each victory.

I'm fully aware that, in general, society expects me to speak diplomatically and not impose my beliefs on others. It's not generally accepted to sound so bossy. My prayer is that you see my heart of love behind it and that you will receive.

There are critical and judgmental spirits. Some are blatant, others appear in the form of the religiously wise. They have the stance that they know everything better than anyone else. I'm thankful to shed that critical spirit. It's my job to keep it away. I want the good stuff instead of being distracted by preconceived ideas.

My firm speech is not against people, but against evil. It may sound like I'm speaking harshly, but please don't be offended. I offer a bit of a shock factor to get the listener's attention. You have seen this in the movies. Someone slaps a person who is in shock and hysterics to snap them out of it for their own wellbeing. I certainly don't want to slap anyone—we have all been slapped too much—but I do want us to wake up!

All my life, I've heard this comment, "Never discuss politics or religion." I ask you, is that doctrine cowardly, self-centered, and apathetic? The very ones who make those statements are the ones who expect their viewpoints to be embraced in the name of modernized self-intelligence. Religion and politics are forces that affect social standards. Many have died to protect them so that others can live freely. In their proper context, they can be beneficial when discussed appropriately and with mutual respect. The word *religion* can be loosely translated. Religious man-made traditions can cause damage, but a true relationship with our loving Lord results in a manifestation of love. It's the fabric that holds society together. Think of the term *politics* as a force that can affect a society for the common good if it is based on laws of God's love. If it is not based laws of love and mutual respect, then show up and get involved. Be an agent of change. Bring the light of Christ to the situation.

Therefore, yes, let's talk about what really matters. Let's talk about life and death and not *only* about what's for dinner and which sports team will take us to the Super Bowl. Those things are fun, but let's definitely also talk about who will take us into eternity and pick us up when we fall down along the way.

Be not deceived by the world's standards. Consider what Paul said, *"and with all deceivableness of unrighteousness in them that perish because they received not the love of the truth, that they might be saved"* (2 Thessalonians 2:10).

Allow me to lovingly, but quite frankly, say that most people are tired of the *fake.* I'm tired of tiptoeing around shallow and fleeting vanity. Perhaps it's our style of dialogue that's ineffective. Perhaps we have lost the guttural groaning of honest human cries and the exhilarating sounds of sheer joy. We have lost those expressions due to fear of what man will think of us. May the Lord make us all bold to remember that it's better to please God rather than to please men.

Therefore, please consider this book as a testimony of a life from despair to peace, from fear to freedom and proof of being forever loved and taught by a very real Savior—a Savior who will do the same for you. Simply stated, my heart burns within me for everyone to encounter the greatest power—one that leaves you breathless and craving more! I want everyone to know by experience, as well as by faith, the real and tangible God who created us! We certainly did not create ourselves.

There is no denying that He *is* absolutely real. I yearn for you experience the incredible joy that comes only from Him and is far beyond any other. Incredible grace and extravagant love comes from an exciting and faithful God who gave His best. He gave His Son, who gave his all. Choosing Christ is not giving up anything, but gaining everything! My greatest hero, Jesus Christ, wooed me with His incredible love, strength, and integrity. He challenged the status quo and continues to turn this world upside down with His radical love, miracles and wonders. That leaves any modern-day video game or movie in the dust!

I'm not the girl who will gently say, "Your philosophy, whatever it is, is okay and whenever you are ready, you might consider leaving the burning building." I guess my style could be considered *tough love,* but I do love you nonetheless. Some people don't believe in eternal life or eternal death. Are you willing to take that chance? My manner of speaking may sometimes seem intrusive, but occasionally it's more loving to scream, "The house is on fire! Get out!"

Are you stuck in the mud, doing the same old thing and wondering why nothing ever changes? I ask what the famous psychiatrist, Dr. Phil, asks, **"How is that**

working for you?" That's a simple and logical question, don't you agree? We cannot expect to think the same ways and do the same things that clearly are not working and expect to achieve different results.

I can no longer be afraid of sounding pushy. We cannot afford to sugar coat it. People are living in bondage and fear. People are dying every moment of every day without the truth. Sometimes we need to be shocked. Snapped out of it! Break the mesmerizing gaze of deception. Allow the Lord to take off the veil. Truth cannot be forever buried. It will resurrect.

There's a point in each of our lives when we come to the end of ourselves—a moment in time when it's the darkest of nights, when we're all alone or perhaps pinned helpless under a wrecked car at the bottom of a remotely hidden ravine. Reality then hits that we are not as intelligent or as strong as we thought we were. We alone are not enough to ultimately save ourselves. There is a higher power. Check out a powerful movie called *The Heart of Man* https://heartofmanmovie.com

Fear, however, is not the best motivator to help us meet and become truly devoted to our Creator. Love and loyalty are much more effective motivators. We love Him because He first loved us. As Paul stated, "...the goodness of God leadeth thee to repentance." (Romans 2:4). Also, James said, "... the wisdom that is from above is first pure, then peaceable, gentle, easy to be entreated, full of mercy and good fruits, without variance, without hypocrisy." (James 3:17, ASV)

Our God is not some far away, made-up escape for the weak minded. He is not someone who is mad at you. He is not some dusty boring story told by someone who, unfortunately, paints the Christian life as one that takes away fun and beats you down with guilt and sin consciousness. No way! Rather, choosing the lordship of Jesus Christ opens up a life beyond your wildest dreams, and we can reign in life with Him.

His word is perfect. You don't have to take my word for it. Try it for yourself. I am alive today because of Him! There's no other explanation. We can avoid lengthy times in the wilderness if we surrender early.

Many others share great indisputable testimonies. You're surrounded by a great cloud of witnesses of faith—faith that produces real life results!

> And I heard a loud voice saying in heaven, Now is come salvation, and strength, and the kingdom of our God, and the power of his Christ: for the accuser of our brethren is cast down, which accused them before our God day and night **and they overcame him by the blood of the Lamb, and by the word of their testimony**... (Revelation 12:10-11 KJV, bold emphasis)

> Fear not, little flock; for it is your Father's good pleasure to give you the kingdom. (Luke 12:32 KJV)

In all thy ways acknowledge him and he shall direct thy paths. (Proverbs 3:6)

Deliver thyself as a roe from the hand of the hunter and as a bird from the hand of the fowler. (Proverbs 6:5)

Be not afraid of their faces: for I am with thee to deliver thee, saith the Lord. (Jeremiah 1:8)

And I will deliver thee out of the hand of the wicked, and I will redeem thee out of the hand of the terrible. (Jeremiah 15:21)

The Lord is good, a stronghold in the day of trouble and he knoweth them that trust in him. (Nahum 1:7)

For anyone who may not yet be convinced and who are *only* scientifically minded, look deeper and see that God is the science behind the science. Have you ever been brave enough to look beyond worldly intelligence and see for yourself? Blindly going along with the crowd applies to both sides of the fence. The scientific method is to discover the truth. Are you willing to discover the Face of God?

For those who still don't believe: are you willing to wait until after death to find the answer? Of course that sounded pushy, but true love pushes people out of a ditch. True love is passionate enough to grab and tackle someone to keep them from jumping off a bridge! Speak the gospel for in it is life everlasting! See John 6:44-47. Allow new light to shine into your lonely places. When we really get honest, we admit there is *more*. When we *really* want answers, we won't stop until we get them. Will you dare to look deeper?

Chapter 41

EVE GOT A BAD RAP

THE DECEIVER DID NOT DISPLAY HIS EVIL FORM when he first approached me. Instead, he was mesmerizing, smooth talking and very subtle. I was temporarily under his spell as though time stood still and switched into another dimension.

We are no different than Eve. We have all been deceived at one time or another. How dare anyone point a finger at her! In fact, we should thank her for teaching us. Jesus said, "He without sin cast the first stone."

One morning while driving to work, I was preoccupied with a *to-do* list that was running through my mind. Suddenly I heard, "Eve got a bad rap!" Stunned, I looked throughout my empty car to see who said that! Instantly, I was flooded with a higher reality and became overwhelmingly aware that Eve has not been recognized for who she *really* was. Society has labeled her. She has been blamed for all of man's troubles. The very mention of her name has been associated with shame and blame. I repented for judging her.

The Lord flooded my spirit with the realization that Eve was an amazingly incredible, beautiful, wise and strong woman whom God created in His image. She was pristine! God saw everything that He had made and said, it was "very good". God does not make junk.

I DO NOT THINK FOR A MINUTE THAT EVE WAS A *PUSH-OVER*.

We don't know how long or how hard the enemy worked to deceive her. She was to multiply and replenish the earth— *God's way.* Many people today say the world is overpopulated and humans have already accomplished the replenishing of the earth, but the context was replenishing the earth with God's children for His kingdom and purpose.

The evil one doesn't want *any* godly woman to succeed in nourishing the church, the men, her fellow-woman or her children in the nurture and admonition of the Lord. It's obvious that the evil one recognizes the capabilities of women and would like to give *all* of us a bad rap.

Eve walked and talked with God. She was a worshipper of our Creator. Then the trap was set by the evil one to steal her away from her spiritual connection with God. Her reputation also became stolen. Did the evil one want Eve to think that God had lied to her about dying so she would trust him more than she trusted God? The evil one wants to discredit God and wants us to worship him instead.

Eve was marked and *blamed* for all of our problems. The accuser accuses everyone of being weak and influences people to accuse other people. The man said, "The *woman* whom **you** gave to be with me, *she* gave me fruit of the tree, and I ate." (Genesis 3:12, ESV, italics and bold emphasis, mine.) Did the man insinuate blame toward God for giving him the woman? Adam could have simply said that the woman gave it to him, but he said that it was the woman *that God* had given to him. He admitted to eating, but he also seemed to be saying that this problem would not have happened if God had not given him the woman in the first place. Fear and shame had entered. (I'm not reading into it or pointing a finger at Adam. I'm just pointing out that once sin entered, Adam's words seemed to be coming from a different place in that moment.)

Of note, in Genesis 1:17, God gave Adam a direct command. He was not to eat of the tree of good and evil. It was not until Genesis 1:22, that woman was made. The evil one attacked through the back door and approached Eve. The woman replied to God that she had been deceived by the serpent. She was deceived! For further insight and study on this section of God's Word, you might consider Katharine Bushnell's biblical research book, *God's Word to Women,* especially pp 28-31. I was led to this book after the Lord spoke to me about Eve and after my hunger was piqued. I asked the

Lord for a greater revelation and understanding of the scriptures. Perhaps there's plenty to learn from God's perspective about the *mother of all living.*

In the dialogue with Eve, it seems that the evil one insinuated blame on God for not being the best provider. He called attention to the fact that God did not allow them to partake of *all* the trees. Did the enemy indicate that he could give Eve more than God would? (*Confusion* came regarding what they should and shouldn't have.) Confusion continues today through the poverty spirit. Some people are afraid of riches as if it's a bad thing, but the scriptures tell us that we are joint-heirs with Christ. We have no lack.

The enemy wanted Jesus to worship him and proposed that he would give Him all the kingdoms of the *world* for such worship in return. Thankfully, Jesus did not fall for his seduction! Jesus obtained far greater riches through His heavenly Father! Those riches now belong to all of us through Christ. **To receive them, deception must be removed and replaced with kingdom thinking.** According to Colossians 1:13, we have *already* been translated into the kingdom of God's dear Son. Why don't we live there?

Detrimentally, too many women carry the derogatory Eve stigma. Some settle for less than God's best. Break free of that! Rise up to be the woman you really are, a daughter of the most high God, freed by Christ, by whom you have all power and authority over the enemy. Be the woman God created you to be! I believe that Eve went on to fulfill her destiny. I don't believe Eve gave up. She regrouped. She was the mother of all living. Christ would eventually be born of a woman! Jesus came! Keep in mind that He indeed came. The enemy also tried and continues to *try* to discredit Him, but we hold high the risen and victorious Lord!

The evil one continues to do everything he can to *discredit* all those who will do great things for God. Sadly, some people don't think that women should be ministers in a Church setting. The trap was set to discredit me and it almost worked, but by the Lord's mercy and grace, truth came and my ministry was renewed! The enemy's lies were exposed and my tongue was loosed to preach the gospel of the Lord Jesus Christ! How sad would it have been for me to keep silent in the body of Christ?

The enemy tried to silence Eve by discrediting her. Why would he stop doing that to any of God's women now? When confusion and doubt remain regarding the woman's place, there's usually more to the story. The veil must come off to see it and we know who removes the veil!

The choice remains. The question remains: to eat or not to eat?

O taste and see that the Lord is good: blessed is the man that trusteth in him. (Psalm 34:8, KJV).

This then is the message which we have heard of him, and declare unto you, that God is light, and in him is no darkness at all. (1st John 1:5, KJV)

Did you catch that? There is no darkness in God. He is good! He separated the light from the darkness. I get so angry when God is blamed for bad things. I get especially angry when it's disguised as a religious doctrine.

Really bad things happen in this present world. So what? God is not doing them! The evil one is still on this earth. Please don't ask why God allows it!

THE REAL QUESTION SHOULD BE, WHY DO WE ALLOW IT?

God already did His part. Good grief! He gave us His very own Son. Therefore, we should not tolerate false words to be spoken against our merciful God or our redeemer! Jesus told us the things that we can do through Him according to the Gospel of John 14:12. There is power in the name of Jesus!

This world is going to end and eternity will begin. Let's look at the innumerable and indescribably *good* things that God is, does and gives! Let's not quickly jump to the blame game. I've heard a minister say, "Sometimes the only exercise we get is jumping to conclusions!"

We lack nothing. If something seems to be out of our sight, that doesn't mean that it's out of our reach! We are complete in Christ. Beware of the liar who introduces something barely noticeable and ever-so-slightly different for us to consider. Don't pause for a second to consider what the enemy says! It's in that instant, that we can get tricked. Therefore, we keep our eyes on Jesus and on God's perfect Word.

We diligently focus on the master of our destiny. Knowing what's at stake, we laser-lock in without wavering. Don't turn to the left or right, but stare straight ahead like a gymnast who is careful not to fall off the beam. Don't listen to the whispered suggestions, "Pssst, look over here." Successful golfers don't take their eyes off the golf ball. The marksman does not blink. **Once our eyes shift, we miss the mark!**

We are to be wise and ever watchful, but not in fear. Fear clouds the mind. The enemy stealthily disguises himself. Knowing this, I constantly ask God to shine His light brightly for me. I have found this to be one of my most powerful prayers. I ask the Lord to expose the lies and show me the truth. Light dispels darkness. Darkness is simply the absence of light. God separated darkness from light. Step into God's light.

We are not to be ignorant "so that we would not be outwitted by Satan; for we are not ignorant of his designs" (2 Corinthians). There are patterns that we must recognize. He likes to catch us off guard. The prey must be snared. The trap can be hidden in many ways, but it always *blinds* the victim to the coming danger. Animals in the jungle know that the lion walks about seeking whom he *may* devour so they dare not walk around willy-nilly. If the prey has not been snared, it may be chased until the the point of exhaustion. Instead of running away from evil, run toward good— run to Jesus the author and finisher of our faith.

We have a Mediator who has gone before us and will help us. We have *not* sweated like Jesus, as it were, drops of blood. For the joy set before him, he endured the suffering. Jesus is acquainted with our pain and is compassionate toward us. We can't do it alone.

The nature of darkness is to cloak the light and to cloak the truth. In reality, neither can be accomplished unless we agree with the darkness.

ONE PINHOLE OF LIGHT CAN DISPEL A ROOM FULL OF THE DARKEST DARKNESS.

See Acts 26:18, II Corinthians 4:6, Ecclesiastes 2:13, Ephesians 5:8, Romans 8:12 and I John 1:5,6.

The light of God shines brightly. He shows us what we need to know.

> ...ye have an unction from the Holy One, and ye know all things. (1 John 2:20, KJV). Eastern Standard Version words it this way, "But you have been *anointed* by the Holy One, and you all have knowledge."

> Wherefore also it is contained in the scripture, Behold, I lay in Sion a chief cornerstone, elect, precious: and he that believeth on him shall not be confounded. (1 Peter 2:6)

Leaning on Jesus, we shall not be confounded and confusion is not from God. We must remain vigilant. We are naked, lost and without hope unless we belong to Father God. The only way to belong to Him is to believe in His Son. Jesus is the *only* way to the Father. Confess with your mouth the Lord Jesus, Son of God, whom God raised from the dead and you shall be saved. (Salvation is also continuous.) Confess Jesus is Lord! (See Romans 10:9,10 KJV.)

Becoming a child of the most high God involves words, but more than words alone. Calling on Jesus is a real thing that comes from our hearts.

WE BECOME TRANSFORMED AS WE WALK UNDER THE *LORDSHIP* OF JESUS.

We thrive under His protective, victorious flesh and blood covenant. We don't merely give lip service. We give love service.

The devil spirits know **who** Jesus Christ is, but He definitely is *not their* Lord. (See the Gospel of Mark 1:24.) Do we merely know *about* Him or do we have a love relationship with Him. Historians know *about* Him. The important question is, "Is He your Lord?"

Sadly, some people perform robotically. As expected, they do a *repeat-after-me* confession, but some don't fully understand it. Specific people have admitted to me that they didn't know what it meant, but simply repeated it in a Church service. We must guard against the *enemy* who tells us that all is well when it is not. We may be well or we may be *half-well*..."And the serpent said unto the woman, Ye shall not surely die" (Genesis 3:4, KJV). Once the seducer gets the prey in the trap, death comes. However, Jesus is risen! When He rose, we rose with Him!

After I asked God to take me deeper into the relationship of the lordship of Jesus, everything changed in my life. Communication became a two-way street. Why not? He said that he would not leave us comfortless and that His sheep know his voice. (See John 16:12-15 and John 14:15-29. This applies to us, as gentiles, who are beyond the flock of Israel! *We are one in Christ if Christ is our Lord.* Thank you Lord!)

While writing this book, I visited a fellow former victim. As we discussed what we had been through, we became heavy hearted and I started to doubt whether I should publish. However, about three hours later, I realized that I had taken my eyes off Jesus and looked at fear. We were temporarily corralled and lassoed, having lost sight of the mark. This is an example of how the deceiver can distract us, but thankfully, my previously abused comrade also realized it. Then she said to me, "Do what the Lord is leading you to do. He will get us through it as always. He is bigger than evil." I was rescued again from the spirit of fear that was knocking at the door. I'm reminded that Jesus suddenly runs up at the cry for help and succors us as a mother does her child who is in need. Thank you, Rev. Tom for teaching me that from a deeper study of Hebrews 2:18.

I've written mostly about women, but I'm not leaving out the men. We've mostly examined Eve, but the principles apply to everyone, children included. There's a need for some women to rise up from where they have been held down. For example, long ago, as Wayne Jackson pointed out in his article...

> Many a Jewish man started the day with a prayer to God, expressing thanks that he was neither a Gentile, a slave, or a woman! A Hebrew man did not talk with women in the street—not even with his mother, sister, daughter or wife! (cf. Lightfoot 1979, 286-287). According to the most liberal view of Deuteronomy 24:1, a Hebrew husband could divorce his wife if she was found "familiarly talking with men" (Edersheim 1957, 157). William Barclay even tells of a segment of the Pharisees known as the "bleeding

and bruised" Pharisees. When they saw a woman approaching, they would close their eyes, hence, were running into things constantly! (1956, 142-143). (Jackson, Wayne. *Jesus and the Samaritan Woman at the Well,* https://www.christiancourier.com/articles/282-jesus-and-the-samaritan-woman, February 3, 2018

Praise Jesus, for blowing the lid off such paganistic thinking. Jesus honored women and all walks of life. There is no racism, gender confusion or discrimination in God's kingdom. He made us just the way He wants us. He made us male and female. Our Father is an equal opportunity God! Let's all see ourselves as God sees us.

> For ye are all the children of God by faith in Christ Jesus. For as many of you as have been baptized into Christ have put on Christ. There is neither Jew nor Greek, there is neither bond nor free, there is **neither male nor female: for ye are all one in Christ Jesus.** And if ye be Christ's, then are ye Abraham's seed, and heirs according to the promise. (Galatians 3:26-29, bold emphasis added)

God created man in his own image, in the image of God created he him; male **and female** created he them. And God blessed them.... And God saw **everything** that he had made, and, behold, it was **very good**. And the evening and the morning were the sixth day. (Genesis 1:27,31 KJV, bold emphasis mine)

Chapter 42

WORDS HAVE POWER

ALL OF US HAVE EXPERIENCED THE EXHILA-rating joy of encouraging words and the crushing blow of hurtful words. There's no denying the power of words. They produce actual physical effects in our bodies, our minds and our spirits. "Death and life are in the power of the tongue and those who love it will eat its fruit." (Proverbs 18:21).

The physical effects are well known, but let's also awaken to the spiritual effects of the spoken word. **Words move kingdoms.** Power comes forth by the spoken word. Let me say that again. These are not mere words; there is an actual power that *calls forth* a change! This will happen because God says so, and the more we actually believe and expect it, the more we will see the results. All of creation was created by God's spoken word. (See Genesis 1:3, 4-11, 14-20, 22-24 and 26.)

Prayer is a manifestation of our hearts, through words to our God. Faith comes by hearing and hearing the word of God. When we audibly pray God's word, we hear those words and our faith builds. They become engraved in our hearts and from our hearts our mouth speaks.

When I pray, I picture Jesus standing beside me and taking me to the Throne Room. The Lord has been teaching me more about the manifestation of His faith. Faith is one of the manifestations of the gift of holy spirit. We speak in tongues much, we prophesy, we manifest the spirit in the other ways; faith is no exception. What? You didn't think we could do it all on our own did you? Jesus was the one who believed the Father big enough and now we have the Spirit of Christ dwelling in us.

THINK OF IT THIS WAY: I BRING MY MUSTARD SEED OF FAITH TO JESUS AND HE MULTIPLIES IT AS HE DID THE BREAD AND FISHES.

His faith manifests. He spoke to the fig tree and so can we! Jesus said...

> For verily I say unto you; that whosoever shall **say** unto this mountain be thou removed and be thou cast into the sea and shall not doubt in his heart, but shall believe that those things which he saith shall come to pass; he shall have

whatsoever he **saith.** (Mark 11:23, bold emphasis mine)

Lots of messages have been taught about the mustard seed. Now look at the second half of that scripture. **Speak** to the mountain! This topic deserves a book of its own, but I'm touching on it because my life has entirely changed since I got a glimpse of this truth. Imagine that! Speaking to the mountains fully expecting them to move, drastically changed my prayer results! (Thank you Rev. Norvel Hayes!) Imagine what will happen when we fully operate in these principles!

We are free to ask God for things (see Matthew 21:22). God's kingdom hears our *words.* (See Psalm 103:20.) You don't have to take *my word* for it. Try it for yourself! Pray the scriptures and see what happens! Ask Daniel and the lions about that one!

God wants our words to partner with His words. Our believing pleases Him. Worship! Worship! Worship! It's through His presence that the power comes.

His kingdom come!

His will be done! Holy Spirit activates a force field because Jesus is seated at the right hand of the Father! God is the Lord of hosts!

Some prayers are spent begging God for things He has *already* given us. For example, let's consider one topic of sickness. We ask to be healed, when in fact,

Jesus healed us a long long time ago when His body was broken, ripped and torn during his scourging. He already healed us.

> He himself bore our sins in his body on the tree, that we might die to sin and live to righteousness. By his wounds you have been healed. (I Peter 2:24 ESV)

> This was to fulfill what was spoken by the prophet Isaiah: "He took our illnesses and bore our diseases. (Matthew 8:17, ESV)

Healing was bought with a great price. Our job is to show the evil one that we know it's true Jesus healed us already and that we won't let go of it. *You won't give up eternal life will you? Don't give up your right to health in Jesus either!*

Would you agree that most Christians believe that Jesus died for our salvation so we can have eternal life? Would you agree that most believe that Jesus paid for our sins? Well, before Jesus was crucified and gave His life, He was tied to the post and beaten severely. He could have been crucified only, but He was first beaten to the extreme. His broken body is the *bread* part of Communion. When we eat the bread (His flesh) we are to agree and receive the fact that Jesus' broken body was for our healing.

We can go through the veil, that is to say His flesh into the place of His healing presence. (See Hebrews 10:20.) We know that Jesus tore the veil, but do we choose to see beyond it and step through it. Jesus will also lift the veil off of our eyes so we can see the truth of all of His finished work. He causes blind eyes to see. We *can* get past our own bodily limitations. *Jesus took dominion over his natural body.* He saw the greater glory that would be his and ours. In other words, He got beyond his own fleshly desires and laid his body down as a sacrifice for us. He saw the spiritual reality in the Garden of Gethsemane. We can get over our-selves and enter into His kingdom where we receive the things of the spirit which are greater than our natural limitations. This applies to all things of the spirit.

CONSIDER TAKING COMMUNION LIKE A POWERFUL MEDICATION. DON'T SKIP ANY DOSES.

The flesh and blood legal covenant is for our healing. It tells satan that he has no right to impose sickness on God's people! Let's enforce it and not leave that truth sitting on a shelf!

We *faithfully* take medications that the doctor pre-scribes and would not dream of missing a dose. (To be very clear, I am *not* telling you not to take prescribed medications from the doctor. I'm simply saying that most doctors will also tell you that they cannot cure everything and pills cannot cure everything.) A nausea pill *can* take away nausea, but not if we don't take the pill. Also, note that placebo's work because we believe they will. Do all that you need to do and remember that believing equals receiving. As often as you take Communion, discern the Lord's broken body.

> For anyone who eats and drinks without **discerning the body** eats and drinks judgment on himself. That is why **many of you are weak and ill, and some have died.** (I Corinthians 11:29,30 ESV, bold emphasis mine).

There was no sickness nor death in the Garden of Eden. The enemy deceived humans and sin entered. When sin entered, consequences came. Sickness and death came. However, Jesus redeemed us from the curse of sin and sickness. He was/is our substitute.

IF THERE IS A SUBSTITUTE, WHY TRY TO DUPLICATE?

A substitute takes our place!

The death sentence was expunged through Jesus. Those who choose Him and are born again are no longer legally condemned. We are exonerated and acquitted by Jesus' perfect spotless flesh and blood sacrifice. *Since Jesus made us not guilty, why do we keep taking costly guilt trips?* Instead, claim a free trip, all expenses paid to Romans 5:10-21.

Some people do not receive healing because they feel *unworthy*. The evil one continues to lie and trick us into staying sick by reminding us of our sin. Two can play that game! We must use our mouths and our words to remind the evil one that the broken body and blood of Jesus paid for our sins!

Our words should match God's words. We can say, "Thank you God for healing me. By Jesus' stripes I am healed. Sickness you leave me now in Jesus' name. Thank you Father for healing me in Jesus' name. Amen." **Stake claim** to your healing. Go to the enemy's camp and take back what he stole from you.

Don't fall into the enemy's camp. Have you ever heard folks say that God made them sick to teach them a lesson, yet they go to the doctor to *get well?* If they think that it's God's will that they are sick, why are they asking a doctor to make them well? Of course, that logic does not make any sense. Go to the doctor if you want to and please don't say that God is making you sick to teach you some sort of lesson! Double mindedness is a clue that there is a lie that is confusing us.

Although doctors have a vast knowledge and do great work which I admire and for which I am thankful, they cannot fix everything. They sometimes tell a patient that they have done all they can do. We all do our best, but God is our sufficiency and He has already provided all our needs according to his riches in glory.

I'm definitely not saying, don't go to the doctor. Assisting doctors is my profession. I am thankful for the skills and knowledge God gave us and the practical things we can do. However, I'm asking, please don't blame God for sickness and please don't blame God for anything bad. He is the One who gave His very own Son to heal us from our diseases. Why would we think He makes people sick? Please don't blame God for the bad things that the evil one afflicts upon us! That is such an insult and another stripe laid on the back of Jesus!

Rather, God is glorified when His children are healed and prosperous! Let's not dishonor our Father! His Son healed everyone who came to Him. This is recorded throughout all four New Testament Gospels and other books of the Bible. It was encouraging to me to see it all in one place. I saw it bigger when I compiled over seventy scriptures that record healing everytime! It's evident that it's not God's will for us to be sick.

GOD IS PLENTY BIG ENOUGH TO TEACH US THINGS
WITHOUT MAKING US SICK TO DO IT.

Would you make your child sick to teach them something? God is much more capable of loving us better than we can love even our own children.

He is a miracle-working God who is full of power and wonder. This has never changed. "Jesus is the same yesterday, today and forever." (Hebrews 13:8) Some Church denominations have stripped miracles from their teachings. As Timothy warned, beware of those, "Having a form of godliness, but denying the power thereof: from such turn away." (2 Timothy 3:5)

We indeed can *expect* power from on high, the Creator of the heavens and earth! However, seeking power from other sources is a very dangerous thing to do. (See Leviticus 19:31.) Don't seek answers and power from the wrong source.

Our Creator's power can be *spoken* forth. Speak it until you see it. Speak it with confidence and authority, knowing the power that backs the words. He gave His Son all power. At the name of Jesus, every knee should bow, of things in heaven, and things in earth, and things under the earth. (Philippians 2:10).

We are never alone. There's a scripture for every situation we face in life. *Find it and speak it.* His kingdom comes and changes the atmosphere!

> Who **hath** delivered us from the power of darkness, and hath translated us into the kingdom of his dear Son. (Colossians 1:13, emphasis mine).

> Behold, I give unto you power to tread on serpents and scorpions, and over all the power of the enemy: and nothing shall by any means hurt you. (Luke 10:19).

Our brains tell our physical bodies what to do. The head is in charge of the body. Sit there and look at your foot. Now tell your big toe to wiggle. Did you *say* to your toe to wiggle? Did it wiggle before your brain told it to move? No. I'm sure it just sat there motionless. Doing nothing affects nothing. We think therefore we speak. Speak to your mountain! Say, "Be it unto me according to your Word!" Sickness must bow to Jesus' name and leave! *Tell* your body to be healed.

We must also be diligent to *keep* all deliverance and healing that we claim. The evil one, who introduced sickness and strife, tries to cheat us out of our healing. He taunts, "Hey, what about that pain? Look how long you've been sick. Look at your bruises. You don't *really* think you're healed, do you?"

What will our answer be when the doubts start creeping in to rob us of the truth? The answer is to *say* what our Lord said when He was tempted. We say, "It is written!" God's word is true, living and powerful. The shield of faith quenches *all* the fiery darts of the enemy. Don't forget the deceptive conversation with Eve. Tell the enemy to leave. Don't listen to that old Liar! Decide who you're going to be and who you are going to believe and never give up! Wait upon the Lord.

A growth about the size of a large grape with three small white spots appeared on my body. I looked at them with a mirror and *said* to them, "Be removed in Jesus' name! By his stripes I am healed!" The first night, nothing happened. The second night, they were half the size. The third night they were gone! **Wimpy, wishy-washy prayers are not impressive.** God is impressed with boldness that shows Him that we believe in Him and what he provided. We must know who we are in Christ and the legal rights that have been given to us. *Say* it like you mean it and don't stop saying it until the victory is manifested.

My brother sustained third degree burns in a kitchen fire. My compassion for him was overwhelming. Burn pain is the worst type of pain, and I couldn't bear to see him suffer. I *knew* that Jesus wanted him to be healed as much or more than I did. John and my sister-in-law joined me in prayer. We laid hands on my brother and *spoke* to the trauma, "Burn trauma, come off of our brother in Jesus' name! I speak light and life into his flesh and skin! I speak the restoration and renewal of the damaged tissue, in Jesus' name. By Jesus' stripes be healed!" Then we thanked the Lord for healing him. I gave him seventy Bible verses on healing and instructed him to speak them out loud every day.

Within a week, his badly burned and swollen face had healed. A few days later, his right arm healed. The last to heal was his right hand which was the most severely burned. He was sent to the burn center at a major hospital. The surgeon saw him on a Thursday and scheduled a full thickness skin graft for the following Tuesday. He told my brother that he had lost the motor function of his hand because he couldn't bring his fingertips together. No matter how his skin looked or his muscles did not work, we all continued to audibly confess that he was healed.

Tuesday came. The surgeon came in to see him before he was to be rolled into the operating room. He unwrapped the dressing from his arm and hand and exclaimed, "Is this the same hand I saw last Thursday?!!! You are healed! I'm cancelling the surgery! You can go home!" So, instead of going to surgery, we went to lunch! While celebrating, I noticed my brother cutting steak with the hand that had no function at all just a few days earlier! Not only that, his diabetes went away and he did not get infected. There's an extremely high risk for infection in a diabetic or a burn patient. My brother had both risk factors, but no infection! His chronic high blood pressure also normalized and we had not even prayed about that! God is good! Praise Jesus!

There was a young woman who developed metastatic lung cancer, although she had never smoked tobacco. We prayed for her and claimed her healing for over two years. She saw great improvement. However, the chemotherapy weakened her immune system and she developed four different infections in her lungs and was admitted to intensive care in respiratory distress. This is a very lengthy testimony, but I will make it as brief as possible.

The family was called in and told she was dying. She could not sustain her breathing and the family was asked if they wanted her placed on mechanical life support. She wore a specialized high-flow oxygen system that forced oxygen into her. However, if she lifted the edge of the mask for just a few seconds, she couldn't maintain appropriate oxygenation and conversations with her were not possible. She became too weak to lift her arms. The medical staff didn't think she would live even five more minutes.

I was in her ICU room while the oncologist told her and her husband that she was dying and there was nothing else they could do for her. Meanwhile my silent prayers were roaring the heavens! In Jesus' name the spirit of death was commanded to leave. Praying the entire time the physician spoke, I claimed her healing. Her family arrived to say goodbye. Suddenly, I realized that her oxygen mask had been off much longer than a few seconds, then longer than five minutes and she was having a long conversation with the doctor and her husband!

I gave the family private time with her, but I stayed behind the curtain and continuing praying. Suddenly, she called for me! She was sitting straight up in bed without the high flow oxygen mask and asked me to pray for her. I spoke to the disease with great authority in Jesus' name. Again, this was no wimpy, wishy-washy prayer. This was bold warfare. We claimed her healing!

At one point God's kingdom was so present in the room that by inspiration, the family spontaneously started singing *Jesus Loves Me*. Everyone could feel the atmosphere in the room literally change. The patient also sang! I repeat, the patient sang with her arms lifted! Remember, just moments previously, she couldn't breathe five seconds unassisted or lift her arms. Now she was singing and had no oxygen on her face! The next thing she did was eat jello and had long conversations with her family! She got out of bed momentarily a couple days later and was eating full meals. She had quality family time. My husband and I stopped by to see her again on our way out of town and she looked so good. We thought she might get to go home in a few days. Two and half weeks had passed. It was a miracle!

Unfortunately, while we were away, she was given morphine and she passed away. This was extremely difficult for me to accept, but I know she *was* healed. What happened? The enemy attacked again. My heart breaks, but she did receive more time with her family than she would have received. Her husband had said, "I want more time with her." He got more time! Her healing manifested for a while and God is good no matter what. We have an enemy and there is a battle. We keep fighting. The troops don't go home when there is a casualty. They regroup and advance.

Always look at the many testimonies of victory! Don't listen to the evil one who loves to remind the sick that sometimes people don't get healed. Don't listen to negative talk! Remember, that for every person that got cheated out of their healing, a multitude more *were* indeed healed! Read the gospels! Trust God! Resist the enemy. No matter what, we will be together in eternity and there will be no more tears. Here is what I do know, healing is absolutely God's will and it is absolutely available. That's the truth! Jesus already healed us. Jesus already made His play. If we strike out, we don't *stay* on the bench or leave the game. No! *We step up to the plate and keep swinging the bat!*

I have another friend who had an aggressive metastatic brain tumor. Most succumb to it within two years. It has been five years since diagnosis and treatment, with consistent, bold prayer. There is now no trace of cancer! A very young nurse, well loved by us all has been delivered by many tragedies. The biggest healing was from bilateral inflammatory breast cancer. This is a fast growing and aggressive cancer. She is alive today!

Another friend was diagnosed with Lupus, which has no medical cure. At age sixty, the doctors predicted that she had about a month of life remaining. She did not accept that! She *spoke* to her body and claimed healing in Jesus' name. That little lady is such a spitfire! She did not back down no matter how sick she was. Daily, she commanded it to leave! She could have given up, but she did this for twelve months. What if she had stopped at the eleventh month? *She didn't lose sight of the victory no matter how much time was passing.* She refused to doubt. At this writing, she remains healed and alive at eighty-eight years old!

The most important thing to do with the power of our tongue is to praise the Lord. God is to be worshipped no matter how things appear. We trust Him. Overall we cannot lose. Obviously, people pass from this present life. However, it is not God's will for folks to die prematurely from sickness or destruction. Until the Lord appears and eternity begins, so what if our bodies get old and we peacefully fall asleep? That's okay, but it is *not* okay for the enemy to steal, kill and destroy. For further insight regarding the power of words, see the records in I Samuel 17:10, 26, 36, 45, 46 and 47. Mark 11:23, Luke 1:37, Romans 8:32, 34 just to name a few. (In addition, you can hear the short audio teachings *Moving the Kingdom, Part 3* and *Two Kingdoms*. See reference page.)

Listen carefully. *Words have power!* The abuser *said* I could never escape. God *said* Jesus made us free.

THE ENEMY HAD ME BRAINWASHED, BUT JESUS MADE ME BLOOD-WASHED.

Chapter 43

WHO WILL DELIVER US?

GOD MAKES A WAY WHERE THERE IS NO WAY. Stop receiving abuse. Let the Prince of Peace reign. See the truth, be protected, be wise, have a safe plan and be free. We are not required to remain in danger. The liar tells us that we can't tell anyone what is happening to us. This is not true because we can always talk to Jesus. **"Who delivered us from so great a death and doth deliver: in whom we trust that he will yet deliver us."** (2 Corinthians 1:10, KJV)

I pray that abusers stop abusing. I pray they receive a revelation of Jesus Christ and truly become delivered from the evil influences. Somewhere along the line, the aggressor became deceived and became a host for darkness. Did they never hear the word of truth or have light shone on them or did they simply refuse it? According to I Timothy 2:4, God would have **all** to come to the knowledge of the truth and be saved. That is what God and all of us would like. Some will choose him, some will not. Unfortunately, some remain committed to the evil one.

In order to protect ourselves and our children, we need to ask the Lord specifically what to do. Abide with Him. He is the Lord of hosts. We are the watchmen. Watch and pray continuously, not only when we are in danger. 2 Corinthians 2:14. It's not the weapons of violence that is the problem, it's the darkness inside that that drives the unthinkable.

> **No weapon** formed against you shall prosper, And every tongue which rises against you in judgment You shall condemn. This is the heritage of the servants of the Lord, And their righteousness is from Me," Says the Lord. (Isaiah 54:17)

Also see all of Psalm 91 please.

In Old Testament battles, God instructed His people not to bring home the heathen to marry. Sometimes, they were told not to take prisoners back from the battle. God separated them. He had good reasons for that. Now, you may say that that's the Old Testament but we are now in the Age of Grace. True, very true, but the Old Testament has lessons to learn and much of it is a foreshadow and physical picture of the greater spiritual battle. There are times when we are to shake the dust off our feet and move on.

310

We read how Pharaoh of Egypt held the Israelites captive, abused them and used them as slaves. God sent Moses to tell him to let His people go (Exodus 7:16 and see all of Exodus for the full story).

The Lord teaches His people how to have full deliverance from an enemy. Don't stop short of fully obeying. You can see this incredible record in II Kings 13:14-19. Trust me, you will find it well worth your time to go read that record. It's a valuable lesson regarding zero tolerance of evil attacks. Not all, but some people from Syria continue, even now, to come against Israel. Some radical terrorists come out of that region and attack God's people.

Evil works in secret and isolates its victims. The true enemy must be exposed. Remember Ephesians chapter six that explains that we do not wrestle against flesh and blood, but against spiritual wickedness in high places.

> Rescue those being led away to death; hold back those staggering toward slaughter. If you say, "But we knew nothing about this," does not he who weighs the heart perceive it? Does not he who guards your life know it? Will he not repay everyone according to what they have done? (Proverbs 24:11,12, NIV)

Have not I commanded thee? Be strong and of a good courage; be not afraid, neither be thou dismayed for the Lord thy God is with thee whithersoever thou goest. (Joshua 1:9, KJV)

And the servant of the Lord must not strive, but be gentle unto all men, apt to teach, patient, In meekness instructing those that oppose themselves; if God peradventure will give them repentance to the acknowledging of the truth and that they may **recover themselves out of the snare of the devil,** who are taken captive by him at his will. (2 Timothy 2:24-26, KJV, bold emphasis, mine)

God is called the Lord of hosts nine hundred and ninety four times in the King James Version of the Holy Bible. Our Father God has innumerable angels. He has a kingdom. Jesus has been given all authority and power. Let's not remain in captivity! Why remain under bondage from any kind?

Angels are not to be worshiped (See Revelation 22:8, 9), but they are a vital part of God's kingdom and of His design. The kingdom of God and God's light are far above the evil kingdom and its angels. God's angels ministered to Jesus at the end of His forty day fast in the wilderness. An angel escorted Peter from prison. An angel came because of Daniel's *words.*

> Then he said to me, Fear not, Daniel, for from the first day that you set your mind and heart to understand and to humble yourself before your God, your **words** were heard, and I have come as a consequence of [and in response to] your words, but the prince of the kingdom of Persia withstood me for twenty-one days. Then Michael, one of the chief [of the celestial] princes, came to help me, for I remained there with the kings of Persia. (Daniel 10: 12, 13 AMPC, emphasis mine)

We need the full benefit of knowing what is available to us. Ask Jesus to open our understanding to the scriptures. Study and rightly divide the whole Word of God with the intent of intimately knowing our Father God and His Son. There is a saying in the medical profession that certain people *know just enough to make them dangerous.* That means that we cannot skim off the top and expect to receive the full benefit.

> And Elisha prayed, and **said**, Lord, I pray thee, open his eyes, that he may see. And the Lord opened the eyes of the young man; and he saw: and, behold, the

mountain was full of horses and chariots
of fire round about Elisha. (2 Kings 6:17,
KJV, bold emphasis, mine)

May the Lord of hosts deliver us all from evil. Jesus, the Christ, is that deliverance. He has done a finished work. We must let the enemy know we are convinced of that and that we aim to take full authority with the name of Jesus that we have been given. Forgive me for repeating this so often, but faith comes by hearing the word of God and the more we hear it (and speak it), the more we remember it.

IF YOU'RE IN A BATTLE OR TAKEN PRISONER, ASK THE
LORD IF YOU ARE TO STAND STILL, FIGHT OR COME
OUT AND BE SEPARATE.

God knows the wheat from the chaff. *He knows the goats from the sheep.* God knows if the aggressor is going to repent or not. God knows the future. We do not. Many abusive people are very subtle in their deception and tell you over and over and over that they are going to stop. Ask the Lord if that is true.

If you abuse people in *any* way, if you have unbridled anger, if you are confused and tormented in any capacity or in any category, ask God to deliver you and instruct you. Ask Him to send you to the people of His choosing to assist you. There are people who know how to speak deliverance in the name of Jesus

Christ. Darkness must go in Jesus' name and by His power! *Jesus is a chain breaker!* This is no joke. This is not wishy-washy religion that I am referring to, this is the real deal.

The victims of abuse need deliverance from the physical, emotional and spiritual trauma of having been closely associated with the darkness that was meant for destruction. I'm thankful to have received deliverance and for the people the Lord placed in my life to help me. I previously described Wendy. Many years later, in 2013, another person came by divine design— Reverend Tom. He asked me a line of questions in a similar way that Wendy had asked. True friends, brothers and sisters in Christ, care enough about us and about our lives to get involved. Like Peter, Tom imparted to me what he had been given, peace. Tom spoke into my life and solidified the grace message. He spoke of the righteousness of Jesus. He ministered to me, and the spirit of fear left! I felt true peace for the first time in my life! How do you properly thank someone for doing that?

I knew the difference now. I had tasted it and I did not want to lose it! Of course, the enemy doesn't want us to hold on to our deliverance. A few months later, anxiety started to tap on my door again. I recognized it immediately. The Lord said call Tonia. The enemy tried to delay our appointment, but I persisted. Reverends Tonia, Mike and Tari ministered deliverance to me in such a powerful way that I could dedicate another entire book regarding the life changing effect that came to me from their willingness to do as Jesus taught them to do! They were relentless in getting me free in Jesus' name. The chains fell off and words of comfort, healing, purpose and power were prophesied. God is a loving Father and the magnitude of it is beyond our comprehension. I was restored that day. The kingdom came! Free in Christ!

How can I ever thank all these people who have taught me so much and imparted such love of Jesus into my life? Reverend Tonia gift ministries have touched many lives other than just mine. Rev. Kevin G. has my appreciation for how he ministers and teaches with impact. Of Rev. Tom, there's much more to say, but he would say Jesus.

I'm thankful to also be fed by other great people in the Body of Christ. Just to name a few: Pastor Bill Johnson, Randy Clark, Joseph Prince, Todd White, Reinhard Bonnke, Heidi Baker, Adrian Rogers, Joyce Meyer, Norvel Hayes, Lance Wallnau, Mahesh and Bonnie Chavda and many more! You can also access their teachings on YouTube, their ministry websites and onsite. I treasure those who went before us, such as Kathryn Kuhlman, Maria Woodworth-Etter, John G. Lake and Smith Wigglesworth. There are so many more to mention and I don't want to leave out anyone, but the Lord knows who you are and I pray that you are greatly rewarded. My hat is off to Katharine Bushnell, who was a doctor, Christian author, missionary to China, biblical scholar and social activist. Marie Monsen who preached fire from the alter as a missionary in China in 1901 and for the next thirty years. She was brave to do that on the skirts of a time when many missionaries had been slaughtered. I'm thankful for the Azusa street revival.

There was a time when I was offended at some of the things that some of the ministers did and taught, but thank God I have learned to listen to all and hold fast to that which is good. God separated the light from the darkness. The deceiver *can* present himself as an angel of light, but our Lord has a much brighter, holy and genuine light. Fear should not prevent us from seeking *all* that God has for us.

Let's not isolate ourselves. Fear prevents us from learning from others or others learning from us. We need to get over ourselves. Preconceived ideas keep us from growing. In the past, I shut out different ministers for fear I would be deceived. It never occured to me that it was the evil one who didn't want me to hear something amazing that God had to say through them. After I let go of fear, and trusted God to show me the truth, He has taught me so much from so many. The following scriptures released me. I realized that God is certainly big enough to protect me.

> When the Spirit of truth comes, he will guide you into all the truth, for he will not speak on his own authority, but

whatever he hears he will speak, and he will declare to you the things that are to come. (John 16:13)

...ye have an unction from the Holy One and ye know all things. (1 John 2:20)

Trust in the Lord to expose the counterfeit. Be vigilant and abide close to Jesus. Try the spirits to see if they are from darkness. To do this, see 1 John 4:1-3.

Beloved, believe not every spirit, but try the spirits whether they are of God: because many false prophets are gone out into the world. Hereby know ye the Spirit of God: Every spirit that confesseth that Jesus Christ is come in the flesh is of God: And every spirit that confesseth not that Jesus Christ is come in the flesh is not of God: and this is that spirit of antichrist, whereof ye have heard that it should come; and even now already is it in the world. Ye are of God, little children, and have overcome them: because greater is he that is in you, than he that is in the world. (1 John 4:1,2,3 KJV).

Trust the manifestation of discernment. God alerts us to false teachings. Glean from others in the *whole* body of Christ. God will show us the bad apple so we can freely eat of all the other trees in the garden!

DON'T MISS THE WHOLE GARDEN OVER ONE
BAD APPLE.

Cut out a little worm and enjoy the rest of the fruit. **Don't let the enemy taint what the Lord is providing.** Thank you Lord for revealing that to me and placing people in my life to help me see it. I praise God for delivering me from the critical spirit and for the grace to keep it away. Strengthen me continuously!

Chapter 44

CUTTING THE CHATTER

IF WE LISTEN TO THE WRONG CHATTER IN OUR heads, we can lose our peace, our joy and our standing. Sometimes we are air boxing long after the threat of evil is away from us. If the chatter does not stop, get help from a fellow Christian. Jesus did not tolerate dark spirits tormenting people. (See all the Gospels and the Book of Acts.)

Once delivered and the floor is swept clean, fill the space with God and keep the light shining brightly. Allow Jesus to keep the door locked and sealed so darkness cannot enter past the "No Vacancy" sign. We can change our habits and get out of our ruts.

We're not *of* this world. What are the lies that prevent us from seeing the kingdom of which we live? The voice of the Good Shepherd can override the chatter of the enemy. The sheep know the shepherd's voice and no other voice will they follow. **Allow the scriptures to ring in your ears and praises roll off your lips and the enemy's chatter will be stilled.** We become a reflection of what we see and hear. Without looking, I touched the cold glass coffee table beside my chair. I instantly figured that the cold table had cooled off my coffee. Not so! The hot coffee cup warmed the table. Which kingdom will you absorb?

An anvil, resists change no matter how hard you pound on it. We can likewise be so solid on the Lord's way, that nothing else can move us from it. Other substances conform to the pressure applied to it. Don't conform to abuse or the ways of the wicked.

Less violence would brew if people stop listening to the voice of anger. Misplaced anger can lead to a spirit of anger, which can turn into bitterness, then into a root of bitterness. Bitterness can grow and invite a spirit of murder. **"...do not let the sun go down on your wrath."** (Ephesians 4:26).

In times past, that scripture bothered me. I used to feel *justified* in going to bed mad or pouting. The chatter would say, "You have a right to be angry." Another voice would say, "Do you *really* want to go to bed angry? Why are you letting so much time go by that is only hurting yourself and the other person?" Still I pouted.

One fine day, I realized that the rebellious spirit had left me. I don't know the exact moment it left. All I know is that it happened after I entered a time where I absorbed the light of God's word more consistently and snuggled closer and closer to Jesus. It was after deliverance that it occurred to me that the scripture no longer bothered me. Now, I liked that scripture!

I understood it! You see, the *Lordship of Christ* had become bigger than the spirit of anger. I realized the trap and its danger. Nothing is worth being in bondage to *misplaced anger*. It can grow like a cancer. It is destructive. Grace overcomes bitterness (Hebrews 12:15). Also, we can speak to bitterness. Tell it to leave in the name of Jesus. Resist it and it will flee. Curse its roots as Jesus cursed the fig tree.

All dark spirits are squatters. They need a host to manifest themselves. They need someone to form habits that agree with them. They are parasites. Don't be friends with them. Let God arise and His enemies be scattered. Would you get rid of a roach invasion or would you let them live in your kitchen? Turn on a light the roaches scatter! A fellow Christian explained that to me and proceeded to speak the name of Jesus Christ on my behalf for my freedom.

In the past, **I** could not get rid of fear no matter what I did and I felt guilty for having it. Do you see how darkness can occupy a mind? It had to be evicted! We cannot be wishy-washy and polite with it. Cast it out in Jesus name with authority! Fear is a *spirit* and it is *not* from God. "For God hath not given us the **spirit of fear**; but of power, and of love, and of a sound mind" (2 Timothy 1:7, KJV bold emphasis mine).

Don't remain in a *mental* prison without bars, fighting an unseen enemy.

Like Israel, I was forty years in a wilderness. I remained fearful forty years after I was physically free from the abuser. Eventually, the lie was completely exposed and I received freedom by the power of the name of Jesus! I'm so thankful for the Christians who spoke His name on my behalf for my deliverance. They obeyed this word, "Heal the sick, raise the dead, cleanse those who have leprosy, drive out demons. Freely you have received; freely give" (Matthew 10:8).

Now that I was free, I had to adjust my thinking to remain free. Having lived under bondage and trauma, my thought patterns had become skewed. I had been used to feeling as though I were on the outside looking in and I had nothing in common with other people. I have a high appreciation for life itself. I couldn't understand why some people seemed to take it for granted. I identification more with the people who were fighting for their lives. I identified with combat soldiers. I understood their fears, their mindsets, and their struggles trying to *fit in* with the civilians. We must cut the chatter from the enemy and direct our thoughts on good things. "Wherefore gird up the loins of your mind, be sober and hope to the end for the grace that is to be brought unto you at the revelation of Jesus Christ" (1 Peter 1:13, KJV).

It's available to find a new reality with new thoughts 2 Corinthians 10:5. There is no benefit in blaming mankind. Take accountability and seek a relationship with our redeemer. Move on and be free. As the song

says, "I'm no longer a slave to fear. I am a child of God."
("No Longer Slaves" by Jonathan Helser, Joel Case, and
Brian Johnson)

In fact, I recommend you listen that that song in
this moment. It's not enough to *only* train our brain.
Reformation and transformation comes from deep
within our hearts and our ability to see Jesus. We *truly*
change as we receive Him and His accomplished work
and levels of grace upon grace.

He removes the darkness. We can't dress it up or
sweep it under the rug. Rotten food in the refrigerator
will stink until you remove it. There is no use to seal
up bags of food in the pantry until you first get rid of
the rats! The rats will keep chewing new holes in the
bags. You can clean up the rat droppings all day long
and throw away the torn food bags, but the rats will
keep eating until you get rid of the rats!

> He delivered me from my strong enemy
> and from them which hated me for they
> were too strong for me. (Psalms 18:17 KJV)

> I sought the Lord, and he heard me
> and delivered me from all my fears.
> (Psalms 34:4)

> The angel of the Lord encampeth round
> about them that fear him, and delivereth
> them. (Psalm 34:7)

O taste and see that the Lord is good:
blessed is the man that trusteth in him.
(Psalm 34:8)

I could have stayed in the trap. I could have blamed God for the bad things that happened. The evil one doesn't want God to receive any glory. He influences people to speak blame toward Him or say there is no God or that if you choose Him you can't have any real fun. He wants you to think that God withholds. That's what he told Eve. Deceived by his lie, she forgot that she *already had more.* She could already eat from all the trees that were beneficial to her. If the liar tells us that he has more to offer than the most high God, The Creator of the heavens and the earth and all that is therein, simply tell him it is written, "For the Lord God is a sun and shield; the Lord bestows favor and honor. No good thing does he withhold from those who walk uprightly" (Psalm 84:11). Jesus became bigger than my fears. He wouldn't let me give up. He rescued me and restored what had been stolen He more than doubled my riches. My reasonable response is worship, praise and joy!

Chapter 45

JOY

ON NEW YEAR'S EVE 2012, I WAS AWAKENED by a revelation that came so strongly to me that I was compelled to write it in my journal. I heard, "Do not let anything steal your joy." Although I didn't understand the fullness of it at the time, I heard it again four years later! Again, on New Year's Eve. Pastor Mahesh Chavda opened his message with the exact same statement. That 2016 night, I couldn't get that statement out of my mind. I knew it was incredibly important and phenomenally deep. He went on to teach that when we lose our joy, we can be more vulnerable to the enemy's devices. Since then, I have learned more about joy. I have much more to learn and I must be quicker at practicing what I am sharing with you.

One day I was looking for some encouragement and decided to read some of my own testimonies. I flipped through my journal and ran across the page where I had written that exact statement about joy four years previously. I instantly knew that God wanted me to get

326

this truth deep inside my spirit! In fact the entire page in my journal was prophetic, but I didn't know it until those other things came true four years later.

Words have power, but one must be ready to receive them. Otherwise we hear only, "yada, yada, yada." Someone who has just fallen in a large pile of wet poop probably does not want to hear a scripture at that moment. They probably would rather have your hand to pull them up and a quick soapy shower. A well-timed word of humor and laughter is good medicine. Sometimes, people have to ask themselves how long they are willing to lie in the poop!

What is the ultimate answer to depression, oppression and heaviness? The scripture tells us that we can exchange mourning for joy. Paise pushes out a spirit of heaviness. God provides the answers. "...oil of joy for mourning, the garment of praise for the spirit of heaviness..." (Isaiah 61:3). A merry heart does good like a medicine: but a broken spirit dries the bones" (Proverbs 17:22, NKJV).

As crazy as it may seem, the sooner we laugh at the enemy who pushed us in the poop, the sooner he stops pushing.

DECIDE TO MANIFEST THE LORD'S JOY NO MATTER WHAT IS HAPPENING.

Of course this is not easy. Those who know me well, know that I allow my joy to be stolen. However, when

I apply the truth, I have extravagant results. You see, nothing changes until we make it our own. It has to become a part of us. Jesus has to become a part of us. It's not our own strength. The *Lord's* joy is our strength. Matthew 25:23 tells us we can *enter into* His joy. It's one of those things that we have *to do* first and results come after we do it! Let it bubble up even if you don't feel like it. It will come, because Jesus said so!

One of the ways to invite joy is in the form of praise, worship and laughter. Doing so is a sacrifice unto the Lord and we benefit from it. An example of this happened to me. One night before I was scheduled to preach, I suddenly awoke very ill with excruciating stomach pain and you know what came with it. I prayed a prayer of thanksgiving claiming that I was healed by Jesus' stripes. I know without a shadow of a doubt that is true and yet the more I prayed, the sicker I got. Suddenly, I started laughing and singing that scripture and in an instant, like flipping a light switch, all the sickness and pain left me! It seemed as though I had to convince the devil that I truly believed what Jesus said. Did I feel like laughing or singing? No, not at first, but after I did it, I felt better! **"Is anyone among you suffering? Let him pray. Is anyone cheerful? Let him sing praise" (James 5:13).**

When Stephen was being stoned, his eyes were fixed on Jesus and he demonstrated joy and hope even as they killed his flesh. They could not take away his interna joy nor his eternal spirit. He won through Jesus, no matter what. (See Acts chapter 7).

The power of praise is no joke. Entire historical wars were won with praise alone. (See II Chronicles chapters 20 and 21.) Those events should be in a movie or a video game. Here are a few *clips*...

As they began to sing and praise, the Lord set ambushes against the men of Ammon and Moab and Mount Seir who were invading Judah, and they were defeated. (2 Chronicles 20:22)

Then he said unto them, Go your way, eat the fat and drink the sweet, and send portions unto them for whom nothing is prepared: for this day is holy unto our Lord, neither be ye sorry; for the **joy of the Lord is your strength.** (Nehemiah 8:10 bold emphasis mine)

Those were old covenant promises. We have the blessings of Abraham plus much more with the new covenant of Jesus Christ!

Looking unto Jesus the author and finisher of our faith; who **for the joy** that was set before him endured the cross, despising the shame, and is set down at the right hand of the throne of God. (Hebrews 12:2, bold emphasis, mine)

And ye now therefore have sorrow: but I will see you again, and your heart shall rejoice, and **your joy no man taketh from you**. And in that day ye shall ask me nothing. Verily, verily, I say unto you, Whatsoever ye shall ask the Father in my name, he will give it you. Hitherto have ye asked nothing in my name: ask and ye shall receive that your **joy** may be full. (John 16:22-24, KJV, bold emphasis mine)

Did you catch that? Joy belongs to us, Jesus said so!

"THESE THINGS HAVE I SPOKEN UNTO YOU THAT *MY JOY* MIGHT REMAIN IN YOU, AND THAT *YOUR JOY* MIGHT *BE FULL*." (JOHN 15:11)

For years, I prayed for peace. I waited and I waited. The problem was, I didn't know that I already had it. All I had to do was *claim* it. Jesus said, "Peace I leave with you, my peace I give unto you: not as the world giveth, give I unto you. Let not your heart be troubled, neither let it be afraid" (John 14:27).

We don't have to accept chaos. We *say*, "Chaos, leave in Jesus' name. I have the peace that Jesus gave me!" I used to wonder how could I have joy when everything

was falling apart all around me. Jesus answered, "...
In the world ye shall have tribulation, but be of **good
cheer**, I have overcome the world" (John 16:33).

Chapter 46

TIME

TIME CAN BE TRICKY. AS DISCUSSED ABOVE sometimes we do wait on the Lord and other times we waste time waiting for something we already have. Let's be careful how we speak. If someone is really hurting, the last thing they want to hear someone say is, "It's all in the Lord's timing." Does the Lord do many things in His own time and His timing is perfect? Absolutely. He also says that we shall have whatever we ask for. The point we are all trying to make is to surrender and trust the Lord. However, there is a way to help someone see that while ministering to their hearts. Beware of making blanket statements without discernment.

Some say that time is your friend, that time heals all wounds and time changes things. Time, itself, is not the answer. If you're looking for real answers, if you're looking for a real friend, there is one. If you have wounds, there is a healer. If you are looking for real change, there is a game changer.

Time can slip away and so can we. We have no guarantee of time and should not take false comfort in it. We can change over time, but time, itself, does not change things. Let's stop making excuses and find real answers. What if we were not bound by time?

Will you settle for cliché or will you speak words of power? Joshua sought *the one* who holds time and time stood still.

> Then spake Joshua to the Lord in the day when the Lord delivered up the Amorites before the children of Israel and he said in the sight of Israel, Sun, stand thou still upon Gibeon; and thou, Moon, in the valley of Ajalon. And the sun stood still, and the moon stayed, until the people had avenged themselves upon their enemies....So the sun stood still in the midst of heaven, and hasted not to go down about a whole day. (Joshua 10:12,13, KJV)

Incredible? Yes! We have the privilege to believe it. Won't you give truth a try? History and science matches up with the Bible. If you're thinking that you're not hearing from God, keep listening. If you haven't seen His power, keep looking. He is speaking, but do we have ears to hear? **Most have seen His power, but didn't recognize it.** Take courage! Suddenly, when least expected, the answer comes! Refuse to quit while waiting. Don't let time make you weary. **Don't allow a veil to cover the glory**.

Our perception of time can be deceptive. For example; sometimes we think time will never end. Other times we feel we don't have enough. While writing this book, I was between jobs. At the first stages, I couldn't seem to accomplish anything, although I finally had free time. This is ridiculous, I thought! We all complain that we don't have enough time, but there are twenty four hours in everyone's day. Why do some people accomplish four times more than another person? We can think of lots of reasons, like they don't have a job or they don't have little kids, or this or that. The fact is, that no matter how many demands or if there are no demands, people respond differently to time itself. The truth is, "Where there is a will, there's a way." We all manage to do what matters to us most.

Regardless of our perceptions, we can take charge of our lives through the one who gave us life. "According as his divine power hath given unto us all things that pertain unto life and godliness, through the knowledge of him that hath called us to glory and virtue" (2 Peter 1:3, KJV).

Let's not allow the thief to steal it from us. I'm determined to stop getting caught in the trap of allowing people who waste time to give me more things to do that they should be doing! Beware of taking on duties for the sake of being a do-gooder. I'm learning to set boundaries. I am writing this to remind myself. If storms come, hold onto Jesus our anchor and speak to the wind and waves! Don't be distracted.

Our time on earth will end. Our physical bodies do have an expiration date. Please don't let time run out before you become born again by the spirit of God. Please don't let someone else die without Jesus. Become his child and receive eternal life which begins now with all power in His name.

Chapter 47

EVERYDAY BALANCE

VICTIMS OF PAST ABUSE HAVE LIVED IN THE extremes. Extremes on either side of the spectrum can alter our quality of life. If struggles and fear are all one has ever known, it can become difficult to function, even when life is going well. The abused are not familiar with normal life. They don't know how to trust. They don't know how to receive good things due to a fear that something bad might happen any minute. Their mindsets are always about survival. Anxiety has taken root, but Jesus can uproot anxiety. There are many approaches to anxiety. I'm not telling anyone not to try various approaches. For me, ultimate and complete transformation manifests each time I receive what Christ died to give me and enjoy an intimate relationship with Him and our Father God.

Do I still get anxious? Of course I do, because there has been a habit of anxiety. If you have been running full blast down a long steep hill, it takes an effort to stop. This momentum is difficult to change using our own strength. The spirit of anxiety must be cast out, and then you can see clearly. After that, decisions must be made to continue in power and truth. We can accomplish that only through the Lord Himself, the author and finisher of our faith. Other tools help, but deep healing is from Jesus our healer.

Sudden distractions and sudden circumstances can temporarily stun us, causing us to *respond to the problem instead of the answer*. However, we can take authority over it by the name of Jesus Christ. He has given us legal power of attorney to use his name! You can take it to the bank (Throne Room). Speak to the mountain. Say, " Anxiety, be removed!" If it lingers and seems to mock you, keep saying it. Refuse doubt. Refuse to allow it to stay!

"BE ANXIOUS FOR NOTHING, BUT IN EVERYTHING
BY PRAYER AND SUPPLICATION, WITH THANKSGIVING,
LET YOUR REQUESTS BE MADE KNOWN TO GOD"
(PHILIPPIANS 4:6)

That's a command actually. Don't be anxious. Some may think, well that's easier said than done, but if it were not available, the Lord would not have said it! Change our thoughts and change our life!

What alternative do we have? Has any other plan consistently worked better alone or worked completely? There is no judgment here. We do what we need to do to be free. Love is patient and powerful. We should encourage each other in every way, but the truth makes us free.

Those who know me well know that I still get caught up in the anxiety snare, but I get to victory faster, the more I abide and trust in The Christ. I do the best I can and depend on His strength. He is our hope. He is our answer. He is the strong one.

I go to the secret place to be with Him. He said, "... And he who loves me will be loved by my Father, and I will love him and manifest myself to him" (John 14:21, ESV). I love to picture Him at my door and I open it at his knocking. "Behold, I stand at the door and knock: if any man hear my voice, and open the door, I will come in to him, and will sup with him, and he with me" (Revelation 3:30). I run to His shelter. "Whoever dwells in the shelter of the Most High will rest in the shadow of the Almighty" (Psalm 91:1).

Past trauma can alter perception of reality, but now we can enjoy a godly balance. We can receive a godly abundance. His extremes are joy unspeakable and we have access to the unsearchable riches of Christ. We decide. Receive the gifts. Make them our own!

Imagine an animal sitting in a cage staring at a closed door, but the lid is off! Oh my, if they would only look up, they could see that they're not actually trapped at all! Escape is only a leap away!

Once out of the trap, some post traumatic survivors make a vow to stay away from chaos and drama. Others who have been accustomed to patterns of violence gravitate toward it. God give us wisdom to break free of mental deceptions! We can *decide* not to expose ourselves to a dark environment.

LET'S REFUSE TO BE USED.

After I escaped from abuse I made a vow, "Never again!" There are many levels of abuse and I was not willing to accept any of it! However, I had to find a healthy way of thinking and interacting with people. I'm still learning to set healthy boundaries. Living in the extremes is costly. The enemy can use the word of God against us (Matthew 4:1-11), but we are not to be ignorant of his devices according to 2 Corinthians 2:11, KJV. We are to ask for the Lord's wisdom and walk in His power. He who overcame!

If we're always hiding, how will others see Jesus through us? People need to see our lights shining brightly. If we don't take risks, how can we grow or help other people grow? Balance heavily on the things of God. We have the written word of God to direct our paths and we have a Living Word who is Jesus Christ and we have the power of Holy Spirit. Care should be taken not to lessen His word, stretch it or take it out of context. We learn in the book of Acts how to be filled with power from on high. We cannot rely on our natural brains alone.

God's natural creation is an example of his perfect balance. The laws of the universe, solar system and gravity are God's design. Look at the balance in our human bodies. One example is the endocrine system. This was a difficult system for me to learn while studying human physiology. However, when I realized that it's all about *balance*, I suddenly understood how the hormones work. In that light bulb moment, I got it! All of our hormones, such as thyroid, insulin, endorphins and others work on a feedback system. The slightest imbalance can wreak havoc on our bodies. While in balance we function like a well-tuned machine.

God also designed us to live in perfect balance with Him spiritually. We become off balance when we are not in alignment with His words and loving plan.

HIS WAYS ARE NOT GRIEVOUS.

Jesus said, *"For my yoke is easy, and my burden is light" (Matthew 11:30).* When Jesus is in the yoke, we are balanced beside Him. He pulls the heavy load.

Being balanced does not mean being wimpy or wishy-washy. It's good to be red hot, one hundred percent in love and involved with the Lord. This is discussed in Revelation 3:15,16 ESV. He does not care for lukewarm followers.

Abused victims who have been under damaging and controlling subjection sometimes find it hard to trust or submit. However, when we submit (willingly surrender) to Father God and the lordship of our good master Jesus Christ, we benefit extravagantly! Don't let the mistrust of the past prevent you from trusting true goodness. Our Lord is worthy of our trust.

Divine balance guides us and keeps us from getting falling off the deep end. The gymnast must remain in perfect balance or risk a fall. This kind of balance comes with diligent practice. Our bodies go where the eyes are looking. We hit or catch a baseball by keeping our eyes on the ball. Our bicycle wobbles if we look backwards. Therefore look forward and resist being double-minded. Fix our eyes on Jesus and go where He leads. He is, of the utmost importance. As Jesus instructs have a single focus.

> The lamp of the body is the eye: if therefore thine eye be single, thy whole body shall be full of light. (Matthew 6:22)

> ....turn not from it to the right hand or to the left, that thou mayest prosper whithersoever thou goest. (Joshua 1:7, KJV)

We fix our eyes on grace. As a favor to me and to you, please read all of chapters eight and nine of the book of Romans. Absorb the higher plane of walking by the spirit and living in grace.

> O foolish Galatians, who hath bewitched you, that ye should not obey the truth, before whose eyes Jesus Christ hath been

evidently set forth, crucified among you?
This only would I learn of you, Received ye
the Spirit by the works of the law, or by the
hearing of faith? Are ye so foolish? having
begun in the Spirit, are ye now made perfect by the flesh? (Galatians 3:1-3, KJV)

One huge mistake that victims tend to repeat is
trying to be a perfect person or become everybody's *fixer*.
Some people don't want to be fixed and never will, and
such involvements may drag you down again. Victims
sometimes find themselves in another relationship that
is unhealthy and detrimental. They unknowingly gravitate to someone else who needs fixing, but their depen-
dence on others only enables them to remain dependent.
Compassion is good, but be aware of those who prey
on your good will. Set boundaries. Have a healthy balance. Ask the Lord to direct your steps. We cannot fix
people. It's not our job to fix people. However, there are
people out there who can be reached, but we need God's
wisdom, discernment and to proceed by His spirit.

After we are free of abuse, let's not go to the other
extreme and form a wall around ourselves. Don't confuse self-preservation with wisdom. Of course, we must
protect ourselves, but not with a skewed sense of living.
Sometimes we need a wall, sometimes we need a bridge.

Fear blinds. Fear can make us run so fast that we
fall into a pit without seeing the hole in the ground.
Allow common sense and the spirit of truth to protect

us from being hurt over and over again. As Rev. Tom asked, "Are our doubts bigger than God's promises?"

> For the weapons of our warfare are not of the flesh but have divine power to destroy strongholds. We destroy arguments and every lofty opinion raised against the knowledge of God, and **take every thought captive** to obey Christ. (2nd Corinthians 10:4,5, ESV, bold emphasis mine)

If it were not possible to choose one thought over another, the scripture would not tell us that we can. Surely we need help! Yes! Leave the harmful thoughts at the cross. Nail the sorrows to the cross and walk away. Lay the burdens at the feet of Jesus who led captivity captive. " ...unto every one of us is given grace according to the measure of the gift of Christ. Wherefore he saith, when he ascended up on high, **he led captivity captive**..."(Ephesians 4:7,8 KJV, bold emphasis mine).

I would like to say that I have mastered my thoughts, but I cannot do that on my own. If I could, I wouldn't need Jesus. Therefore, I press into Him. When I fall, He picks me up again. In my fifties, I am still learning to walk this out. I pray and declare that you receive these life giving words now and reap the benefits early. Break old habits of negative thinking. Know and use your authority in the name of Jesus Christ. Fight in the spirit, not by the flesh.

> Finally, my brethren, be strong in the Lord, and in the power of his might. Put on the whole armor of God, that ye may be able to stand against the wiles of the devil. **For we wrestle not against flesh and blood,** but against principalities, against powers, against the rulers of the darkness of this world, against **spiritual wickedness** in high places. Wherefore take unto you the whole armor of God, that ye may be able to withstand in the evil day, and having done all, to stand. Stand therefore, having your loins girt about with truth, and having on the breastplate of righteousness; And your feet shod with the preparation of the gospel of peace; Above all, taking the shield of faith, wherewith ye shall be able to quench **all** the fiery darts of the wicked. And take the helmet of salvation, and the sword of the Spirit, which is the word of God: Praying always with all prayer and supplication in the Spirit, and watching thereunto with all perseverance and supplication for all saints. (Ephesians 6:10-18 KJV, bold emphasis mine)

Chapter 48

LOVE AND GROW IN GRACE

AT THE END OF THE DAY, HAVE WE LEARNED to love? What is love? It's easy to love the lovable. It's easy to love those who speak kindly to you. So here comes the toughest test: do we completely separate ourselves from them? Can we learn how to be around them, still love them and protect ourselves? I'm not talking about staying with a dangerous person who is ruled by evil. I'm talking about learning to love again, in general, for the remainder of our lives. How do we love all types of people? Jesus died for everyone. He showed grace and mercy. We are commanded to love people, but we are not commanded to love evil.

God is good. We are to be *living* sacrifices, not dead ducks. We cannot praise God from the grave. Our lives should reflect all the benefits of children of the King! Our lives are to glorify God by reflecting the exceeding good quality of His Fatherhood.

Some people may judge me and say that I should have stayed in the abusive marriage. I did pray for him the entire time I was there. I have prayed for him since I escaped. However, he also has a responsibility to Christ. He has free will to choose.

Some do truly accept Christ and change. Others carry on with the deception. They say they are sorry, even quote scripture only to repeat the abuse over and over again. I cannot walk their walk for them. It's between them and the Lord, but staying in an abusive marriage is as ridiculous as inviting a terrorist into your home! It's terrorism.

Would we dismantle all of our military and allow anybody to do anything to our country, all in the name of turning the other cheek? Please take an extensive look at what Jesus meant by that. Take the entire Bible cover to cover and you will see that evil itself was not to be tolerated. Look deeper at what Jesus was saying. He also turned over the money changers' tables. Jerusalem had walled cities. God had protective armies.

Please don't tell me that you are staying in a marriage for the children's sake. Children who witness abuse are living in fear. Children who witness abusive behavior sometimes grow up to repeat that behavior. They often become abusers themselves or they become the abused even into adulthood. Children learn what they live.

I'm aware that we are to pray for others to come to Christ. I believe God's mercy and grace is available for absolutely everyone. I believe and I pray this promise from Romans 8:28: "and we know that all things work

346

together for good to them that love God, to them who are the called according to his purpose."

I believe all things are possible with God and that His ways are not our ways. It is beyond my brain to explain all that, but it's true. I'm aware that sometimes abusers change. **However, I would not advise you to put your life in danger waiting around for something that may or may not happen!** We can stay alive somewhere else, in a safe place, at the right time, under a protective, well-thought-out and divine plan. If the person truly changes, then reevaluate the situation, but make sure they have truly changed instead of merely continuing to deceive. Ask the Lord for the absolute truth. Only He truly knows for sure.

Sometimes, we have no choice but to love from a distance. Sometimes, we have no choice but to put our time and energy into other people who *want to receive* the goodness of God and behave accordingly. "and whosoever shall not receive you, nor hear your words, when ye depart out of that house or city, shake off the dust of your feet" (Matthew 10:14).

Do not be deceived into accepting abuse in the name of *religious* ideology. It's important that we understand what the Lord was *really* saying. Listen closely. God is a good God and in Him is no darkness at all. He parted the Red Sea so His people could pass to safety. The evil did not pass through. He empowered His armies against the heathen. He instructed them not to marry the heathen.

The sanctity of marriage must be honored and maintained, but first we have to define a marriage. Is it a godly marriage or one *you* put together? God does not *put together* a marriage of abuse. The head of the woman must have Christ as his head and must love the woman as Christ loves the Church and gave Himself for it. Likewise the woman loves the man and does not abuse him. I'm not picking on men. Men, women and children suffer abuse, and it must not be tolerated.

If you are connected with someone by a piece of paper called a marriage license, ask yourself if that is the person you chose or the person God chose. Did you *really* consult the Lord before marrying? I'm not demeaning a commitment or a vow. God can deliver, heal and bless married people, but they *both* have to want to be healed and delivered. I don't believe God wants any person to be harmed or killed by their spouse.

Don't forget that the enemy twists and tweaks God's word to deceive. In his attempt to trick Jesus, he quoted one of the scriptures exactly, but he took it out of context. Jesus did not fall for the devil's lies. He exposed them. As Rev. Tom says, "We cannot let the devil's badness be spoken of more than God's goodness." We must fully know the goodness of God. After we see that, the evil will be easy to distinguish and it will look very small compared to God Almighty and His Victorious Son! Evil is no match for the goodness of God.

We are to magnify our God, and be vigilant. This word of power is also to the many people who are devastated by alcohol addiction. Lord, "I speak against the spirit of addiction. I also pray that we all are sober in the true meaning of that word." Everyone must be seriously kingdom minded to stand against the wiles of the wicked. The scripture says, "Be sober, be vigilant; because your adversary the devil, as a roaring lion, walketh about, seeking whom he may devour (1 Peter 5:8).

I'm thankful that we dwell in the shadow of the most high God. We are to feed our minds and our hearts with goodness and love. Our new way of thinking is critical.

> Finally, brethren, whatsoever things are true, whatsoever things are honest, whatsoever things are just, whatsoever things are pure, whatsoever things are lovely, whatsoever things are of good report; if there be any virtue, and if there be any praise, think on these things. (Philippians 4:8)

> This is how we learn to love others when we have not been loved by others. We know we have been and always will be loved by God. We are not doormats! However, we also must *not let the evil one trick us out of our capacity to love.* He knows how important love is and how important love is to God. If we allow it, the enemy will rob us of love by making us afraid to take risks. Deep

inside there is a person; try to find out if that person wants to be rescued from darkness. Otherwise, light has no fellowship with darkness (see Ephesians 5:11).

We fight *from* victory, *not toward* victory. Christ already won the war. We put on the whole armor of God and fight while at rest. We do not have to spend forty years in the wilderness.

For unto us was the gospel preached, as well as unto them: but the word preached **did not profit them, not being mixed with faith** in them that heard it. **For we which have believed do enter into rest,** as he said, As I have sworn in my wrath, if they shall enter into my rest: although the works were finished from the foundation of the world. (Hebrews 4:2,3 bold emphasis mine)

We can enter into His rest now. Giving the battle to Christ helps us love. Love is the great commandment, above all else. Where, then, does the lie come in on this mind battle? Remember, whatever the true God does, the devil wants to counterfeit. His version of God's Word sounds so sugary nice, but if we look closely and seek the Lord for wisdom and revelation, we will see the ultimate truth.

The abuser has been spoken of in a highly negative way, but his faults were not described to condemn him as a person, but to expose the darkness that consumed him. We don't know how the darkness got access to him, although I do know some of the open doors. This story is not told to glorify darkness, but to awaken to the truth. The truth can free both the abuser and the abused. Grace is big enough to set the abuser free. Grace is big enough for the victim to be set free. Mercy is for everyone. We choose. However, God does He *approve* of abuse or neglect on any level. He does not expect us to live in it. Jesus freely laid down His own life for our freedom.

Chapter 49

FORGIVENESS

FORGIVENESS IS REQUIRED. OFFENSE IS DANgerous. Offense may be understandable, but it backfires on the person who is offended. We should have zero tolerance for evil, but forgive the person and move on, otherwise we are not really free.

The enemy uses offense to trick us into opening a door for him to come in and live as a squatter. Once he moves in, he sets up his furniture. He wants to install the same sort of bad spirits that the abuser carries. In other words, the goal of evil is to have a legal right to ultimately destroy both the abuser and the abused.

No matter the form or level of abuse, we have to guard our hearts. Otherwise the trauma goes beyond the original insult and extends the damage. It's kind of like a burn injury. The hand can be removed from the heat source, but it the flesh is not cooled immediately, the burn keeps going deeper. Permanent scarring can occur.

Unforgiveness keeps the bad memories stirred up which also causes further damage.

Genuine forgiveness is the ultimate act of godly love. It's extremely hard to do without the Lord's help. Two things can help us get there: 1) Picture what they did to Jesus, yet He forgave them. 2) Jesus forgave us when we didn't deserve forgiveness. When we look at it that way, we can't help but forgive.

No matter what has happened to us, we were never treated like Jesus was and he was a perfect man who certainly didn't deserve any of what was done to Him! He endured the worst of the worst and yet He overcame! He shed his perfect blood to forgive us of all our sins.His forgiveness demands that we also forgive. When we look at His sacrifice, we are moved in our hearts to forgive others because we have been forgiven for so much.

Let's remember to put on the whole armor of God as mentioned earlier in Ephesians chapter six. This battle is fierce, especially for those who have been under repeated assaults. Our best bet is to let Jesus stand in front of us.

A huge part of my deliverance was forgiving the abuser. I said out loud that I forgave him, but I didn't *fully* forgive him until I heard the testimony of forgiveness from one of my fellow victims. It was the best *sermon* on forgiveness that I have ever heard even from any pulpit of any Church in my whole life! Coming from her, especially from her, I saw incredible humility and strength. It rocked my world. If she can do it so can we.

When we forgive, it does not mean that we will allow it again! It does not mean that we agree with what happened. It definitely does not mean that it was okay or that we accept it! We cast our cares upon the Lord because He cares for us. He cares for us and that is the most important place to be. Under the Lord's caring embrace. Forgiveness means that we turn it over to Jesus. It's between the person and the Lord.

We have to let go of unforgiveness, otherwise we remain in chains.

FORGIVENESS DOES NOT GIVE THE ABUSER PERMISSION TO DO IT AGAIN.

Forgiveness does not say, "Come on in, evil, and sit on my couch. I'll make you a sandwich and bring you a beer." No, that's not what the Lord is asking. We are to forgive because we are forgiven, but as mentioned earlier, **light has no *fellowship* with darkness.**

If they truly *want* to be helped, there is spiritual and physical help for those who are under the influences of darkness. You may have heard the old adage, "You can lead a horse to water, but you can't make him drink." I'm well aware of the Mental Health Professionals that have practical and medicinal treatments for organic and psychiatric brain disorders. I'm not advocating abandonment or rejection of that care. Those who have been under that care for many years without any progress at all may consider looking at Jesus Christ who is the ultimate deliverer. The physically ill with an incurable illness has also been helped by the Lord. There are innumerable validated testimonies out there as proof of that.

It's recorded all through the Gospels that Jesus released the afflicted from their afflictions. This is not only documented in the Bible, but also documented by historians. What do you have to lose? If you have already lost it all, why not seek Jesus? If you need to forgive someone, ask the Lord to help you. If all you have is the Lord, then you have everything!

Chapter 50

DENY DEATH BY DECEPTION

JESUS CHRIST CAME TO "DELIVER THEM WHO through fear of death were all their lifetime subject to bondage." (Hebrews 2:15). Three and a half years I lived with the relentless abuser. It was an intense time that seemed like forever. I was blinded to the freedom that could be mine.

Many have endured much longer, but many have escaped only by death. Women are not the only ones who are abused. Children are the most victimized as they fall under the subjection of adults. Men are abused as well, and they especially keep it a secret due to shame.

> Every nine seconds in the United States, a woman is assaulted or beaten. Around the world, at least one in every three women has been beaten, coerced into sex or otherwise abused during her lifetime. Most often, the abuser is a member of her own family. Nearly one in five teenage girls who have been in a relationship said a boyfriend threatened violence or self-harm if presented with a breakup. Every day in the US, more than three women are murdered by their husbands or boyfriends. The costs of intimate partner violence in the US alone exceed $5.8 billion per year: $4.1 billion are for direct medical and health care services, while productivity losses account for nearly $1.8 billion. Men who as children witnessed their parents' domestic violence were twice as likely to abuse their own wives than sons of nonviolent parents. (http://domesticviolencestatistics.org/domestic-violence-statistics/)

Those of us who have escaped, physically, must not remain bound. We cannot stay in a prison without walls. I received and continue to receive help from my Christian brothers and sisters who remind me of the power of God and His protection. I trust in the Lord who saved me and is faithful to continue to save.

> If thou faint in the day of adversity, thy strength is small. If thou forbear to deliver them that are drawn unto death, and those that are ready to be slain; If thou sayest, Behold, we knew it not; doth not he that pondereth the heart consider it? and he that keepeth thy soul, doth not he know it? and shall not he render to every man according to his works?" (Proverbs 24:10-12 NIV)

> Lay not wait, O wicked man, against the dwelling of the righteous; spoil not his resting place; for a just man falleth seven times, and riseth up again: but the wicked shall fall into mischief. (Proverbs 24:15,16, KJV)

> ...for the testimony of Jesus is the spirit of prophecy...(Revelation 19:10)

And they overcame him by the blood of the Lamb and by the word of their testimony and they loved not their lives unto the death. (Revelation 12:11)

There is life beyond the flesh. "...through the veil that is to say his flesh." Hebrews 10:20). We can enter into the very manifest presence of God. True living is not bound by the flesh. We live unto Christ. Forgiveness was bought with the precious blood of Jesus Christ.

The enemy lied to me saying, "You will never get away from me. You will never get out of the driveway alive." He continues to lie and tell me not to write this book. He whispers that there might be consequences. This is a pivotal moment. Do I keep the dark secrets silent by fear? What is the cost? What is the cost of a potential life saved? I choose life. I choose life for me and others. Yes! I declare in the name of Jesus Christ that there will be consequences— the following consequences.

> I speak a blessing on you. I speak life, light and truth into your lives. I speak a deeper revelation and a true relationship with the Lord Jesus and that you grow in grace! Jesus open their eyes and their ears. There will be forgiveness, healing protection and freedom!

Chapter 51

WHAT LIES HAVE YOU BELIEVED?

A LIE IS LYING AT THE BOTTOM OF ALL THINGS opposite of the abundant life that Christ came to give us. Ask yourself, what lies you have believed. Think about it. How much did it impact you? Did it prevent you from doing whatever you needed to do or did it cause you to react in a way that was totally unnecessary? Were you paralyzed needlessly with anxiety, only to find out later that it was all a lie? Perhaps you *seemingly* have everything the world offers. The liar tells you, "You're good. You don't need anything." However, at the end of the day, there is an empty place that has not been filled.

A lie (deception) is like a street drug. It appears good at first. It promises you everything, but it only gives you pleasure until you are in bondage and in debt to it. No matter how much you have, there is never enough to fully fulfil you. You must have more until the insatiable false pleasure finally destroys you completely.

Say no to false hope, seductions, deceptions, confusion, chaos, false security and false happiness. Instead, become a joint heir with Jesus who truly has been given everything and He shares it with us. It's a life far more exciting, genuine, dependable, eternal and prosperous and satisfying than the world offers. Jesus made you accepted in the beloved. He is the one who paid the price for sin and washed you in His very own perfect blood. **Jesus is the one who sticks closer than a brother when everyone else abandons you.** "God so loved the world, that he gave his only begotten Son, that whosoever believes in him should not perish, but have everlasting life." (John 3:16)

> ... if Christ be in you, the body is dead because of sin; but the Spirit is life because of righteousness. (Romans 8:10, KJV)

> And their sins and iniquities will I remember no more. (Hebrews 10:17)

> For if these things be in you, and abound, they make you that ye shall neither be barren nor unfruitful in the knowledge of our Lord Jesus Christ. (2 Peter 1:8)

> These things have I written unto you concerning them that seduce you, but the anointing which 'you' have received of him

'abides' in you, and 'you' need not that any man teach you, but as the same anointing 'teaches' you of all things and is **truth** and is **no lie** and even as it has taught you, **you shall abide in him.** (1 John 2:26-27) Remove the false way from me, and graciously grant thy law (vs 32)

Knowing that a man is not justified by the works of the law, but by the faith of Jesus Christ, even we have believed in Jesus Christ, that we might be justified by the faith of Christ, and not by the works of the law: for by the works of the law shall no flesh be justified. (Galatians 2:16)

I do not frustrate the grace of God: for if righteousness come by the law, then Christ is dead in vain. (Galatians 2:21)

Jesus said unto him, Thou shalt love the Lord thy God with all thy heart, and with all thy soul, and with all thy mind. This is the first and great commandment. (Matthew 22:37-38) And the second is like unto it, Thou shalt love thy neighbor as thyself. On these two commandments hang all the law and the prophets. (Matthew 22:39-40)

If a line is drawn vertically on a page, you could place everything in your life under two columns: Truth or Lie. Remember that all was well in the Garden of Eden until the liar appeared and spoke. Don't listen to him. How do you know when the enemy has arrived? Measure everything by the truth.

> In hope of eternal life, which **God, that cannot lie**, promised before the world began. (Titus 1:2)

> **God is not a man, that he should lie;** neither the son of man, that he should repent: hath he said, and shall he not do it? or hath he spoken, and shall he not make it good? (Numbers 23:19)

> Who is he that 'overcomes' the world, but he that 'believes' that Jesus is the Son of God? (1 John 5:5)

> Jesus saith unto him, I am the way, the truth, and the life: no man cometh unto the Father, but by me. (John 14:6)

> Then said they unto him, What shall we do, that we might work the works of God? Jesus answered and said unto them, This

is the work of God, that ye believe on him whom he hath sent. (John 6:28-29)

Howbeit when he, the **Spirit of truth**, is come, **he will guide you into all truth**: for he shall not speak of himself; but whatsoever he shall hear, that shall he speak: and he will shew you things to come. (John 16:13, KJV)

Nevertheless **I tell you the truth**; It is expedient for you that I go away: for if I go not away, the Comforter will not come unto you; but if I depart, I will send him unto you. (John 16:7)

We are never alone. Search all the holy scriptures for in them you find Jesus. God's words are life, power and truth. You will see all the benefits from the love letter God wrote to you.

Chapter 52

WOMEN IN MINISTRY

JUST AS JESUS SPOKE OF HAVING OTHER SHEEP (Gentiles) beyond the flock of Israel, He also included women. Remember, Jesus did not restore *only* what Adam lost. He also restored Eve.

> There is neither Jew nor Greek, there is neither bond nor free, there is neither male nor female: for ye are **all one** in Christ Jesus. (Galatians 3:28).

Together we stand, divided we fall. The enemy knows that and seeks to divide and discriminate. He certainly seeks to squelch *any* powerful voice for the Lord. It's time we recognize that the enemy continues his effort to keep women silent.

However, women were active during Jesus' earthly ministry. Women ministers have undeniably impacted His Church since that time and continue to do so. There's a long legacy in the Old Testament of impactful women. It seems obvious that the evil one knew the value of women, and so he quickly tried to discredit them—starting with Eve. God designed the entire family to carry out His purpose. The enemy has worked to destroy families and or change their dynamics.

The Lord has called women to rise up in His Church and it is He who makes them able ministers for His purpose. The fruit is evident for those who will be humble enough to look. I encourage any who may be under the deception to the contrary to take it up with the Lord. Jesus Christ decides who He calls and we can see who bears the fruit no matter what the gender, educational background, age or color. This chapter will dispel some deception regarding women's place in the Church. Let's look at what God says. "The Lord gives the word [of power]; the women who bear and publish [the news] are a great host" (Psalms 68:11, AMP).

Anna the Prophetess had a place in the temple and declared the baby Lord Jesus to be the long sought redemption of Israel. She was not silent in the Temple. Read about her in Luke 2:36 through 38. Also, enjoy the record in John 20:16-18 record of Mary's proclamation after leaving the sepulchre. The women were the first to preach the gospel, declaring the Lord was risen from the dead!

It was Mary Magdalene, and Joanna, and Mary the mother of James, and other women that were with them, which told these things unto the apostles. **"And their words seemed to them as idle tales, and they**

believed them not. Then arose Peter, and ran unto the sepulchre; and stooping down, he beheld the linen clothes laid by themselves, and departed, wondering in himself at that which was come to pass" (Luke 24:10-12, bold emphasis).

Clearly, women were still striving for credibility, which I presume continued since Eve. Some people continue thinking that women should not be ministers in a formal Church. Some have said that its okay for them to be missionaries. What does that mean? That they can do a job that others *might* not want to do?

Women have made some advancements in society. However, equality remains inconsistent in the workplace. Some employers pay a woman less than a man, even though they are doing the exact same job. It hasn't been all that long since we received the right to vote. Some countries treat women as slaves, without a voice at all, and consider them to be lesser than a dog. In those countries dogs are considered to be worthless and lowly and certainly not treated as esteemed house pets.

Hallelujah, the Lord gave women credibility! He gave them a place in His ministry. He showed them love. Jesus was radical in the culture of His day. He was a friend to women and certainly remains so. He treated everyone with equal loving compassion.

> How long will you waver and hesitate [to return], O you backsliding daughter? For

the Lord has created a new thing in the
land [of Israel]: **a female** shall compass
(woo, win, and protect) a man. (Jeremiah
31:22, AMPC emphasis mine)

God created women to fulfill His purpose in many
ways. Here are a couple of fun facts that you may
not know: Women invented bullet proof vests and
fire escapes.

Women leaders are mentioned throughout the Bible.
Many powerful women since the 1800's have led huge
revivals with powerful evangelism, miracles and healings. The genealogy in the Gospel of Matthew lists a few
women who were not perfect, but their role in God's
plan and the coming of Christ was important.

No human is perfect. Remember the sure mercies
of David? Remember Saul who became Paul? Really
and truly consider why Eve got such a bad rap. Male
ministers are not perfect and neither are we, but that
doesn't mean that the Lord is not building HIS Church,
His way. The Lord is building His Church and the gates
of hell shall not prevail against it.We put our trust in
the Lord and not in humans no matter what the gender.
Let everything that has breath praise the Lord. We are
to ask the Lord for truth no matter who it is doing
the speaking.

I'm not rewriting the Bible. I'm not adding to or sub-
tracting from the word of God. I'm simply testifying
of what the Lord has done for me. I used examples of

scripture that have produced victory in my own life. This has been only an *introduction* to the word of God. Each person should search the matter out for himself. God answers all who are truly hungry for the whole truth and willing to lay down preconceived ideas.

> It is the glory of God to conceal a thing, but the honor of kings is to search out a matter. (Proverbs 25:2)

> Be diligent to present yourself approved to God, a worker who does not need to be ashamed, rightly dividing the word of truth. (2 Timothy 2:15)

The word of God is to be treasured in its entirety. Honor its integrity. These are not simply words on a page, but life and power. Try it for yourself with a pure heart. It's impossible not to see a change. We learn with the goal to *know* our Creator and our redeemer in an intimate relationship.

Women have the God-given nature *to nurture* all kinds of relationships. Several women remained at the foot of the cross until the Lord was taken away. **I would call that an act of pastoral care.** They also nurture children in the admonition of the Lord, which raises up a generation unto God. Mother Lois and Grandmother Eunice are matriarchs of the ministry spoken of in

II Timothy 1:3-6. This is one of women's divinely appointed ministries that can change the world.

Further study has been researched regarding women's role in the Church. What was the actual meaning behind the statement for women to keep silent in the Churches? What was the whole picture? Didn't Paul clearly say that all may prophesy. Was one scripture taken out of context or misunderstood? What was the culture? What was law? What was grace? We get clear understanding by looking at the entire Word of God, being humble and asking the Lord Jesus for understanding of the scriptures. Women (nor anyone else) were to be allowed to cause confusion, jealousy, distractions or disrupt the order of Church meetings. The purpose of a teaching should not be compromised by *anybody*. The truth is available for those who wish to see the truth. May we *all* be humble and in submission to the truth. Extensive Biblical research on this topic is found in pages 84 to 98 in Katharine Bushnell's book *God's Word to Women*.

Wasn't Miriam called by God to minister with Moses? Would squelching the ministry of women in the Church cause a great void? Women worship and praise without inhibition. Miriam, at an elderly age, led the whole congregation in a dance of praise. David was one of the few men who danced before the Lord uninhibited. I believe more men are now learning to surrender, let go of pride and release their sacrifice of praise without shame of what others may think. Surely if our Lord raised his arms on the cross, the least we can do is raise our arms in praise to Him! Let **every** voice (women included) proclaim his Gospel and lift him high! He was on display. We can certainly display our ministering and our praises!

GODLY WOMEN SURRENDER TO THE LORD WITH GRACE, BOLDNESS AND HUMILITY. WITH SURRENDER COMES REVELATION WHICH EQUIPS THE CHURCH.

Godly women submit with gladness. Gracious men protect and honor the women who submit and who are powerful through Christ. Men have their own unique God-given ministerial qualities. Both men and women are necessary and complementary. It seems that God had that all figured out when He said that it was not good for man to be alone. **Women and men are better together, even in the Church.** All scripture must be considered for the complete picture. Any confusion must be resolved with defined biblical research and revelation. Search the matter out with the Lord. (Extensive research is also described in Katharine Bushnell's book, *God's Word to Women*.)

Ruth, Deborah, Sarah, Rahab and many more are a testament to the value of women in ministry. The woman at the well has stood out to me since childhood. Now I know why the Lord called my attention to her so strongly. Not only was I drawn to the water that Jesus gives, but also to another scripture that captured my heart as an seven year old. Obviously this record is about worship. It's the main point and it's a point that I want to do with all that is within me and with all my heart. The fact that Jesus said,

> But the hour cometh, and now is, when the true worshippers shall worship the Father in spirit and in truth: for the Father seeketh such to worship him. God is a Spirit: and they that worship him must worship him in spirit and in truth. (John 4:23, 24)

It is noteworthy that Jesus, himself, revealed who He was to her, a woman. Jewish men were not to speak to women in public and certainly not to a gentile woman. All of my life, I have only heard this pivotal record spoken of with a focus on how many husbands she had. However, worship was the main point of the conversation. Jesus was not shaming the woman, per se, but probably pointing out that the Samaritans had become adulterous having other gods than the true God. Also, it showed the woman and her people that the Lord knew things without having been told. Do you see how the manifestation of Holy Spirit is powerful? She in turned preached the good news and evangelized her people. "And many of the Samaritans of that city believed on him for the saying of the woman, which testified, He told me all that ever I did." (John 4:39).

Church is not limited to the inside a building made by hands. Two or three can be gathered (Matthew 18:20). Looking at the potential effectiveness of women ministers, it's easy to see why the enemy worked quickly to deceive Eve, perhaps hoping to discredit her and all of her daughters.

Chapter 53

EVE IS FREE

"BUT SEEK YE FIRST THE KINGDOM OF GOD, and his righteousness; and all these things shall be added unto you" (Matthew 6:33). That is a direct and true promise from a faithful God that cannot be changed. No matter what we're facing, we must not allow the enemy to trick us out of all God is and gives! While waiting for the pieces to fall into place, don't be surprised if the opposing kingdom *tries* to block your freedom or any of God's promises. He wants to prevent God from getting any glory. We know by now that we can speak God's truth more loudly than the enemy roars, and refuse to give up.

All things have been added to me. This is my testimony. Remember to worship God and not the *all things*. All that I have comes down from the Father of Lights and through His Son Jesus. He has given me the desires of my heart, and He will do the same for you.

Delight thyself also in the Lord; and he shall give thee the desires of thine heart. Commit thy way unto the Lord; trust also in him; and he shall bring it to pass. (Psalms 37:4,5).

Through him then let us continually offer up a sacrifice of praise to God, that is, the fruit of lips that acknowledge his name. (Hebrews 13:15).

To truly live is to live in Christ. May He be magnified and glorified. When I lay my head down on my pillow, I thank God that I am safe. There was a time when all I wanted was to close my eyes and sleep. Now, I rest. Now, I awake. Awaken!

Let there be an awakening! God **is** real. The manifest presence of our Lord is literally tangible. Absorb verse twenty-one in chapter fourteen of the Gospel of John. He says He will **manifest** Himself. Jesus said that if we have seen Him, we have seen the Father. There is historical proof that Jesus was seen both before and after His resurrection from the dead. When He ascended to the Father's right hand, He said that it was expedient that He should go because He would send the Comforter to us.

Also, God *showed up* all through His Word. The weight of his glory was so heavy in the Holy of Holies that the High Priest could not remain standing. The

Red Sea actually parted, a pillar of fire by night and a cloud by day was visible to the Israelites in the wilderness, a donkey talked; on and on are records of God visiting His people. Seek Him with all your hearts and you will find Him. Worship Him because He is worthy of all our praise and worship. I declare and decree in the name of Jesus that you will do so!

"But I fear, lest by any means, as the serpent beguiled Eve through his subtilty, so your minds should be corrupted from the **simplicity that is in Christ**" (2 Corinthians 11:3).

Let Christ and His peace rule in your hearts, and don't be entangled with the pressures or temptations to be righteous by your own works. Don't make things complicated. We don't need to be *afraid* of deception, but rather take authority over it in Jesus' name.

> For there shall arise false Christs, and false prophets, and shall show great signs and wonders; insomuch that, **if** it were possible, they shall deceive the very elect. (Matthew 24:24)

We will trust in the spirit of truth to alert us of the spirit of deception. The scripture said *if* it were possible. So, it is possible *not* to be deceived if we are abiding with the spirit of truth. Don't be afraid of the *manifest presence* of our Lord, and don't be afraid of the genuine signs, miracles and wonders. We must not guess about such things or hold on to our preconceived ideas. **There has to be a genuine in order to have a counterfeit, so seek the genuine.** Ask and trust God to show you the counterfeit. "For God hath not given us the spirit of fear; but of power, and of love, and of a **sound mind**." (2 Timothy 1:7, bold emphasis mine)

The enemy wants to confuse us, strike fear, destroy love and make us think we are crazy or weak. He sets the world against us to mock us. He wants to distract us from worshiping God. He competes for worship. He wants other things to become our idols.

If other things, activities, people, family, children or careers consume us to the point that we cannot be satisfied without them, that is a red flag of idolatry. All those things are very important to us and should be, but nothing should be more important than our Father God and our Lord Jesus Christ. Remember, God gave us everything, he gave us our families, His Son, even life itself. He is *the* source for *all* that we have.

If God, His Son and Holy Spirit are *all* you have, is it enough? If so, then true freedom manifests because we have no idols. It doesn't matter what the enemy suggests. We say, "No, satan! Go away! We already have *all* that we want or need!" Jesus restored what was lost in the Garden of Eden. The scourged, crucified and risen Christ redeemed us all, including *Eve.* She is forgiven and so are we. May we not label Eve. May we not judge her or anyone else. Judge evil not people.

> I waited patiently for the Lord and he inclined unto me and heard my cry. He brought me up also out of an horrible pit out of the miry clay and set my feet upon a rock and established my goings and he hath put a new song in my mouth, even praise unto our God: many shall see it, and fear, and shall **trust in the Lord.** (Psalms 40:1-3, KJV emphasis mine)

Let us shed the guilt-mentality. In Hebrews 10:17, God said that he remembers our sin no more, so why should we? Let's see Eve for who she really was, a beautiful, wise and amazing woman that God created and said it was very good. Let every man, woman and child rise up to be all that God created us to be.

When people have abused us, we tend to have a mindset that we are constantly being attacked. We feel that a lot of people and circumstances are against us. This is bondage and a lie. That cloak that must be taken off. Instead, put on the whole armor of God (Ephesians 6:13), put on Christ (Galatians 3:27) and put on the new man (Ephesians 4:24). Speak out loud that God's kingdom *is for us.* Don't live below par.

No matter what it looks like at the moment, the Lord is working things for our good. When the storm descends upon us, we labor to enter into His rest. This is a daily ongoing choice, but if God be for us, who can be against us?

When we look in the mirror, let there not be any confusion as to who we truly are. Jesus is not confused. Jesus can take the pain that we cannot bear. Actually, He already took it. Because He lives, we can live and face tomorrow. He is our only true relief.

My prayer is that the youth will become strong against seduction into violent behavior patterns. Break those chains by the power of Jesus' name! I pray that parents and teachers will identify bullying and have a zero tolerance for it. You cannot fight this in your flesh, but you can take spiritual authority over it by speaking to the mountain with bold prayer and believing. Bullying can be recognized in the very young child and can become more dangerous as the child grows up. Abusive spouses were usually childhood bullies. Childhood bullies sometimes become abusive parents. Child abuse should be entirely eradicated! Identify the rebellion spirit early and address it with the Lord's help. This can be a challenge, but ask the Lord how to do it. Love is stronger than evil. People of any age won't be as frustrated and angry if they know they have hope, real answers to life's problems and that grace is enough!

My prayer is that the youth will be aware of red flags of dangerous people who are under the influence of darkness. If your boyfriend or girlfriend has anger, jealousy and control issues, then beware. My prayer is for prevention of becoming trapped in bad relationships. My prayer is for men and women to avoid marrying destructive people. Prevention is better than damage repair.

MY HEART IS CRYING OUT LIKE ABEL'S BLOOD
FROM THE GROUND FOR THOSE WHOM
HAVE BEEN KILLED BY EVIL.

I am screaming, "Watch out for the traps!" If you are already in a trap, ask God what He wants done about it. Ask Him when and how. Obey Him. He is the only One who truly knows you, the other person, your circumstances and the future.

No matter your background or who you are, life is tough, but we all can be more than conquerors through Jesus who loved us and gave Himself for us. **You see, ladies, there is a man whom we can trust and His name is Jesus.** Ask for a revelation of Him, grace and truth. For those who know this already, we share in His joy. The best is yet to come. **He is coming back!** Let us watch and pray and love His appearing! In the meantime exalt Him!

> "Let the redeemed of the Lord say so, whom
> he hath redeemed from the hand of the
> enemy" (Psalms 107:2, KJV)

I am redeemed! I pray this book fulfills what I claim as my job description listed in Matthew 10:7,8: "And as ye go, preach, saying, The kingdom of heaven is at hand. Heal the sick, cleanse the lepers, raise the dead, cast out devils: freely ye have received, freely give."

For I determined not to know anything among you, save Jesus Christ, and him crucified. (I Corinthians 2:2, KJV)

Now thanks be unto God, which always causeth us to triumph in Christ, and maketh manifest the savour of his knowledge by us in every place. (2 Corinthians 2:14)

That at that time ye were without Christ, being aliens from the commonwealth of Israel, and strangers from the covenants of promise, having no hope, and without God in the world: but now in Christ Jesus you who sometimes were far off are made nigh by the blood of Christ. (Ephesians 2:12-13 bold emphasis)

Now the Lord is that Spirit: and where the Spirit of the Lord is, there is liberty. (II Corinthians 3:17)

And you shall know the truth, and the truth shall make you free. (John 8:32)

Be free!

REFERENCES

Bushnell, Katharine C. *God's Word to Women* First publication 1921, 2nd publication Christians for Biblical Equality cbeinternational.org 2003

Dill, T. Covenant Provision, audio teaching, *https://cffm.org/multimedia-archive/covenant-provision/* August 22, 2017

Dill, T. *Moving the Kingdom, Part 3, audio teaching, https://cffm.org/multimedia-archive/moving-the-kingdom-part3-seeking/* ,February 15, 2017

Dollar, Creflo. *What's Your Motive?* https://www.youtube.com/watch?v=sA3UXT3ASEU Published on YouTube March 2, 2015

Domestic Violence Statistics. *Let's Put a Stop to Domestic Violence and Abuse,* http://domesticviolencestatistics.org/domestic-violence-statistics/, 2018

Guigou, K. *Sent With The Sender*, audio teaching, *http://cffm.org/multimedia-archive/sent-with-the-sender/* ,August 13, 201

Harper Collins Christian Publishing, Inc. *Olive Tree Bible Study App Version 6.0.14 Holy Bible, ASV, ESV,* KJV, NIV, NKJV translations, App updated January, 8, 2018 https://itunes.apple.com/app/id332615624?&referrer=click%3D96a93bae-2851-400d-ab13-c48a06ab859f

Jackson, Wayne. *Jesus and the Samaritan Woman. ChristianCourier.com.* Access date: February 3, 2018. https://www.christiancourier.com/articles/282-jesus-and-the-samaritan-woman

Jesus Gives Us Understanding, audio teaching, *http://cffm.org/multimedia-archive/jesus-gives-understanding/* July 3, 2016

Shroyer, T. *Two Kingdoms,* audio teaching, *http://cffm.org/multimedia-archive/two-kingdoms/* May 25, 2014

The Heart of Man https://heartofmanmovie.com Copyright 2018

APPENDICES

Benefits of speaking in tongues
(Heavenly Language)
Acts 1:5, 2:4 and 2:38

1. To edify you: I Corinthians 14:4, Jude 20. Isaiah 28:11 & 12
2. To speak to God divine secrets: I Corinthians 14:2 (I Cor 14:14 Praying in the spirit)
3. To speak the wonderful works of God: Acts 2:11
4. To magnify God: Acts 10:46
5. To pray perfectly: Romans 8:26 and 27
6. To give thanks well: I Corinthians 14:17
7. To have the Spirit bearing witness with our spirit: Romans 8:16
8. To know you are a joint heir with Christ: Romans 8:17
9. To strengthen you with might in your inner man: Ephesians 3:16, II Corinthians 4:16
10. To be a sign to unbelievers: I Corinthians 14:22 and Mark 16:17

11. Rest to the soul: Isaiah 28:11 and 12, I Corinthians 14:21
12. To bring a message from God or for God to people (when interpreted): 1 Corinthians 14:39 Therefore, my brothers and sisters, be eager to prophesy, and do not forbid speaking in tongues.
13. John 4:24
14. John 7:38,39
15. Job 29:23 Psalm 81:10
16. Acts 8:18
17. I Peter 4:10
18. Mark 16:17
19. I Corinthians 14:2 and 5

Some people don't like to think about speaking in tongues because they haven't yet experienced it. Therefore, they assume that it's not for them, but we clearly see that it is for all God's people. We speak by taking action to manifest it. Humans tend do dismiss things they don't yet understand. If they can't explain it, they discard it, speak against it or sometimes judge others. Some assume speaking in tongues died with the apostles. That is not true; it simply *started* with the apostles.

...APPENDICES P 2

SPEAKING IN TONGUES HAS SO MANY BENE-
fits from God to you. Natural man cannot understand things of the spirit. Receive the baptism of Holy
Spirit. Become a spirit filled Christian by confessing
Jesus Christ and asking for it.

Speaking in tongues is spirit to spirit. It connects
us with our Father God. TRUST God and enjoy the gift
that Christ died to make available. It's a form of perfect
prayer and praise. It builds up our inner man (spirit).
It's worshiping in spirit and in truth.

We praise and speak in tongues because we choose
to do as God instructs. We recognize the benefits of it.
We realize it is pure. We do it also as inspired by Holy
Spirit. Our heavenly language is an awesome privilege!
Don't allow the lies of the enemy to trick you out of this
powerful manifestation of the spirit. Deception keeps
us from God's best! Ask Eve!

~ ~ ~ ~ ~ ~ ~ ~ ~ ~ ~ ~ ~ ~ ~ ~ ~ ~ ~